CONTEMPORARY
Black
Biography

ISSN-1058-1316

CONTEMPORARY Black Biography

Profiles from the International Black Community

Volume 53

Detroit • New York • San Francisco • San Diego • New Haven, Conn. • Waterville, Maine • London • Munich

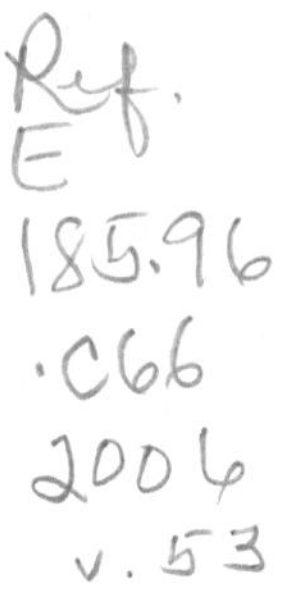

THOMSON GALE

Contemporary Black Biography, Volume 53

Sara and Tom Pendergast

Project Editor
Pamela M. Kalte

Image Research and Acquisitions
Jillean McCommons, Robyn V. Young

Editorial Support Services
Nataliya Mikheyeva

Rights and Permissions
Lisa Kincade, Kim Smilay, Andrew Specht

Manufacturing
Dorothy Maki, Rhonda Dover

Composition and Prepress
Mary Beth Trimper, Gary Leach

Imaging
Lezlie Light, Mike Logusz

For more information, contact
Thomson Gale
27500 Drake Rd.
Farmington Hills, MI 48331-3535
Or you can visit our internet site at
http://www.gale.com

ISBN 0-7876-7925-9
ISSN 1058-1316

Printed in the United States of America
10 9 8 7 6 5 4 3 2 1

Advisory Board

Contents

Introduction

Contemporary Black Biography provides informative biographical profiles of the important and influential persons of African heritage who form the international black community: men and women who have changed today's world and are shaping tomorrow's. *Contemporary Black Biography* covers persons of various nationalities in a wide variety of fields, including architecture, art, business, dance, education, fashion, film, industry, journalism, law, literature, medicine, music, politics and government, publishing, religion, science and technology, social issues, sports, television, theater, and others. In addition to in-depth coverage of names found in today's headlines, *Contemporary Black Biography* provides coverage of selected individuals from earlier in this century whose influence continues to impact on contemporary life. *Contemporary Black Biography* also provides coverage of important and influential persons who are not yet household names and are therefore likely to be ignored by other biographical reference series. Each volume also includes listee updates on names previously appearing in *CBB.*

Designed for Quick Research and Interesting Reading

- **Attractive page design** incorporates textual subheads, making it easy to find the information you're looking for.
- **Easy-to-locate data sections** provide quick access to vital personal statistics, career information, major awards, and mailing addresses, when available.
- **Informative biographical essays** trace the subject's personal and professional life with the kind of in-depth analysis you need.
- **To further enhance your appreciation** of the subject, most entries include photographic portraits.
- **Sources for additional information** direct the user to selected books, magazines, and newspapers where more information on the individuals can be obtained.

Helpful Indexes Make It Easy to Find the Information You Need

Contemporary Black Biography includes cumulative Nationality, Occupation, Subject, and Name indexes that make it easy to locate entries in a variety of useful ways.

Available in Electronic Formats

Diskette/Magnetic Tape. Contemporary Black Biography is available for licensing on magnetic tape or diskette in a fielded format. Either the complete database or a custom selection of entries may be ordered. The database is available for internal data processing and nonpublishing purposes only. For more information, call (800) 877-GALE.

On-line. Contemporary Black Biography is available online through Mead Data Central's NEXIS Service in the NEXIS, PEOPLE and SPORTS Libraries in the GALBIO file and Gale's Biography Resource Center.

Disclaimer

Contemporary Black Biography uses and lists websites as sources and these websites may become obsolete.

We Welcome Your Suggestions

The editors welcome your comments and suggestions for enhancing and improving *Contemporary Black Biography.* If you would like to suggest persons for inclusion in the series, please submit these names to the editors. Mail comments or suggestions to:

The Editor

Contemporary Black Biography

Thomson Gale

27500 Drake Rd.

Farmington Hills, MI 48331-3535

Phone: (800) 347-4253

Arnez J

1966?—

Comedian

Diverging from the hard-edged raunchy and streetwise observational styles of other contemporary African-American comedians, Arnez J offers comic routines reminiscent of an earlier era of comedy. His improvisational comic style is primarily physical, with a strong reliance on impressions and exaggerations of familiar personalities. "J is a whirling dervish on stage—he runs, jumps, spins, slides, slips, and mugs through a performance, acting out many of his bits while describing them," wrote Doug Kaufman in the *St. Louis Post-Dispatch.* His idols are the classic television comedians of the 1960s: Flip Wilson, Red Skelton, and a performer who might be considered an unlikely inspiration for a modern African-American male artist. "There was never a nicer and funnier comedian to me than Carol Burnett," Arnez J explained to Daniel Neman of the *Richmond Times Dispatch.* "*The Carol Burnett Show,* to me, will never be replaced."

Arnez J has been close-mouthed about his age and, in recent years, about much of his background including his full name. But various media have given his name as Arnez Johnson, and the *Times Dispatch* reported that he was 12 years old when *The Carol Burnett Show* went off the air in 1978, which would place his birth date in the middle of the comedy golden age that shaped his own style. Some newspapers reported that he was born in Atlanta, but he grew up in a military family and never called one place home for long. That fact, according to Arnez J, shaped his choice of career. "I think most people remember things beginning when they were seven," he told Neman. "But I remember things from when I was four, because when I was four I was in Germany, in Hannover. My father was in the military, and I remember he was in the field a lot. I think I was more of a studier of human nature."

Television had a strong impact on Arnez J. After watching *Superman* one time, he tied a towel around his neck and jumped off the roof of his family's home, landing in some bushes. He was a convincing enough liar to land a job at a gas station when he was 14. Spending part of his teenage years in the Denver area, though, Arnez J excelled not in performing arts but in sports. He attended Aurora High School, where he was both a baseball star (at third base) and a strong professional basketball prospect. Baseball was his first love. But a criminal act that Arnez J refuses to discuss landed him in prison for a year in the early 1980s and scuttled his chances to win a spot with the Philadelphia Phillies organization. "All I'll say is that I was young and stupid and somebody got hurt and I did some time," Arnez J told Ed Condran of the Bergen County (New Jersey) *Record.* "It hurt real bad, because I was being scouted, and you only get one or two chances to play serious baseball."

After his release from prison, Arnez J thought about his broken dreams of sports stardom and sank into what he described as a two-year depression. In the late 1980s, however, he put his life back together, going through training and landing a job as a Continental Airlines flight attendant. His talent for getting a laugh from passengers wedged into jets made him think about a new career. "I entertained the passengers—always," he recalled to Bruce Westbrook of the *Houston Chronicle.* "If I went to San Francisco, I'd be a gay

At a Glance . . .

Born c. 1966; grew up in military family and traveled frequently; married; children: JeLaney (son).

Career: Continental Airlines, flight attendant, late 1980s-early 1990s; comedian and actor, 1990s–; Harlem Globetrotters, basketball player, 1995-96.

Selected awards: Bay Area Black Comedy Competition, finalist, 1992.

Address: *Agent*—Patterson & Associates, 20318 Hiawatha St., Suite 100, Chatsworth, CA 91311.

flight attendant, or for Boston, I'd be real hard and snobby. But people knew I was putting them on." His talent for impressions carried over into his career as a comedian, and he boasted to Kaufman that "I can basically do anybody I study."

Arnez J began trying out his comedy skills at Atlanta-area clubs, making his debut at the Comedy Act in 1990. At first he was booed, but he stuck with it. Three months after he started doing comedy, a performance he gave at Zanie's in Mount Prospect, Illinois, was taped for broadcast on cable television's *Showtime Comedy Club Network*. Five months after that, he was booked into Lake Tahoe, California, for the network's *Comedy Club All-Stars* special—and found himself a fish out of water. "My live comedy was about what my life was in the inner city," he told Allan Johnson of the *Chicago Tribune*. But at Lake Tahoe, he faced audiences "45 and above, and white."

Finding a more comfortable niche on programs like Black Entertainment Television's *Comic View* and becoming a finalist in the 1992 Bay Area Black Comedy Competition, Arnez J also began to appeal more and more to racially mixed audiences. One factor in his broad-based appeal was his avoidance of profanity in his shows, which attracted family-oriented fans of all races. "I'm not going to sell myself short by [cursing]," he told Kaufman, "because No. 1, I have a son. I'm just not going to do that. And No. 2, I don't curse in my daily life, why would I do it on stage? Then I'm contradicting myself."

In 1995, Arnez J got a chance to combine his ambitions as an athlete and performer: he was recruited by scouts for the famed Harlem Globetrotters basketball team. In 1996 he joined the team, but three months later a knee injury ended his Globetrotters career. "Apparently I'm meant to make a living as a comedian, which is fine," he observed to Condran. In the late 1990s, Arnez J became a familiar face on the comedy circuit and landed plum television spots on *Russell Simmons' Def Comedy Jam* A&E's *An Evening at the Improv*, and Comedy Central's *Make Me Laugh*, among other shows. After a half-hour solo special on BET, Arnez J became the host of *Comic View* in 2002.

As his career developed, Arnez J branched out into new activities. He toured with actor Billy Dee Williams in a play called *The Maintenance Man*, playing a nightclub owner, and he performed as an opening act for the Artist Formerly Known as Prince. Arnez J moved to Los Angeles, and indeed film seemed to offer the best new potential avenue for his talents. He starred in the independent film *Up Against the 8-Ball*, and hoped to make more movies. "We've missed good slapstick comedy," he told Westbrook. An enterprising director might find in Arnez J an ideal performer for the revival of a type of comedy that had gone out of fashion.

Selected works

Films

Up Against the 8-Ball, 2004.

Plays

The Maintenance Man, 2004.

Television

Showtime Comedy Club Network, 1990.
Comic View, 1992–.

Sources

Periodicals

Chicago Tribune, September 28, 2001, p. 8.
Columbus Dispatch, September 5, 2002, Weekender sec., p. 11.
Commercial Appeal (Memphis), July 9, 2004, p. G34.
Houston Chronicle, June 19, 2003, Preview sec., p. 16.
Post-Tribune (Gary, IN), April 23, 2004, p. D4.
Record (Bergen County, NJ), May 28, 2004, p. G16.
Richmond Times Dispatch (Richmond, VA), July 31, 2003, p. D30.
Sacramento Observer, July 8, 1998, p. E3.
St. Louis Post-Dispatch, August 1, 2002, Get Out sec., p. 29.
Tennessean (Nashville), November 29, 2003, p. E6.

—James M. Manheim

Jean Augustine

1937—

Politician

Augustine, Jean, photograph. AP/Wide World Photos. Reproduced by permission

In 1993 Jean Augustine made Canadian political history as the first black woman ever elected to the nation's House of Commons. Nine years later, Augustine achieved yet another historic advance when she became the first woman of African heritage to serve as a cabinet minister in Canada. "Being the first black feels good, yes, but more than that, it says to others and to ourselves that blacks can be in every place in society," she told Vernon Clement Jones of Toronto's *Globe & Mail* newspaper in the spring of 2002, not long after being appointed Canada's newest Secretary of State for Multiculturalism and the Status of Women. "It's important that no one be able to say that blacks can't perform in every segment of Canadian society because we can."

Never Knew Her Father

Augustine is one of a large number of Caribbean immigrants who came to Canada in the years following World War II. She was born on September 9, 1937, in Grenada, an island nation in the southeastern Caribbean Sea that was then still part of the British colonial empire. She grew up in a village called Happy Hill near Grenada's capital of St. George's. Her father, Ossie Simon, was a sugarcane-plantation worker, but he died before she was a year old after a deadly bout with tetanus, which he contracted during a visit to the dentist.

Augustine's mother, Olive, was already expecting a second child when her husband died, and the entire family was adopted by an older woman in the village, whom they called "Granny." Granny had no children of her own, but owned some property and was moderately well-off. Such communal and charitable arrangements were more commonplace in West Indian society during Augustine's youth. Granny's was a household in which Augustine was encouraged to excel in school, and she did. She won a scholarship to a local Roman Catholic school, where she earned top grades. During her high-school years, she founded an all-girl band and also hosted her own youth program on a local radio station before graduating a year early.

Augustine's first job was as a schoolteacher in Grenada, but her pay was less than $10 a month. On Sundays she would write letters for other Grenadians who had never learned to read or write, but wanted to keep in

At a Glance . . .

Born on September 9, 1937, in Happy Hill, St. George's, Grenada; daughter of Ossie and Olive Simon; married Winston Augustine, 1968 (divorced, 1981); children: Valerie, Cheryl. *Education:* Earned degree from Toronto Teacher's College, 1963; earned M.Ed. from the University of Toronto. *Politics:* Liberal Party of Canada. *Religion:* Roman Catholic.

Career: Elementary school teacher in Grenada; nanny for a Toronto family, c. 1959, and clerk in a medical-billing firm; became elementary school teacher in the Toronto public school system, and then vice principal and principal; named chair of the Metro Toronto Housing Authority, late 1980s; Canadian House of Commons, Member of Parliament, 1993–; served as Parliamentary Secretary to the Prime Minister, c. 1995-2005; Secretary of State for Multiculturalism and the Status of Women in Canada, Canadian government, 2002-04; Special Advisor for Grenada, Canadian government, 2004–.

Selected memberships: York University, board of governors; The Hospital for Sick Children, Toronto, board of trustees; Donwood Institute, board of directors; Harbourfront Corporation, board of directors; Metro Toronto Housing Authority, Chair; Congress of Black Women of Canada, national president.

Selected awards: YWCA Woman of Distinction Award; Kaye Livingstone Award; Ontario Volunteer Award; Pride Newspaper Achievement Award; Rubena Willis Special Recognition Award; Toronto Lions' Club Onyx Award. .

Addresses: *Office*—Rm. 433, West Block, House of Commons, Ottawa, ON K1A 0A6, Canada; *Home*—80 Rayside Dr., Etobicoke, ON M9C 1T1, Canada.

touch with relatives living overseas. This experience exposed Augustine to people who had left the West Indies in search of better economic opportunities, and at the age of 22 she herself moved to Toronto, Ontario, Canada, to take a job as a nanny. She arrived on a special visa the Canadian government gave out to citizens of other nations inside the British colonial realm, which required her to work one year as a domestic servant. After that period was finished, she would then be free to stay in Canada permanently if she wished.

Earned Teaching Degree

Augustine was fortunate, however, for she had been placed with a Toronto pediatrician's family who were of a generous spirit, and they recognized that the new caretaker for their children was overly qualified for the job. They helped her find an office job at a medical-billing firm, and she took night-school classes at the Toronto Teacher's College and babysat for the family in her spare time. After earning her teaching degree, Augustine taught elementary school in the Toronto public school system. She eventually became one of the first black school principals in the country.

Augustine had long been active in black political and social organizations in Toronto, which began to emerge as a richly multinational and multicultural hub during the 1960s. The very first meeting of the Grenada Association was held in her apartment, and she also served on a committee that helped to organize the city's first Caribana Festival in 1967, which later became one of Toronto's most important annual tourist events.

Augustine's community service work led her into politics. She served on municipal task forces on drug abuse and crime, and became active in the Liberal Party, one of Canada's two main political parties. In 1985 she was named to the transition team for new Ontario premier David Peterson. As thanks for her service, Peterson made her chair of the Metro Toronto Housing Authority, the largest landowner in Canada. Augustine served in that post for six years, and came to the attention of the national Liberal Party leadership as a result.

Stunning Victory at the Polls

In 1993, Liberal Party leader Jean Chrétien nominated her for a place on the party ticket for the coming general elections, which allowed her to bypass the usual party nomination process. She was the Liberal Party candidate for a seat in the House of Commons from Etobicoke-Lakeshore, a section of Toronto. Her victory at the polls that year was all the more significant given the fact that her riding, or electoral district, did not have a strong black political base; in fact, of Etobicoke-Lakeshore's 65,000 voters, just 700 were black Canadians.

Augustine became the first black woman to serve in the House of Commons, and joined one other African-Canadian there, Ovid Jackson, a fellow Liberal Party MP (member of parliament) also of Caribbean heritage. She earned some unfavorable publicity, however, when reporters asked her on election night about how it felt to be Canada's first black woman parliamentarian. "I didn't run as a black politician," *Chatelaine* writer Cecil

Foster quoted her as saying. "I ran as a competent woman who is Canadian." Though some viewed her statement as a rebuff to the black community in Canada, Augustine's supporters pointed out that she had long been active in serving the African-Caribbean émigré community in Ontario.

Appointed to Cabinet

Chrétien had become Prime Minister thanks to the Liberal Party's victory at the polls in that 1993 election. He named Augustine to a two-year stint as his Parliamentary Secretary, which gave her a prominent place during legislative sessions in the House of Commons with a seat located just behind the Prime Minister's. Her duties included responding to questions on behalf of Chrétien or his cabinet ministers when they were unable to attend House of Commons sessions. She also earned high marks for her primary role representing Etobicoke-Lakeshore, and she went on to serve on the foreign affairs committee in the House of Commons. Her constituency returned her to the House of Commons in the 1997 and 2000 elections. In May of 2002, Chrétien made Augustine Secretary of State for Multiculturalism and the Status of Women in Canada. She was the first black woman in the cabinet in the 135-year history of Canada's federal government and served until 2004. She was reelected to the House of Commons that same year by a large majority.

Augustine is divorced and has two grown children. Back in Grenada, she is a well-known figure and object of national pride. After her impressive first House of Commons win, Grenadians presented her with a plaque that read simply, "From Happy Hill to Parliament Hill." She remains grateful to Granny, who died in 1967, and to her other family members and friends who have also passed away. "I know they would have been so proud to know that I've come to this country," she told Foster in *Chatelaine,* "and I've reached the highest place in the land."

Sources

Periodicals

Chatelaine, November 1994, p. 52.
Globe & Mail (Toronto, ON), June 7, 2002.

On-line

"Jean Augustine," *Liberal Party of Canada,* www.liberal.ca/bio_e.aspx?&id=35023 (July 6, 2005).

—Carol Brennan

John Barnes

1963—

Professional soccer player, soccer analyst

Barnes, John, photograph. © Rune Hellestad/Corbis.

During his stellar career as a professional soccer, or football, player in England, John Barnes played for England 79 times, scoring 12 goals. He was a member of the Liverpool team that won the league title in 1988 and 1990, the Football Association (FA) Cup in 1989 and 1992, and the League Cup in 1995. He was the first black player to win the Football Writers' Association Player of the Year award in 1988; he also won the prestigious Professional Footballers' Association (PFA) Footballer of the Year award that same year. His professional career lasted 18 years, all but one season of it as a member of teams in the highest league division. Two images of John Barnes are remembered most clearly by English soccer fans; the first being his stunning individual goal for England against Brazil in 1984, and the second his dismissive back-heeling of a banana thrown onto the pitch by racists.

John Barnes was born in Kingston, Jamaica, on November 11, 1963, and moved to England as a child. He was spotted by a talent scout from Watford FC while playing soccer in a park and made his professional debut for the team in 1981. By the following season Watford had been promoted to the English first division (now the Premiership). Watford flourished under manager Graham Taylor and so did Barnes. He was a member of the team's impressive 1983 European Cup campaign and in the following year enjoyed second place to Liverpool in the league as well as collecting an FA Cup finalist's medal.

By then he had come to the attention of England coach Bobby Robson, making his international debut in 1983. But it was in 1984 that Barnes became an England regular when he scored a remarkable individual goal against Brazil on June 10, 1984, at the Maracana stadium in Rio de Janeiro. Barnes collected the ball at the halfway line and beat five Brazilian defenders to score one of the most memorable goals ever achieved by an England player. He went on to play 79 times for England, scoring 12 goals, but despite some notable contributions his best performances always seemed to come at club level.

Even so, Barnes's England career was long and at times dramatic. As a player he could turn games around with his power and pace and had the ability to energize a whole team. For example he was brought on with 15 minutes to go against Argentina in the 1986 World

At a Glance . . .

Born John Charles Bryan Barnes on November 11, 1963, in Kingston, Jamaica; children: Jamie, Jordan, Jemma, Jasmine.

Career: Watford FC, 1981-87; Liverpool AFC, 1987-97; Newcastle United FC, 1997-98; Charlton Athletic, 1998-99; Glasgow Celtic (as manager), 1999-2000; TV football (soccer) analyst, 1998–.

Memberships: Save the Children, ambassador.

Awards: English Football League Championship winner, 1988, 1990 (Liverpool); FA Cup Winner, 1989, 1992 (Liverpool); FA Cup runner-up, 1984 (Watford), 1988, 1996 (Liverpool), 1998 (Newcastle); League Cup Winner, 1995 (Liverpool); Football Writers' Association Player of the Year award, 1988, 1990; Professional Footballers' Association (PFA) Footballer of the year Award, 1988.

Cup quarterfinals when England was 2-0 down and Barnes single-handedly dismantled the Argentine defense, setting up a goal and a missed chance for teammate Gary Lineker. But by the early 1990s England was a team of underachievers and Barnes became the focus for the fans' discontent.

When Graham Taylor moved away from Watford in 1987 Barnes also left and joined Liverpool, one of the most successful English clubs of the decade, for a fee of £900,000. His time at Liverpool brought him many awards and accolades, including two league titles (1988, 1990), two FA Cup winner's medals (1989, 1992), two runner's up medals (1988, 1996), and a League Cup winner's medal (1995). In his most successful season, 1989-90, he made 34 appearances and scored 22 goals, an outstanding tally for a midfield player. He was rewarded for this performance in 1990 when he was named Football Writers' Association Player of the Year for the second time. Two years earlier in 1988 he had been the first black player to receive award and also picked up the Professional Footballers' Association Footballer of the Year award.

In all Barnes scored 70 goals for Liverpool in the 10 years he spent at the club. He also performed an ill-advised rap on the team's traditional FA Cup final single in 1989, a skill he demonstrated again with greater success on the England World Cup 1990 record, "World in Motion" with the band New Order. "World in Motion" made the number one spot in the British charts. But Barnes was not always happy at Liverpool; when he first arrived he was the target of some vicious racist abuse. Like most black players, Barnes was accustomed to racism among football fans—his remarkable individual goal against Brazil in 1984 took place in front of abusive far-right National Front activists who were outraged that he had been picked for the England team. But the issue became big news when Liverpool played local rivals Everton in 1988 and Barnes was abused with "monkey" noises and had bananas thrown at him. One well-known image was captured by a press photographer who spotted Barnes dismissively back-heeling a banana off the pitch. Barnes told BBC Sport: "Because Liverpool v. Everton was a very high-profile game a lot was made of it, but that sort of thing had been going on for years and years." Barnes has since been outspoken about the problem of racism in the soccer world, saying that British society has to change, not just soccer.

Another dark period in Barnes's career at Liverpool came in the aftermath of the Hillsborough Stadium disaster, which took place during the 1989 FA Cup semi-final between Liverpool and Nottingham Forest. Barnes was on the pitch when 96 Liverpool fans were crushed to death during a crowd surge and he was heavily involved with comforting survivors and relatives in the hospital, and attending funerals of the victims. He explained in his autobiography: "Before Hillsborough, I had always tried to keep things in perspective but what happened on the Leppings Lane terraces made me question so much in my life. When I struggled to get in the team at Liverpool and then Newcastle United, I said to myself, 'Does it really matter?'"

For the part he took in helping fans recover from Hillsborough, and for his long service to the club, Barnes became one of Liverpool's biggest heroes. But in 1997, at age 34, he moved to Newcastle United, where he was reunited with Kenny Dalglish, a former Liverpool manager and playing star. Barnes featured in over 40 games for Newcastle, boosting their European Champions' League squad and appearing in yet another FA Cup final, losing to Arsenal in 1998. But by then he was struggling to win a place in the team and moved to London-based Charlton, where he ended his playing career in 1999.

After leaving Charlton Barnes took the common step of entering soccer management. But rather than beginning with a small club where he could learn away from the glare of the media, he joined one of Scotland's top teams, Celtic, alongside his mentor Kenny Dalglish, who was by then director of soccer. Despite some success early in the season, Barnes was criticized for his team selections and tactics and left within a few months. He then became a sports broadcaster on the British television channel ITV and later on Channel 5. Besides working in television, he is also involved in education projects to promote the anti-racist message and is an ambassador for the charity Save the Children.

Selected works

Books

John Barnes: The Autobiography, Headline, 1999.

Sources

Books

Barnes, John, *John Barnes: The Autobiography*, Headline, 1999.

Periodicals

Guardian (London, England), February 10, 2000; March 12, 2004.

On-line

"Barnes Is on the Ball," *Children's Express*, www.childrens-express.org/dynamic/public/barnes_is_191101.htm (March 22, 2005).

"John Barnes," *AFIWI: Your Caribbean Online*, www.afiwi.com/people2.asp?id=163&name=John+Barnes&coun=0&cat=1&options=&keywords=&alpha_index=&offset= (March 23, 2005).

"John Barnes," *ITV Football*, www.itv-football.co.uk/The_ITV_Team/The_Pundits/story_67776.shtml (March 23, 2005).

"John Barnes Autobiography," *Hillsborough Football Disaster*, www.contrast.org/hillsborough/history/barnes.shtm (March 22, 2005).

"Society Has to Change—Barnes," *BBC Sport World Football*, http://news.bbc.co.uk/sport1/hi/tv_and_radio/world_football/2399629.stm (March 22, 2005).

—Chris Routledge

Fantasia Barrino

1984—

Vocalist

Barrino, Fantasia, photograph. Evan Agostini/Getty Images

The third-season winner of television's *American Idol* singing competition in 2004, Fantasia Barrino, stood out from tough competition for two reasons. Above all, she was a vocal powerhouse, a singer with the kind of raw vocal talent the program's voting audience hadn't encountered before. And she made a strong emotional connection with that audience, showing a human side in addition to sheer vocal virtuosity. In both respects, Barrino's triumphant performances on *American Idol* were rooted in her pre-stardom life in High Point, North Carolina: as a gospel singer at Mercy Outreach Church of Deliverance, and as a single mother enduring and then overcoming domestic abuse.

Barrino was born in High Point on June 30, 1984. Music-making ran through both sides of her family. Her father Joseph Barrino sang in gospel quartets beginning in his teenage years. Her mother Diane, co-pastor at Mercy Outreach, also sang, as did two of her brothers, one of whom served as a church choir director. Barrino told interviewer Elizabeth Vargas of ABC television's *20/20* that "I've been singing ever since I was five years old. I would go in the bathroom and put my mom's clothes on, get something, act like it was a microphone, and just make my own videos." Tasia, as relatives called her, toured with the family gospel group, the Barrino Family, from the time she was nine or ten years old, performing as far away as Maryland and Florida.

Grew Up in "Shouting Church"

"Everybody that we talk to makes the comment that 'she seems so confident,'" Joseph Barrino told *Winston-Salem Journal* reporter Tim Clodfelter. "Well, yes, because she's been [performing] since she was a child." Even when performing for a national television audience, Fantasia Barrino told Clodfelter, she was never nervous. "I'm in a zone," she said. "When I'm singing, I'm in my own little world. I just tune [the audience] out. I really don't see them." The transcendent quality of Barrino's performances came partly from the worship style of Mercy Outreach, which Raleigh *News & Observer* writer Thomasi McDonald described as a "'shouting church,' led by pastors who stoke a holy fire and members who don't mind laying their burdens down." Barrino herself became choir director and praise team leader at Mercy Outreach.

At a Glance . . .

Born on June 30, 1984, in High Point, NC; daughter of Joseph (a gospel singer) and Diane (a preacher) Barrino; children: one daughter, Zion. *Education:* Studied toward GED while competing in *American Idol. Religion:* Served as praise team leader and choir director at Mercy Outreach Church of Deliverance, High Point.

Career: Won *American Idol* television singing competition, 2004; hosted *Soul Train* awards show, 2005.

Addresses: *Label*—c/o J-Records, LLC, 745 5th Ave., 6th Floor, New York, NY 10151. *Other*—c/o American Idol, P.O. Box 900, Beverly Hills, CA 90213-0900. *Web*—www.fantasiabarrinoofficial.com.

At High Point's Welborn Middle School, Barrino made the all-county chorus. Shortly after she entered Andrews High School, however, she became pregnant and dropped out to give birth to her daughter, Zion. Barrino struggled financially, singing at weddings or wherever else she could to help pay the bills. And she was physically abused by her partner, Brandel Schauss, who was arrested at one point for punching and choking her. Barrino told Vargas that "things just started going really downhill for me. You know, I don't talk about it a lot.... Sometimes that abuse feels like love to you. Sometimes that's all you know."

Studied During Early *Idol* Rounds

Wanting to set a positive example for her daughter, Barrino finally mustered the strength to leave her abuser. She made plans to enroll in a community college to earn a high school equivalency degree (and she brought books to Los Angeles and studied high school course materials during the run of *American Idol*). Her up-and-down experiences gave her a depth and a level of self-confidence that many of her *American Idol* competitors lacked. Friends and family members persuaded her to enter the contest, an idea Barrino resisted at first because she was intimidated by the show's caustic British host, Simon Cowell. But Cowell was impressed by Barrino in the early rounds and set his usual critical style aside. "You have a lot of terrible people turn up," he told Vargas. "And then when one person comes in with what I call the 'X' factor, you just know you've seen somebody special. She just nailed it."

Controversy flared as Barrino advanced to the final rounds of the competition. Some viewers questioned whether Barrino's past made her a good role model. Her onstage confidence sometimes came off as cockiness. And in a well-publicized incident, singer Elton John leveled charges of racism against the show's organizers when Barrino and several other African-American contestants were grouped in one round in such a way that one was sure to be eliminated. Barrino, deciding that a dramatic move was needed, prepared a song that she had never heard prior to the *American Idol* competition. Her favorite music was gospel, and she also enjoyed the music of the rock group Aerosmith. But she selected the George Gershwin classic "Summertime," from the 1937 opera *Porgy and Bess.*

Won *American Idol* Competition

The effect on audiences was electric. "And so, on 'Summertime,' I was like, I'm going to go out and I'm gonna sit on that stage and I'm gonna humble myself. And people were actually crying in the audience." The normally unflappable Barrino gave in to tears herself. She advanced to the final round against Georgia teenager Diana DeGarmo, niece of 1980s Christian rock vocalist Eddie DeGarmo. Barrino delivered powerful performances in the final rounds and edged DeGarmo in nationwide voting on May 26, 2004. A record 65 million votes were cast. "I been through some things but I worked hard to get to where I'm at," Barrino said after winning (as quoted in the Memphis *Commercial Appeal*).

The victory brought Barrino ongoing fame. She went on a concert tour and made several special appearances, including one in a tribute to Elton John at the Kennedy Center Honors in Washington, D.C., in December of 2004. "There were so many awesome people in the house," she told Janice Gaston of the *Winston-Salem Journal.* "The president was there!" Closer to home, she was able to buy her mother a $500,000 home in Charlotte, North Carolina—and her daughter Zion a Barbie Jeep that she had been unable to afford the previous Christmas. In February of 2005 she hosted the annual *Soul Train* televised music awards program.

Barrino's debut album, *Free Yourself,* was released (with the artist billed simply as Fantasia) in November of 2004 on the J-Records label, with direction from music industry veteran Clive Davis. Unlike earlier releases by *American Idol* winners, Barrino's was a cutting-edge affair that drew on creative contributions by hot hip-hop artists and producers such as Missy Elliott, Jermaine Dupri, and Rodney "Darkchild" Jerkins. Her debut single, the gospel-flavored "I Believe," debuted at Number One on *Billboard* magazine's Hot 100 singles chart, and another track, "Baby Mama," seemed to draw on Barrino's experiences as a single mom. Teen listeners identified with the song, Barrino told Gaston; they came up to her and told her, "I'm a baby mama." "That's cool," Barrino would respond. But then she would ask: "What are you doing to try to better yourself?"

Selected works

Albums

(as Fantasia) *Free Yourself,* J-Records, 2004.

Books

Life Is Not a Fairy Tale (memoir), Touchstone Fireside, forthcoming.

Sources

Periodicals

Commercial Appeal (Memphis), May 27, 2004, p. A1.

Essence, September 2004, p. 292.

Jet, June 14, 2004, p. 56; January 10, 2005, p. 54.

News & Observer (Raleigh, NC), May 26, 2004, p. A1; July 5, 2004, p. C1.

People Weekly, December 6, 2004.

Winston-Salem Journal, March 14, 2004, p. E1; February 5, 2005, p. B1.

On-line

Fantasia Barrino Official Site, www.fantasiabarrinoofficial.com (June 29, 2005).

Other

20/20 (ABC News Transcripts), November 12, 2004.

—James M. Manheim

Tritobia Hayes Benjamin

1944—

Art historian, educator

Benjamin, Dr. Tritobia Hayes, photograph. Photo by Jarvis Grant.

A distinguished art historian and champion of black artists, Tritobia Hayes Benjamin has been a member of the Art Department at Howard University since 1970. She was made full professor of art history in 1993 and is associate dean of the Division of Fine Arts and director of the Howard University Gallery of Art. A respected authority on black American women artists, she has written many articles and exhibition catalogues. Benjamin is the author of an acclaimed book about African-American artist Lois Mailou Jones, has won many awards and fellowships, and is a member of many prestigious organizations. She has been responsible for seeking and developing a new building to house the Gallery of Art with the aim of making the permanent collection more accessible to students, faculty, and the wider public.

Born in Brinkley, Arkansas, on October 22, 1944, Tritobia Hayes Benjamin attended Howard University, where she received her bachelor's degree in art history in 1968 and her master's degree in 1970. In 1991 she was awarded a Ph.D. in art history at the University of Maryland. She is married to Donald S. Benjamin and they have three children, Zalika Aminah, Aminah Liani, and Anwar Salih.

Benjamin's academic career began in 1970 when she was employed as an instructor in art history at Georgetown University. At the same time she worked as an instructor at Howard University, and she went on to become an assistant professor in the Art Department in 1973, associate professor in 1977, and full professor in 1993. In the meantime she served at Howard and elsewhere in other capacities. In 1978 she was named Cafritz Guest Lecturer, a position funded by the Cafritz Foundation, which seeks to enhance the lives of Washington, D.C., residents by awarding grants that support artistic and cultural projects. In this period she was also guest curator at the Afro-American Institute, where she delivered an exhibition entitled "African Artists in America."

Benjamin's career has been focussed in particular on the work of African American women artists and she has done a great deal to promote their work in the United States and abroad. The painter Lois Mailou Jones, who was also Benjamin's teacher, colleague, and friend at Howard, has been the subject of several of her articles. Benjamin's book, *The Life and Art of*

At a Glance . . .

Born Tritobia Hayes on October 22, 1944, in Brinkley, Arkansas; married Donald S. Benjamin; children: Zalika Aminah, Aminah Liani, Anwar Salih. *Education*: Howard University, BA, 1968; MA, 1970; University of Maryland, PhD, 1991.

Career: Georgetown University, instructor, 1970; Howard University, instructor, 1970-73, assistant professor, 1973-77, associate professor, 1977-93, professor, 1993–, associate dean, Division of Fine Arts, 1993–; Howard University Gallery of Art, curator of exhibits and director.

Memberships: National Conference of Artists; College Art Association; Smithsonian National Associates; Studio Museum, Harlem; National Museum of American Art.

Awards: National Endowment for the Humanities, Fellowships-in-Residence for College Teachers, 1975-76, National Endowment for the Humanities Fellowship for Faculty of Historically Black Colleges and Universities, 1984-85; Howard University School of Education, Spencer Foundation Research Award, 1975-77; Eta Phi Sigma, honorary member, 1986; United Negro College Fund, PEW Humanities Fellowship Grant, 1986-87; Howard University, Office of the VP for Academic Affairs, Faculty Research Grant in the Social Sciences, Humanities, and Education, 1988-89.

Addresses: *Office*—Associate Dean, Division of Fine Arts, College of Arts and Sciences, Howard University, 2455 6th St NW, Washington, DC 20059-0002.

Lois Mailou Jones (1994), was widely praised for having rediscovered an artist unjustly ignored. As the reviewer in *American Artist* put it, until Benjamin's book appeared Lois Mailou Jones had "fallen through the cracks," while Donna Seaman, writing in *Booklist*, states that Benjamin "covers each stage of Jones' 'triumphant' life with knowledgeable enthusiasm and deep respect."

Benjamin has written on other black artists, including sculptor Selma Hortense Burke and painter Annie E.A. Walker, and has contributed to the organization and presentation of many exhibitions. In 1989 she served as cultural consultant for a Washington-Moscow cultural exchange and throughout her career has worked tirelessly to serve the academic and artistic communities through her work in various committees and organizations. In particular she is a member of the National Conference of Artists, the College Art Association, Smithsonian National Associates, The Studio Museum in Harlem, and the National Museum of American Art.

Benjamin reached the highest academic level in 1993 when she became full professor, and later was named director of the Gallery of Art at Howard. In addition, she has also received many awards, including a National Endowment for the Humanities Fellowship-in-Residence for College Teachers, which she held in 1975-76, and the Fellowship for Faculty of Historically Black Colleges and Universities from the National Endowment for the Humanities in 1984-85. Her work in exhibiting and developing the work of black American artists has been recognized at an international level throughout her distinguished career of over 30 years.

Selected writings

Books

The Life and Art of Lois Mailou Jones, Pomegranate Artbooks, 1994.

Periodicals

"Color, Structure, Design: The Artistic Expressions of Lois Mailou Jones," *The International Review of African-American Arts,* 1991.

"Selma Hortense Burke, American Sculptor" and "Lois Mailou Jones, American Painter," in *Black Women in America, An Historical Encyclopedia*, Carlson Publishing Inc., 1992.

"Annie E.A. Walker, Painter," in *Dictionary of American Negro Biography*, W.W. Norton, 1993.

"Lois Mailou Jones: The Decorative Patterns of Her Life," *American Visions*, June-July 1993.

Sources

Periodicals

American Artist, September 1995, p. 88.

Booklist, February 15, 1995, p. 1050.

On-line

"AAWI Profiles: Tritobia Hayes Benjamin, PhD," *African American Women's Institute*, http://ora.howard.edu/centers/aawi/benjamin.htm (June 8, 2005).

Howard University Gallery of Art, www.howard.edu/CollegeFineArts/gallery_final/galleryofart.html (June 8, 2005).

"Tritobia Hayes Benjamin," *Howard University*, www.coas.howard.edu/chairsbios/tobibio.pdf (June 8, 2005).

—Chris Routledge

Lamont Bentley

1973-2005

Actor, rapper

Bentley, Lamont, photograph. UPN/Landov.

Known for his charisma and talent, actor Lamont Bentley stole the hearts of television and movie viewers from the time he was a teen. Debuting on a 1986 Starburst commercial, the young actor went on to play bit parts in several television series and movies. His first recurring role came in 1994 on the short-lived, but critically acclaimed show *South Central.* But he was best known for his role on the popular mid-1990s television series *Moesha*, where he played Hakeem Campbell opposite award-winning rhythm and blues singer Brandy. At the height of his acting career and at the start of a promising rapping career, Bentley was tragically killed in an automobile accident near Simi Valley, California, on January 18, 2005, at the age of 31. His mother and two young daughters were living with him at the time of his death.

Artimus Lamont Bentley was born in Milwaukee, Wisconsin, on October 25, 1973, to Loyce Bentley and Donald L. Gardison. Bentley and his sister grew up on Milwaukee's north side of town and attended Webster Middle School. Bentley was bent on stardom from an early age, and his friends recalled him preparing for stardom by practicing his autograph when he was 12 years old, according to the *Milwaukee Journal Sentinal.* Known by most as Lamont, he was also affectionately called "Cuz" and "My Guy" by his friends. Although Bentley moved to the west coast in his early teens, Milwaukee stayed close to his heart. After Bentley became famous, he would lavish attention and kindness on anyone he met from Milwaukee. His winning personality made many consider him "a cousin, a brother, a son, a friend," as local Milwaukee radio personality Reggie Brown recalled at his funeral service, according to the *Milwaukee Journal Sentinal.*

Bentley's mother, Loyce, moved her family to Los Angeles to pursue her own singing career when Bentley was 13 years old. But whenever she would audition for a part, her son stole the show. His own goals to become a star and his ability to make people laugh eventually caused someone to suggest that he become a child comic—which he did. His first role was cast in a 1986 Starburst commercial. He went on to portray juveniles in a variety of circumstances: most notably, he played a teenage father who opted to stay home with

At a Glance . . .

Born Artimus Lamont Bentley on October 25, 1973, in Milwaukee, Wisconsin; died in a car accident on January 18, 2005; children: Artesia and Brazil.

Career: Actor, 1986-2005; rap musician, 1990s-2005.

his child instead of turn out for the high school football team in a public service television announcement.

Hooked on acting, Bentley dropped out of high school to pursue his career. But success came slowly, and Bentley had to take odd jobs in movie theaters, a fish market, and a grocery store, among other places as he waited for his big break. Bentley's youthful appearance enabled him to play the part of teens even into his twenties, and he landed a variety of small parts in television series and movies before landing bigger roles.

His first feature film role came in the 1995 horror movie *Tales from the Hood.* The movie, about the inner-city ganglands, is an anthology of four stories focused on the consequences of the gang lifestyle. Bentley's persona in the movie was cold and angry—a far cry from the young child comic of his youth. His portrayal of Crazy K was impressive, according to film critics. With chameleon-like acting qualities, Bentley proved that he could perform in horror, drama, and comedy.

In 1996 Bentley acquired a leading role on the television sitcom *Moesha.* For his comic portrayal of Hakeem Campbell, the always hungry friend of "Moesha," Bentley quickly gained recognition. He remained a favorite among dedicated viewers of the show until it was canceled in 2001 after six seasons. As the end of *Moesha* came close, Bentley related to the Indianapolis, Indiana, *Recorder* that his memories of the show were sweet: "The show gave me a lot of exposure and it has enabled me to realize some of my wildest dreams. Now I have stronger footing to go back into feature films and take on other TV roles, because I've proven that I can play both drama and comedy."

As *Moesha* played in syndication, Bentley went on to pursue both acting and musical opportunities. He landed a variety of parts in films and television movies, and formed a hip-hop duo called Uprise with partner Tyson. Before he became an actor, he had dabbled in rapping, so his musical focus was not a complete surprise. He was recording an album under rapper Coolio, and was in the process of releasing it at the time of his death.

When Oakland rapper Habitt released his new album *Talk of the Town* in May 2005, he dedicated it to Bentley, who was a close friend. Bentley had recorded a skit with Habitt for the new album titled *Shakin" It Up.* "It was such a shock to lose someone who is a friend like that," Habitt said. "I dedicated my album to Lamont. He was a true friend, and we all miss him a great deal," he said on the *Spokesman* Web site. Bentley's own hip-hop project Uprise had not secured a record deal at the time of his death, but his involvement in the rap and hip-hop culture was just another facet of his energy and talent as an entertainer.

Even after finding fame in California, Bentley did not forget his Wisconsin roots. He returned occasionally to host events for his own charitable organization, the Lamont Bentley Foundation, Inc., which distributed funds to local non-profit groups including Strive Media Institute and the Pentecostal Church School of Wisconsin. "He wasn't pompous" and he never flaunted a "big-star type attitude," attorney John Carlson commented in the *Milwaukee Journal Sentinal.* According to comedian D-Rock in the same article, "It wasn't about fame for Lamont. It was all about love."

Selected works

Films

Tales from the Hood, 1995.
The Breaks, 1999.
The Wash, 2001.

Television

South Central, 1994.
Moesha, UPN, 1996-2001.
Buffalo Soldiers (television movie), 1997.
The Parkers, 2000.
Too Legit to Quit: The MC Hammer Story (television movie), 2001.
Shards (television movie), 2004.
Sucker Free City (television movie), 2004.

Sources

Periodicals

Michigan Chronicle, November 20, 2001, p. D3.
Recorder (Indianapolis, IN), November 16, 2001, p. C1.
Variety, January 31-February 6, 2005, p. 69.

On-line

"Hakeem Killed in Car Crash," *The Spokesman*, www.msuspokesman.com (June 4, 2005).
"Milwaukee's Bentley Dies in Car Crash, *Milwaukee Journal Sentinal*, www.jsonline.com/enter/.asp (June 4, 2005).
"Sitcom Star Dreams Big," *Milwaukee Journal Sentinal,* www.jsonline.com/news/sunday/lifestyle/0817lunch.stm (August 30, 2005).

"Talents of Milwaukee Native Remembered," *Milwaukee Journal Sentinal*, www.jsonline.com/enter/tvradio/jan05/296222.asp (June 4, 2005).

—Cheryl Dudley

Beverly Bond

1970—

Disc jockey

Beverly Bond was born to DJ. Though her looks propelled her down fashion runways, it was music that set her heart flying. "Eventually the music chose me and I had to become a DJ," Bond told *Contemporary Black Biography* (*CBB*). Since setting up her turntables in 2000, Bond has captivated jet-setters, stylebreakers, and baggy-panted beat makers with her ingenious mixes. "People call me a hip-hop DJ, but really I play a lot more than that," she told *CBB*. Whether playing for thousands at a televised awards ceremony, or scratching out a more intimate vibe at a New York club, Bond's goal as a DJ and producer is simple. "I want to take the crowd on a journey when I DJ and not lose sight of what great music really is," she told *CBB*.

Became Model Record Collector

Beverly Bond was born on December 19, 1970, in New York City, though she was raised all over Maryland by her mother Mary Burroughs. "My mom was something of a rolling stone, she liked to move around," Bond told *CBB*. "So sometimes I lived with her, sometimes with other relatives." Throughout the moves, one thing stayed constant—music. "My mom really influenced me because she loved music," Bond told *CBB*. "She collected albums and was always really informed about music of all types, from Kurtis Blow to Hugh Masekela to Gladys Knight. She loved soul, African music, world music. She tried to really educate me on music."

Bond picked up her mother's habits and started collecting her own albums as a child. Soon it became an obsession. "For hip-hop [vinyl], you gotta get your old-school hip-hop, for soul you gotta go diggin' through every little record shop you can find, little mom-and-pop stores, thrift shops," she explained to the *Village Voice*. By the time she moved to New York, Bond had amassed hundreds of albums. "Everybody that came to my house thought I was a DJ cause they would see my record collection is crazy," Bond told the on-line hip-hop magazine, *SOHH*.

Despite her passion for music, Bond told *CBB*, "I didn't want to DJ because I thought it was such a huge responsibility, to keep all the people dancing, satisfied, and to keep the music interesting." Instead, at the age of 17 Bond moved to New York to pursue modeling. Her lithe, five-foot-nine frame and honeyed complexion landed her contracts at Elite New Faces and Wilhemina. She was soon strutting down runways and posing for clients such as Diesel Jeans, Guess, and Nike. Like a lot of New York models she was also a regular on the club scene; unlike most she was not there to be seen. "My mom loved to dance and was known as a dancer. I caught a lot of that too," Bond explained to *CBB*. "When I was modeling I'd go out at night dressed down in baggy pants and tennis shoes, real comfortable, and just dance. I was right out there battling with the guys on the dance floor."

Dug Deep to Find DJ Dreams

As Bond's modeling career blossomed, so did her

At a Glance . . .

Born on December 19, 1970, in New York, NY; married Bazaar Royale, November 29, 2004.

Career: Elite New Faces, Wilhelmina, New York, NY, model, mid-1990s; disc jockey, New York, NY, 2000–.

Awards: Justo Mixed Tape Awards, Best Female DJ, 2002.

Addresses: *Agent*—dGi. Management, 9 Desbrosses St., 2nd floor, New York, NY 10013.

record collection. Eventually she bought a professional set of turntables. It was an ear-opening move. "The reason I bought my turntables wasn't cause I wanted to be a DJ; it was because my regular record player broke down and I couldn't play my vinyl," she told *SOHH*. "When I bought [them] and started practicing I was like, 'I'm kinda nice.'" All her nights spent dancing had given Bond an ear for what sounded good. "I was like a club head, the person who the DJ played for," Bond told *Village Voice*, "so it was kinda easy for me to absorb what they did, and taking it to finding my own flow."

Still not ready to step up to the decks, Bond did like many models and turned to the stage. She enrolled in an acting academy where one of her classes focused on the Meisner Technique. "The essence of that program was to be true to yourself, to find the truth of yourself by digging deep," Bond told *CBB*. By the time she graduated in 1999, Bond had become a good actress and her classmates assumed she was destined for Hollywood. "But by that time, I had found the truth," she told *CBB*. "I wanted to be a DJ."

In 2000, Bond became DJ Beverly Bond and started lugging crates of records down from her fifth-story walk-up to play small gigs around the city. Her style was a throwback to the varied sounds her mom played for her as a child—from old school hip-hop, soul, and funk to African drummers, Brazilian grooves, and classic jazz. "I know that I have set myself apart from girls who are models, who are trying to be DJs and trying to be trendy," Bond told *Village Voice*. "I like to surprise people. I changed the game in a way."

Spun Records to Fame and Respect

Within a year of her debut, Bond became one of New York's most sought-after DJs. Her music resonated with a club culture famous for its finicky pursuit of the hottest and hippest. Bond landed on the A-list, performing for high-flying clients like Sean Combs, Prince, and Kimora Simmons. Soon she was playing big gigs such as the VH1 Fashion Awards, the ESPN X-Games, the New York Planet Hollywood opening, Playboy parties, and D'Angelo's *Voodoo* album release party. "I guess my commercial appeal happens because of the whole modeling thing," she told *SOHH*. "I guess that's where people would wanna automatically see me."

Bond found more success in her two years as a DJ than she had in nearly a decade as a model. "I stopped modeling because when I started DJ-ing, my career started blowing up as a DJ," she told *SOHH*. "As I became more famous for what I did it didn't make any sense for me to continue to go on my castings." Though off the runway, Bond still made appearances at fashion events, spinning for clients like Chanel, Hugo Boss, and Diesel. Known for her six-inch high afro and funky mix of street wear and haute style, Bond was named one of "New York's Most Fashionable Females" by the *New York Daily News*.

Cynics ready to dismiss Bond's sudden fame as hype were silenced in 2002 when she was named the Best Female DJ at the Justo Mixtape Awards—a recognition that is considered one of the most credible evaluations of a hip-hop DJ's skills. Mixtapes are actually CDs that serve as a DJ's aural press kit. Songs from other artists are sampled, mixed, and re-mixed to express the DJ's unique vision. "I was so shocked when I was nominated," Bond told *CBB*. "I felt like I had just started out and I didn't know that there were that many people aware of me."

Poised to Produce Own Beats

In just a few years as a DJ, Bond had become a celebrity. She spun on television shows including BET's *Rap City* and *106 & Park*, and MTV's *Total Request Live* and *Direct Effect*. She also co-hosted an episode of NBC's *Weekend Vibe*. On the road, she made worldwide DJ appearances with The Roots, Floetry, Musiq SoulChild, and Erykah Badu. She was also the official DJ for the Courvoisier tour and was the celebrity DJ for Eileen Ford's Super Model of the World contest in Puerto Rico. *Village Voice* named Bond a "Clubland MVP," *Honey Magazine* called her one of the "Hot 100 People to Watch," and *Vibe Magazine* tagged her a "Future Urban Icon."

Not content to just play music, Bond turned to producing it. In addition to the collection that pulled down her Justo award, Bond put out *Word Iz Bond*, a highly acclaimed 34-track CD which featured remixes of 50 Cent's "Many Men" and Nas's "One Mic." Bond was also the music director for Comedy Central's *Comic Groove*. She later teamed with Grammy winner Alicia Keys to produce an exclusive track for Baby Phat Fashions. Despite her skill at the mixing boards, Bond has had to confront sexism as a producer. "What I do find is that it's very difficult for females as far as people believing that you actually made your beats," she told *SOHH*. "A lot of times it's almost like people think that somebody else co-did it for you or that you just took some sample that nobody else happens to have and all it is, is a sample."

By 2005, Bond was on her way to becoming as renowned a producer as she was a DJ. She had an album in the works and was collaborating with several musicians to produce tracks and mixtapes. She told *SOHH*, "I really expect to be a serious contender as a producer." She was also keeping her finger on the vinyl with DJ gigs, both high and low brow. "It's natural for me to…spin at a little underground spot…as it is for me to do Chanel or the VHI Awards," she told *SOHH*. There was no shortage of venues looking to book her. As she told *CBB*, "My career is exploding. Check back with me in a year, I'll have a lot more to say by then."

Sources

On-line

"Ladies First Female DJs Got a Foot Through the Door, Ain't Goin' Nowhere," *Village Voice*, www.villagevoice.com/news/0129,cepeda,26472,1.html (May 15, 2005).

"Model/DJ Beverly Bond Dances To Her Own Beat, Now She Sells Them!" *SOHH*, www.sohh.com/thewire/read.php?contentID=6801 (May 15, 2005).

Other

Additional information for this profile was obtained through an interview with Beverly Bond on June 26, 2005.

—Candace LaBalle

Oscar Brown, Jr.

1926-2005

Entertainer

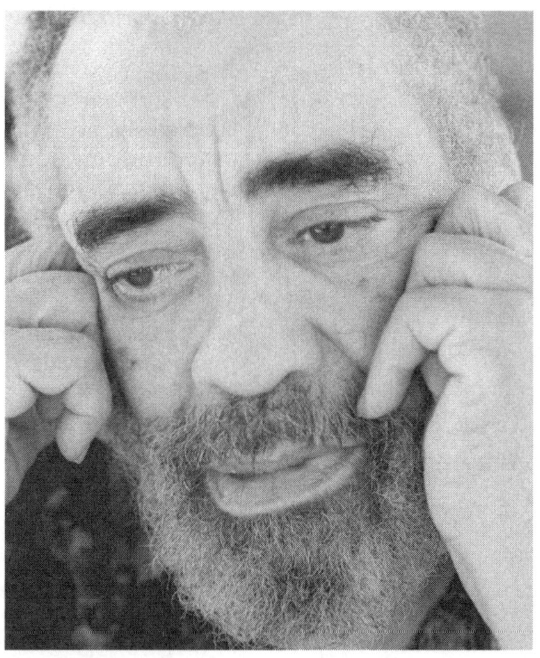

Brown, Oscar, Jr., photograph. AP/Wide World Photos. Reproduced by permission.

Oscar Brown Jr. was not a man easily defined. Labels like songwriter, composer, actor, singer, director, producer, playwright all fit, but not quite. He was also an activist, a visionary, and a social commentator. As influenced by the Harlem Renaissance as he was by the Civil Rights Movement, Brown had a desire to create and to communicate. "I wanted to present a picture of black culture to anyone who could hear it," the *Los Angeles Times* quoted him as saying. In doing so he penned over 1,000 songs, recorded 11 albums, and wrote several plays. Though he never received the recognition many felt he deserved during his life, his music and words have had a continued influence on a whole new generation of artists and activists.

Took to Airwaves as Teen

Oscar Cicero Brown Jr. was born on October 10, 1926, in Chicago, Illinois. His father, Oscar Sr., was a lawyer and real estate agent and his mother, Helen Clark Brown, taught school. Though African Americans were legally, socially, and economically second-class citizens throughout most of the country, Brown and his sister Helen enjoyed a comfortable middle-class upbringing. "I really enjoyed growing up in Chicago, you could say I was fat, dumb and happy," Brown told *Black World Today*. "I wasn't aware of a lot of the problems." However, Brown soon learned about activism by example. His father was a leader of the Chicago branch of the NAACP and both of his parents were active church-goers, committed to giving back to their community.

At the age of 15, Brown got his first taste of show business when he landed a role on the national radio series, *Secret City*. He recalled in "Legend: Moments in the Spotlight," an essay posted on the *Oscar Brown Jr.* Web site, "My father was an attorney and had wanted me to follow in his footsteps. However, when I obtained employment as a radio actor in high school, making sixty four dollars and sixty cents a week for only six hours of work at a time when others were making forty dollars a week for forty hours of work, the choice to get involved in the arts was a no-brainer."

Brown eventually bowed to his father's wishes and gave college a shot. During his early education, Brown had been an excellent student. "I was smart enough to have

At a Glance . . .

Born on October 10, 1926, in Chicago, IL; died on May 29, 2005; married Irene Brown, 1948 (divorced); married Maxine Brown, 1954 (divorced); married Jean Pace, mid-1960s; children: Napoleon, Maggie, Donna, Iantha, Africa, Oscar. *Education*: Attended University of Wisconsin, University of Michigan, and Lincoln University. *Military Service:* US Army, mid-1950s.

Career: Actor, director, playwright, producer, singer, writer; *Secret City*, Chicago, IL, radio actor, 1941; WJJD and WVON, *Negro News Front,* radio announcer, 1947-52; Columbia Records, singer, 1961-65; *Jazz Scene USA,* television host, 1962; Verve Records, singer, 1965; Atlantic Recrods, singer, 1972-73; Howard University, Washington, D.C., artist-in-residence, 1970s; *From Jump Street: The Story of Black Music,* PBS, host, 1980; University of California at Riverside, regents professor, early 2000s.

Memberships: Communist Party, 1947-52; American Authors' League.

Awards: Chicago/Midwest Regional Emmy Awards (2), both for *Oscar Brown Is Back In Town,* 1975; City of Chicago, Senior of the Year Award, 2002; California State Legislature, "Oscar Brown Day," early 2000s; Pan African Arts Society, Gordon Parks Maverick Award, 2004; Pan African Film and Arts Festival, Lifetime Achievement Award, 2005.

been 'double promoted' twice in grade school so I was only sixteen years old when I enrolled at the University of Wisconsin in the fall of 1943," Brown wrote in "Legend." For the next few years Brown bounced from Wisconsin to the University of Michigan to Lincoln University in Pennsylvania. With the exception of English, Brown was a failure in college. "I never got out of my college freshman year," Brown told *Global Black News.* "However, I was turned on to writing."

Fought Racism with Politics and Revolution

After returning to Chicago in 1947, Brown landed a broadcasting job with Chicago's first African-American radio news show, *Negro News Front*. It brought him face-to-face with the current events affecting the black community. "[That] sort of pivoted me," Brown told *Black World Today*, "it changed me around and made me not only an actor but also an activist." He became involved with the Civil Rights Congress, a movement led by Chicago activist Will Patterson that openly accused the U.S. government of genocide against black peoples. Brown also joined the Communist Party. "[It] was the only outlet available to participate in the struggle for black people," he wrote in "Legend."

At the age of 21, Brown decided to go into politics. He joined the Progressive Party and ran for Illinois State representative. "Undaunted by an overwhelming defeat, I ran again in 1952 in the Republican Primary for 1st District Congressman," he recalled in "Legend." He lost that bid as well. As Brown became more politically active, his on-air commentaries became increasingly radical. By 1953 the white station owners had had enough and *Negro News Front* was cancelled. By the mid-1950s the Communist Party had also had enough. "I got kicked out for being a black nationalist....We were too black for the Reds," he was quoted in *Black World Today*.

Over the next few years Brown served in the U.S. Army and worked for his father. He also married and divorced his first wife, Irene Hebert, and was headed towards divorce from his second wife, Maxine Fleming. Eventually he returned to his first love—writing—and started to compose songs. In order to get them heard, he began singing in local night clubs. In turning to music, he did not abandon politics. "The liberation of black people from the domination of racist whites can only be achieved by application of the necessary force. Can music provide this force? Yes, it can, due to its matchless ability to stir the human spirit," he wrote in an essay entitled "Music: The Liberating Force," published on his Web site.

Found Jazz Fame with First Album

In 1959 Brown attended the Chicago opening of Lorraine Hansberry's play, *A Raisin in the Sun*. There he met the playwright's husband, Robert Nemiroff, a music publisher from New York. Impressed with Brown's music, Nemiroff made an introduction to executives at Columbia Records. Columbia promptly offered Brown a recording contract. Brown was not so sure. "When they first sent me the contract for a singer, I wanted to go in as a writer," he told *Global Black News*. "I let a year go by before I realized that was the best offer I was going to get so I signed as a singer."

Brown's 1960 album *Sin and Soul* debuted to critical acclaim and made Brown a national celebrity. The 12 songs moved from hard-hitting social commentary to light-hearted humor, all bound by the rhythmic flow of classic jazz. "Bid 'Em In" offered a somber look at slave auctions delivered with a lyrical style that many critics have called a foreshadowing of rap. "Signifyin' Monkey" was a humorous reworking of an old black folk tale. "Brown Baby" was a lullaby written for his newborn son, Oscar III. It was later made famous by gospel legend Mahalia Jackson. Several songs were instrumentals by other jazz artists to which Brown added lyrics, including Mongo Santamaria's "Afro Blue," Nat Adderley's "Work Song," and Bobby Timmons' "Dat Dere."

The success of *Sin and Soul* introduced Brown into the world of jazz greats. Brown's performance style made him an instant sensation. "He was really a dramatist," long-time friend Joe Segal told *Chicago Tribune*. "He was more than a vocal artist because his shows were very easy and dramatic at the same time." Brown was soon sharing the stage with names like Dizzy Gillespie, Miles Davis, and John Coltrane. He teamed up with drumming great Max Roach to pen lyrics for Roach's 1960 Civil Rights album, *We Insist! Freedom Now Suite*. In 1962 he headlined a sold-out show in London called *Oscar Brown Entertains*.

Produced Plays for Broadway and Gang Members

Even as *Sin and Soul* was cementing his fame as a singer, Brown remained a writer at heart. Making the rounds of New York's music scene he always had a copy of his musical, *Kicks and Company,* in hand. Dealing with racism and revolution, *Kicks* was both timely and riveting. Determined to produce the show on Broadway, Brown embarked on a string of fundraisers including private performances for guests from Martin Luther King to Harry Belafonte. In an unprecedented—and never repeated—display of support, NBC's *Today Show* dedicated a full-two hour program to Brown and *Kicks*. Though the play never made it to Broadway, it did have a brief run in Chicago in 1961.

In 1962 Brown moved to Los Angeles to host the television program *Jazz Scene USA*. There he met singer and dancer Jean Pace. The two would eventually marry and collaborate on dozens of projects during a 30-plus-year partnership. Back in Chicago, Brown wrote and produced the musical *Opportunity Please Knock*. It was success, not only for its music but for its performers—members of the notorious Chicago street gang, Blackstone Rangers. The *Washington Post* wrote that Black originally confronted the gang members about "steppin' on my hustle, scaring my audience." Eventually he recruited them to appear in the show. The result was a reduction in gang violence and national fame. Members of the gang were invited to perform on the popular TV show *The Smothers Brothers Comedy Hour*. Brown was also recruited by Gary, Indiana, officials to launch a talent search in that town's troubled inner-city. Among his early discoveries were five brothers known as the Jackson Five.

Brown produced several other plays during the 1960s, including *Joy 66, Summer in the City,* and *Buck White*. The latter, a musical based on themes of black power and militancy, made it to Broadway with Muhammad Ali in the title role. At the time Ali was under a government-enforced hiatus from boxing due to his refusal to join the Vietnam War draft. Meanwhile Brown continued to write and record music including the albums *In a New Mood…*, *Between Heaven and Hell,* and *Tells It Like It Is!,* all for Columbia. In 1965 he moved to Verve and recorded the critically hailed *Mr. Oscar Goes to Washington*. Like *Sin and Soul*, this album showcased Brown's vocal dexterity and ability to swing from politically confrontational songs such as "Brother Where Are You" and "Forty Acres and a Mule" to lighthearted humor as in "Living Double in a World of Trouble," about having two girlfriends at once.

Performed Until the End

By 1972 Brown had recorded nine albums and collaborated on dozens more. Though jazz aficionados considered him a visionary, Brown could not get a new recording contract. "I think I was a bit too political for them," he told *Global Black News*. Nonetheless, Brown stayed active in music and theater. He served as artist-in-residence at Howard University in Washington, D.C., where he produced *Slave Song,* a musical drama told in rhyme. He produced a television special, *Oscar Brown Is Back*, that won two Chicago Emmy awards. In 1983 his play *Great Nitty Gritty* debuted in Chicago, once again with local youth in the cast. Brown also made television appearances, hosting music specials such as the 13-week PBS series *From Jump Street: The Story of Black Music,* and guest starring on shows like *Brewster Place* and *Roc*. He also regularly performed onstage, often with his daughter, jazz singer Maggie Brown. His son Oscar III had also shared the stage with his father until his 1996 death in an auto accident.

Brown made a comeback in 1995 with the album *Then and Now*, a compilation of old and new songs. Despite his age, his voice was still commanding and his message still relevant. Three years later, Brown recorded the live album *Live Every Minute* during a tour of Europe. He was 72 at the time. Over the next few years Brown toured worldwide, headlining shows and appearing at political rallies, including several against the Iraq War. He also became an honored guest on the Russell Simmons show *Def Poetry Jam*. In 2003 the show *Serenade the World: The Music and Words of Oscar Brown Jr.* debuted to packed houses in New York. In 2004 a documentary about his life, *Music Is My Life, Politics Is My Mistress*, premiered.

In 2004, when asked by NPR radio host Tavis Smiley what he gets out of performing at the age of 78, Brown responded, "Same thing I got out of it at 38…people are applauding." He added, "That's the best of all possible worlds. And so, you know, the more I can keep that going…." Brown did keep it going, all the way to May 29, 2005, when he died of respiratory failure. The loss was great, but as his daughter Maggie said in a statement quoted in the *Chicago Defender*, "he has left a wealth of works that will continue to touch the world."

Selected works

Albums

Sin and Soul, Columbia, 1960.
In a New Mood..., Columbia, 1962.
Between Heaven and Hell, Columbia, 1962.
Tells It Like It Is!, Columbia, 1963.
Mr. Oscar Goes to Washington, Verve, 1965.
Finding a New Friend, Fontana, 1966.
Movin' On, 32 Jazz, 1972.
Brother Where Are You, Atlantic, 1973.
Fresh, Atlantic, 1972.
Then and Now, Weasel, 1995.
Live Every Minute, Minor Music, 1998.

Plays

Kicks and Company, 1961.
Joy 66, 1966.
Summer in the City, 1960s.
Opportunity Please Knock, 1967.
Slave Song, 1970s.
Great Nitty Gritty, 1983.

Sources

Periodicals

Chicago Tribune, May 31, 2005.
Los Angeles Times, May 31, 2005.
Washington Post, May 31, 2005.

On-line

Oscar Brown Jr., www.oscarbrownjr.com (July 6, 2005).
"Oscar Brown, Jr.: The Man, His Music and His Words," *Global Black News,* www.globalblacknews.com/OscarBrown.html (June 12, 2005).
"Oscar Brown Jr., Legendary Patriarch of Culture, Dies," *Chicago Defender,* www.chicagodefender.com/page/local.cfm?ArticleID=925 (June 12, 2005).

Other

"Oscar Brown Jr. Discusses Why He's Still Performing at 78," interview with Tavis Smiley, "The Tavis Smiley Show," *National Public Radio,* December 14, 2004.

—Candace LaBalle

Byron Cage

1965?—

Gospel singer, praise leader

Cage, Byron, photograph. © Laura Farr/Zuma/Corbis.

Known as the "Prince of Praise," celebrated gospel singer Byron Cage has been performing and recording songs since the 1980s and has become known for a self-described "cross-cultural, mass-appeal praise and worship" style that has kept his albums in the Billboard Gospel Top Ten almost continuously since it began in 2003. Cage is minister of music at the mega church, Ebenezer African Methodist Epsicopal (AME) Church in Fort Washington, Maryland. Since releasing his debut album, *Dwell Among Us,* in 1995 he has helped "praise and worship" music to become a major force among gospel musicians. Cage has served in two mega churches, helping them to grow and sustain large congregations with his charismatic style. In his ten years at Atlanta's New Birth Cathedral, Cage helped expand the church from a small congregation of 700 worshippers into a mega church of over 16,000 members.

Born in Grand Rapids, Michigan, Byron Cage grew up in a Christian family and attended church as a child, being influenced in particular by Bishop Abney. He spent his early years in Grand Rapids before moving to Detroit, Michigan, with his family at the age of 12. He recalled for *Christianity Today* that it was in the Pentecostal church there that he first experienced the form of worship that would become known in the 1990s as "Praise and Worship." He attended Oakland University in Rochester, Michigan, and at age 23 won a scholarship to attend Morehouse College in Atlanta, Georgia. There he also began attending Bishop Eddie Long's church, the New Birth Cathedral, then known as the New Birth Missionary Baptist Church. Bishop Long later presided over Cage's marriage to Sonya Windham Cage, a pediatric dentist, in 2004.

Cage's career as a gospel singer began when he was still in his teens and he held the role of choir director at the Greater Grace Temple in Detroit. He was invited to join the group "Commission," then known as the "Disciples of Christ," but his studies at the University of Oakland stood in the way. After moving to Atlanta, Cage joined the New Birth Cathedral and persuaded Bishop Eddie Long to make changes to the traditional form of service. As well as touring with the late Thomas Whitfield, a gospel star ten years his senior, whom he lists as his musical mentor, Cage spent a decade at the New Birth Cathedral and became musical director. In

At a Glance . . .

Born Byron Cage in 1965?, in Grand Rapids, MI; married Sonya Windham Cage, 2004. *Education:* Oakland University, Rochester, MI; Morehouse College, Atlanta, GA. *Religion*: Christian.

Career: New Birth Cathedral, music director, 1980s-1990s; recording artist, 1990s–; Ebenezer AME Church, Fort Washington, Maryland, music director, late 1990s–.

Awards: Four Stellar Awards, for Male Vocalist of the Year, Best Song (with Kurt Carr), Best CD, and Best Contemporary CD, 2004; Soul Train Award, for Best Gospel Album, 2004, for *Byron Cage.*

Addresses: *Agent*—Flipside Agency, c/o Sean Pennington, 276 Fifth Ave, Suite #403, New York, NY 10001.

his time there he gradually transformed the traditional old-style Baptist church into a gospel-oriented, charismatic style. While he acknowledges that the process was difficult and painful for some, in the same period the membership increased from a modest 700 to over 16,000.

In the late 1990s Cage accepted the position of minister of music at Ebenezer AME Church in Fort Washington, Maryland, where the pastor is Rev Browning. Ebenezer is one of the largest AME churches in the area with over 12,000 members. Cage admitted to *Christianity Today* that it was difficult bringing his contemporary style of music and worship to a conservative AME church. He also noted that the cultural divide between black and white congregations that he experienced early in his career is being broken down by music. Cage has since become senior minister of church worship and music administration at Ebenezer.

By 2003 Cage was a senior member of the Ebenezer ministry team, with a growing reputation as a charismatic musician and worship leader, and performing regularly at large venues. But it was the 2003 album *Byron Cage* that brought him to the attention of the wider public and to the mainstream music industry. Recorded at New Birth Cathedral the album won four Stellar Awards at the gospel music industry's 19th annual awards ceremony in 2004, including "Best Male Vocalist," "Best Song," with Kurt Carr, "Best CD," and "Best Contemporary CD." Carr, his long-time collaborator and producer, picked up an award for "Producer of the Year." The album also won a Soul Train Award for "Best Gospel Album, 2004."

Since the late 1980s Cage has been at the forefront of developments in praise and worship music, which represents a break with more traditional gospel music in that it brings contemporary styles and new songs to the old format. Along with performers like Ron Kenoly and others he has helped to broaden gospel's appeal; he has also been part of a movement within the American Baptist churches that is changing the traditional style of services. Cage claims credit for inspiring the Full Gospel Baptist denomination churches to adopt "praise and worship" more widely. But Cage is also aware that his music has spread beyond traditional gospel congregations. As one of the best-known exponents of "praise and worship, " Cage is an influential figure: his music is used by worshippers in a wide range of different churches and settings.

Selected works

Albums

Dwell Among Us, 1995.
Transparent In Your Presence, 1996.
Byron Cage, 2003.

Songbooks

Byron Cage: Folio, 2004.

Sources

Periodicals

Ebony, February 2005, p. 60.
Grand Rapids Press, (Grand Rapids, MI), January 12, 2004, p. B8.
Houston Chronicle (Houston, TX), August 16, 2003, p. 1; March 27, 2004, p. 1.
New York Times, March 28, 2005, p. E5.
USA Today, February 5, 2004.

On-line

"Breaking Barriers: An Interview with Byron Cage," *Christianity Today*, http://www.christianitytoday.com/music/interviews/2004/byroncage-0104.html (June 23, 2005).
Byron Cage, www.byroncage.com/ (June 16, 2005).
"Byron Cage," *Detroit Gospel*, www.detroitgospel.com/DG-Byron-Cage.htm (June 23, 2005).

—Chris Routledge

Mariah Carey

1970—

Singer, actor

Mariah Carey has displayed each of the characteristics that commonly describe a diva. She possesses both a five-octave vocal range and award-winning music business skills. She co-wrote all but one of her No.1 songs (which was a cover of a Jackson 5 song) and co-produced of all of her chart-topping hits. She was named the world's top selling female artist of the millennium. By the summer of 2001, the talented, classically trained, and hardworking singer had come full circle and reached a breaking point, but quickly rebounded.

Carey was born March 27, 1970, in Long Island, New York, to Patricia Carey, who was a soloist with the New York City Opera, and Alfred Roy Carey, an aeronautical engineer. And since the tender age of four, she knew she wanted to sing. By the time she was 18, Carey had a tape ready for the moment that opportunity came knocking. A brief meeting with Sony executive Tommy Mottola at a party was the catalyst to her successful career. Mottola told *Ebony* magazine that he knew right away that she had star potential. "When I first heard and saw Mariah, there was absolutely no doubt she was in every way destined for stardom," he said.

Made Chart-Topping Entrance

Carey burst onto the scene with the rich and soulful single "Vision of Love," in 1990. The first single from her first album *Mariah Carey* hit number one on the charts. The incredible freshman effort led Carey to become the third artist to be nominated in the same year for best album, best song, and best new artist. *Mariah Carey* earned 22 weeks at Billboard's number one, sold more than seven million copies, and was responsible for four number one singles: "Vision of Love," "Love Takes Time," "Someday," and "I Don't Wanna Cry."

On her second album, *Emotions*, in 1991, Carey produced a record-breaking fifth consecutive number-one single with the album's title track. Two other songs from her sophomore release reached the top five in the charts. The next album for Carey was a live effort, *MTV Unplugged*, and it also produced a number one song—a cover of the Jackson 5 single "I'll Be There."

In June of 1993, Carey wed Tommy Mottola at the historic St. Thomas Church in New York. The grand wedding sparked even more comparisons of Carey's success to a fairytale. Mottola, then 43, served as the prince who swept the young songstress off her feet. She also released *Music Box* in 1993, which sparked more chart-topping success. This album produced the hit singles "Dreamlover" and "Hero."

While Carey suffered poor critical reviews of her first tour, the bad reviews did not deter her. She released *Merry Christmas* in 1994. Although this was one of the three albums that did not produce a number one hit, the single "All I Want for Christmas Is You," was a bright moment.

Mixed Musical Styles

In 1995 Carey released *Daydream,* and its lead single,

At a Glance . . .

Born on May 27, 1970, in Long Island, New York; daughter of Patricia Carey, (a former soloist with the New York City Opera) and Alfred Roy Carey, (a former aeronautical engineer); married Tommy Mottola (divorced).

Career: Singer, 1990–; actress, 2000–.

Awards: Grammy, Best New Artist, 1990, Best Female Vocalist, 1990; World Music Award, Best-Selling Female Artist of Millennium, 2000; Lady of Soul Awards, nominated for Best R&B/Soul Single, for "We Belong Together" and for Best R&B/Soul Album, for *The Emancipation of Mimi,* 2005.

Addresses: *Record Label*—Island Records, 825 Eighth Avenue, New York, NY 10019.

"Fantasy," debuted at number one. The single was a duet with embattled rap star, O.D.B. of the Wu Tang Clan. In spite of the strangeness of the combination, the two produced what was the beginning of Carey's hip-hop pop sound. Years later *Variety* magazine would attribute Carey's musical brilliance to "her ability to stay ever-so-slightly ahead of the teen beat curve." This single represented one of the trends in fusing the ever-growing popularity of hip-hop and rap with the pop music sound—a practice that has become standard in the music industry. She also scored another hit from *Daydream* with "One Sweet Day," a collaboration song that paired the singer with Boys II Men. The song saw a good measure of success and remained at the top of the charts for four months.

Despite the continuing success musically, Carey's personal life was becoming troubled. She separated from Mottola in 1997 and was finally divorced in 1998. She spent the time immersing herself in what she called the music of her youth. Though best known for her pop sound, her next effort *Butterfly* was the most hip-hop laden of her releases. Carey was still topping the charts but critics questioned her leanings towards hip-hop and R&B. Carey told *Newsweek International* that critics "don't understand that I'm someone who grew up with this music. It's exciting to be able to work with [today's leading [h]ip [h]op artists.]"

To mark the many years of number one singles and success with music, Carey's next album, *#1,* was a compilation of her first 13 number-one hits. It also highlighted a few duets, including "Whenever You Call" with Brian McKnight and "When You Believe" with Whitney Houston. "When You Believe" was featured on the soundtrack of Disney's animated film, *The Prince of Egypt,* and met with worldwide success. With so many record-breaking successes under her belt and an album of greatest hits that included 13 number one singles, it seemed that Carey had accomplished all that any one person could in music. However, 1999 proved to be a very good year for the star as well. She released her eighth album *Rainbow* and became the first artist to have hit songs at the top of the charts for each year in the 1990s with the single "Heartbreaker."

Life Took a Turn

The new millennium was looking bright for the artist after being honored as the best-selling female artist of the millennium at the 12th annual World Music Awards. Carey broadened her work to include acting in 2000. She made her film debut in a small part in *The Bachelor.* At the same time, Carey launched another singing tour and began work on the semi-autobiographical film *Glitter,* and soon started filming the movie *Wise Girls,* with Mira Sorvino. Carey was on her way to becoming the world's highest-paid recording artist with a five-year, $100 million deal with Virgin records.

But Carey's nonstop hit making schedule would catch up with the diva by mid-2001. In addition to the music news, Carey had been making the headlines with bizarre behavior in the early months of the year. She performed an impromptu striptease that revealed a tank top and short shorts on MTV's *Total Request Live* and stories of minor arguments on the set of *Wise Girls* were making their way into headlines. In late July Carey was hospitalized for extreme exhaustion. She had always described herself as hard working with need for little sleep, but according to her publicist, Cindi Berger, the fast pace caught up with the star. A *Time* article quoted Berger saying that Carey had "an emotional and physical breakdown." The star ultimately took time off of her busy schedule for recuperation at a hospital in Connecticut and later in the year at another hospital in Los Angeles.

Carey's *Glitter* landed with a thud in theaters and "Loverboy," the first single from her *Glitter* soundtrack, topped at number two. Although the road looked a little rough for the star, Carey remained many steps ahead of her competition. She regained her health and soon began working again. In 2002 she released *Charmbracelet* that topped the charts at number two, followed by an album of remixed favorites.

By 2005 Carey had regained her momentum. With the release of *The Emancipation of Mimi,* Carey enjoyed record sales in the album's first week and had her first number one album on the Billboard charts since 1997. As *Billboard* magazine wrote: "Go ahead and call it a comeback."

Selected works

Albums

Mariah Carey, Columbia, 1990.
Emotions, Columbia, 1991.
MTV's Unplugged, Columbia, 1992.
Music Box, Columbia, 1993.
Merry Christmas, Sony, 1994.
Daydream, Columbia, 1995.
Butterfly, Columbia, 1997.
#1's, Columbia, 1998.
Rainbow, Columbia, 1999.
Glitter, Virgin, 2001.
Charmbracelet, Columbia, 2002.
The Remixes, Island, 2003.
The Emancipation of Mimi, Island, 2005.

Films

The Bachelor, 2000.
Glitter, 2001.
Wise Girls, 2002.

Sources

Periodicals

Allure, July 20, 2005.
Billboard, April 23, 2005, p. 6.
Business Wire, October 7, 1999.
Entertainment Weekly, August 10, 2001, p. 8.
Jet, February 7, 2000, pp. 60; May 29, 2000, p. 24; September 24, 2001, April 25, 2005, p. 58.
Money, June 1, 2001.
Newsweek International, November 22, 1999, p. 92.
New York Times, August 5, 2005.
Teen People, October 1, 2001.
Time, August 13, 2001, pp. 56.
Variety, March 27, 2000.

On-line

All Music Guide, www.allmusic.com.
Mariah Carey, www.mariahcarey.com.

—Ashyia Henderson, Leslie Rochelle, and Sara Pendergast

Ken Carter

1959(?)–

Basketball coach, motivational speaker, entrepreneur

Coach Ken Carter's 1999 lockout of his Richmond (California) High School basketball team seemed like a story made for the movies. And indeed, when the story was brought to life by actor Samuel L. Jackson in the 2005 hit film *Coach Carter,* a fresh new round of publicity came to the man whose daring form of discipline had set a group of young people on course to positive futures. Coach Carter's own story, it turned out, exemplified the values of dedication and accomplishment that he tried to instill in his players.

Born in tiny Fernwood, Mississippi (near McComb) around 1959, Carter grew up in a close-knit family and community. He had seven sisters and one brother. "When you hear that statement *it takes a whole village to raise a child,* I am that child," he told *Christianity Today.* "My family is extremely close." Having grown up with both parents in the home, Carter often pointed out to interviewers that only seven of the 45 students in his basketball program at Richmond could say the same. His life was stable enough that he could dream big dreams. "When I was a little boy...," he was quoted as saying in the *Seattle Times,* "I was in the kitchen with my mama, and I took this big wooden spoon she was using to stir some cake batter and talked into it like it was a microphone and said 'Someday they're going to make my life into a movie.'"

Carter's small-town roots stuck with him. One educator who worked with Carter later described him to *San Francisco Chronicle* writer Chip Johnson as "a little country bumpkin who has a lot of stories and a unique way of telling them." But his family later moved to the troubled city of Richmond, north of Oakland, California. When he was a teenager, he recalled, his classmates might try to steal sodas from a neighborhood shop, but he was more likely to find the store's owner and ask whether he could sweep the floor or do something else to earn the soda.

Set Records on Court

A gifted athlete himself, Carter played basketball for the Richmond High School Oilers from 1973 to 1977. He set all-time school records for scoring, assists, and steals, all of which remained standing when he took over as Richmond's coach 20 years after graduating. (His son Damien later broke the assists and steals records.) He was a high school All-American on not only the basketball court but also the baseball diamond, where he played shortstop.

Carter attended George Fox University in Oregon on a scholarship. He later returned to Richmond and took further courses at San Francisco State University. A born entrepreneur who realized the power of the Internet early on, he also took e-commerce courses at Contra Costa College in San Pablo, California, near Richmond. Carter invested in his home community, opening a sporting-goods store, a barbershop, and a hair salon in a block of downtown buildings that he eventually purchased. Married and with a son coming up on high school and college, Carter was proud of these accomplishments but looked to wider horizons. Even before the Richmond lockout put him much in

At a Glance . . .

Born ca. 1959 in Fernwood, MS; moved with family to Richmond, CA; children: Damien. *Education:* Attended George Fox University, Oregon; San Francisco State University; and Contra Costa College.

Career: Operated sporting goods store, barbershop, and salon, Richmond, CA, late 1970s–; Richmond High School, head boys' basketball coach, 1997-2002; Prime Time Publishing and Prime Time Sports, founder and CEO, 2001–; The Rumble (SlamBall team), Los Angeles, CA, head coach, 2002–; Coach Ken Carter Foundation, founder and chairman, 2002–; consultant for film *Coach Carter,* starring Samuel L. Jackson, released 2005.

Memberships: Scholar-Athletes Organization.

Selected awards: San Francisco Bay Area Entrepreneur of the Year, 2001; Torchbearer, 2002 Winter Olympic Games, Salt Lake City, UT; *CityFlight* magazine award as one of Ten Most Influential African Americans in the Bay Area; NAACP Impact Citizen of the Year; Leadership Award from San Francisco Mayor Willie Brown; California Unsung Heroes Award.

Addresses: *Office*—Coach Ken Carter Foundation, 641 S. 15th St., Richmond, CA 94804; *Web*—www.coachcarter.com.

demand as a motivational speaker, he had begun taking seminars and giving talks on the path to success.

In 1997, Carter accepted an offer to coach the high school boys' basketball team at his alma mater. The school and the community had both deteriorated since his days as a Richmond star. Drug abuse and high unemployment plagued the town, and Richmond High had a graduation rate of only around 50 percent. "The fact is this, sir," Carter said in an interview quoted in the *Seattle Times.* "A kid in Richmond is 80 percent more likely to go to jail than to college." Carter agreed to take the Richmond coaching post only on the condition that he be given full control over the basketball program.

Led Trips to Offices, Redwood Forests

When he took the reins, the school's basketball team wasn't in much better shape than its student achievement record, which ranked in the bottom ten percent of California high schools. The two decades since Carter's glory days had been marked mostly by losing seasons. Carter turned things around in a hurry. Part of his success was due to the interest he took in his players off the court. He took them on field trips to the offices of high-tech firms in the Silicon Valley, across San Francisco Bay 60 miles from Richmond, trying to impress on them that despite all the headlines that came with sports stardom, education was a surer route to success. "There's less than 5,000 jobs in all of professional sports that you can make a living," Carter pointed out to *Christianity Today.* "But one company, Microsoft, has over 10,000 millionaires in that one company." His students, he added, "do the math real quick." Carter also took his students, some of whom didn't realize that there were forests in California, on a trip to one of the state's preserves of giant redwood trees.

With educational goals in mind, Carter had all his players sign a contract in which they promised to maintain a 2.3 grade-point average, higher than the state-required minimum of 2.0. They also pledged to keep perfect class attendance records, sitting in the front row at all times, to address men and women as "sir" and "madam," to study for ten hours a week, to turn in homework on time, and to wear shirts and ties on days when games were scheduled. The new level of discipline Carter demanded worked wonders on the court. By January of 1999, perennial loser Richmond had amassed a 13-0 record and was regarded as a contender for the state championship. "Go Oilers!" signs sprouted in the windows of businesses in the economically hard-hit town.

But all was not well from Carter's point of view. Fifteen of the 45 players in the program had failed to meet the terms of the contract, falling short in various ways. So, in early January, he padlocked the doors of Richmond's gymnasium, locking out not only members of the varsity squad but also the likewise undefeated junior varsity and freshman players, including his 16-year-old son. He marched the players down to the school library, where tutors were waiting. Carter chose to punish the entire team rather than just the offending players because, he reasoned, that was the only way to make peer pressure work in favor of academic accomplishment rather than against it. "At that point," he told Dixie Reid of the *Sacramento Bee,* "I was prepared to forfeit the whole season."

Carter's action, which the Richmond High student body termed the Great Lockout, gained widespread publicity. Praise for Carter crossed the liberal-conservative divide, with both Democratic California governor Gray Davis and right-wing radio host Rush Limbaugh weighing in with commendations for his stance. In Richmond, however, opinions were much more mixed as two games were forfeited and the team's undefeated season evaporated. A brick was thrown through the window of Carter's sporting-goods shop, and a passer-by spat on his car. The Richmond school board questioned whether he had the right to unilaterally lock the gym facility and reopened it at one point. The players, however, after talking to Carter, honored the lockout. "I give them three minutes" to talk, Carter explained to Suzanne Espinosa Solis of the *San Francisco Chronicle.* "They can say anything they like. Being the coach I am, I cut them short at two."

Players Went on to College

After a week, Carter relented, although several players were once again benched later in the season. The team finished with a 19-5 record and lost in the state playoffs—something Carter insisted be accurately represented in *Coach Carter,* over the objections of studio executives who wanted to give the film a storybook ending. The ultimate outcome of Carter's crusade, however, was inspiring enough to carry the film on its own: half the players on Carter's 1998-99 Richmond squad were admitted to college, as compared with only two dozen of the school's 200-member graduating class in 2000. Several attended big-name schools such as the University of California and the University of Nevada at Las Vegas, and Carter's son Damien enrolled at the U.S. Military Academy in West Point, New York.

Lynne Oliver, mother of Richmond player Wayne Oliver, credited Carter with her son's success after he enrolled at California's West Hills College and played on a team that reached the state junior college tournament. "At first I was upset [about the lockout]," she told the *Chronicle*'s David Steele. "But when I understood what the coach was doing, I was happy. And now look at my baby." Carter once again demonstrated his commitment to education in 2000 when he rode a human-powered kick scooter 90 miles from Richmond to Sacramento during a state school funding debate.

The Great Lockout made Carter famous. Lucrative lecture opportunities came his way, and he was paid a consulting fee for *Coach Carter,* personally approving the casting of Samuel L. Jackson as himself and spending four months on the set of the film. In 2002, Carter became the head coach of the Rumble, a SlamBall team in Los Angeles; SlamBall was a new team sport that combined basketball, football, and gymnastics, being fought out on a floor-level trampoline surface. Carter founded a publishing company, Prime Time Publishing, and authored several motivational print and audio products including *101 Ways to Earn a Higher GPA.* Among his many awards was his selection as torchbearer in advance of the 2002 Winter Olympic Games in Salt Lake City, Utah.

Some charged Carter with opportunism, but he plowed many of the profits from his new enterprises back into the Richmond community. In 2002 he established the Coach Ken Carter Foundation, a nonprofit that provided educational opportunities for minority youth, promoting projects designed to further student achievement in math, science, and technology. In 2005 he announced plans to return to coaching in Richmond—this time at the junior high school level. "I want to catch them a bit earlier," he explained to Christa Turner of the Columbus, Alabama *Ledger-Enquirer.* "We're noticing the kids now need influence earlier and earlier. By the time they get to high school, they're already set in their ways." Richmond's young basketballers would have a famous coach—the film *Coach Carter* grossed over $29 million in its first week of release in 2005 and topped American box-office lists—but it didn't seem likely that his tough philosophy would change. As he had told the *Chronicle*'s Steele several years earlier, "Raise the standards, and the kids will meet them."

Sources

Films

Coach Carter, 2005.

Periodicals

Jet, January 17, 2005, p. 54.
Ledger-Enquirer (Columbus, AL), June 15, 2005.
Sacramento Bee, January 20, 2005, p. E1.
San Diego Union-Tribune, January 13, 2005, p. E1.
San Francisco Chronicle, January 8, 1999, p. A19; March 1, 2000, p. E1; July 14, 2001, p. A15.
Seattle Times, February 2, 2005, p. F5.
Sports Illustrated, January 24, 2005, p. 29.

On-line

Coach Carter, www.coachcarter.com (June 18, 2005).
"Just Call Him 'Sir,'" *Christianity Today,* http://www.christianitytoday.com/movies/interviews/kencarter.htm. (June 18, 2005).

—James M. Manheim

Perry Christie

1944—

Politician

Christie, Perry, photograph. AP/Wide World Photos. Reproduced by permission.

Perry Gladstone Christie became prime minister of the Bahamas in May of 2002 after a long career in his Caribbean island-nation's main legislative body, the National Assembly. Christie heads the Progressive Liberal Party (PLP) of the Bahamas, which dominated the political landscape even before the country won independence from Britain in 1973. His rise to leadership of the Bahamas reflects the socially committed character of the relatively affluent island nation, which has a majority black population but whose economy is heavily dependent on tourism. "The mark of a country, and the measure of a society," Christie declared in his inaugural address, according to *Miami Herald* journalist Jacqueline Charles, "is the extent to which it is committed to helping the most unfortunate."

Christie was born in 1944 in Nassau, the Bahamian capital on the most populous island in the 700-island archipelago. Once known as a haven for pirates and even deemed a "Privateers' Republic" with Edward Teach, the pirate known as Blackbeard, as its chief magistrate, the Bahamas officially became part of the British Empire in 1717. New England loyalists to the British crown arrived after they were given land grants there during the American Revolutionary War, and they established cotton plantations. Slaves were brought from Africa to work the land, but the cotton crops failed to thrive in the tropical soil, and Britain outlawed slavery in the early 1800s in its territories. After that point, vessels of the Royal Navy would intercept slave ships bound for North America and take the human cargo to freedom in the Bahamas instead.

Christie's family was part of the 85-percent black majority in the country, a population that expanded over several generations. His father owned a taxi, and his mother was trained as a nurse. He was a lackluster student at Eastern Senior School in New Providence, but an outstanding track athlete who took part in 1960 West Indies Federation Games and even won a medal in the triple jump at the Central American and Caribbean Games in 1962. Ousted from his school because of poor grades, Christie eventually finished his academic credentials through the University Tutorial College in London. He went on to study law at Britain's Inner Temple, one of the four Inns of Court in London, and earned his law degree from the University of Birmingham, where he headed its debating society.

At a Glance . . .

Born on August 21, 1944 (some sources say 1943), in Nassau, Bahamas; son of Gladstone L. (a taxi owner) and Naomi (a nurse; maiden name, Allen) Christie; married to Bernadette Hanna (an accountant and attorney); children: Steffan, Adam, Alexandra. *Education:* Attended University Tutorial College; University of Birmingham, law degree (with honors), 1969; also studied at the Inner Temple, London. *Politics:* Progressive Liberal Party of the Bahamas. *Religion:* Anglican Church.

Career: McKinney Bancroft and Hughes, Bahamas, attorney, from 1969; Christie Ingraham and Company law firm, co-founder; appointed to the Bahamas Senate, 1974-77; elected to the National Assembly, on the Progressive Liberal Party (PLP) ticket, 1977–; Minister of Health and National Insurance, 1977-82; Minister of Tourism, 1982-84; Minister of Agriculture, Trade and Industry, 1990-92; elected co-deputy leader of the PLP, 1993, and party chair, 1997; Prime Minister of the Bahamas, 2002–.

Memberships: Board member, Broadcasting Corporation of the Bahamas, 1973.

Addresses: *Office*–Office of the Prime Minister, Sir Cecil Wallace-Whitfield Centre, West Bay Street, Nassau, N.P., Bahamas.

After being granted his degree from Birmingham in 1969, Christie returned to the Bahamas. He joined the law firm of McKinney Bancroft and Hughes, and in 1973 was named to the board of directors for the Broadcasting Corporation of the Bahamas. With another attorney, Hubert Ingraham, he established his own practice, Christie Ingraham and Company; Ingraham would later serve as prime minister from 1992 to 2002, though he and Christie had parted ways professionally and politically by then.

The Bahamas has a parliamentary system similar to Britain's. A party leader whose party has won the majority in the National Assembly elections becomes the prime minister, though technically he or she is appointed by the governor general, who represents the British monarch. The governor general also appoints members of the 16-member Senate, some with the advice of the prime minister. In November of 1974, Prime Minister Lynden O. Pindling recommended Christie for a Senate seat. Barely 30 years old, he was thought to be the youngest-ever member of the Bahamian Senate.

In 1977, Christie ran for a seat in the National Assembly, whose members are directly elected. He ran from Centerville on the Progressive Liberal Party (PLP) ticket and won. The PLP had dominated Bahamanian politics since the 1950s, and Pindling, its longtime leader, was known as the "Black Moses" in the Bahamas for leading the country to independence from British colonial rule. During that first term, Pindling gave Christie a cabinet post as minister of health and national insurance, which he held for five years. Re-elected in 1982 to his second term, Christie was made Pindling's minister of tourism, a key economic and goodwill job, but the PLP and Pindling were soon to become embroiled in a deep political scandal. There were charges of widespread corruption inside Pindling's government and even hints of ties to drug traffickers. In 1984 Christie resigned from Pindling's cabinet to distance himself from the political fracas, and he publicly chastised those in the PLP tainted by bribery.

Christie still held onto his National Assembly seat, however, and was re-elected in 1987 as an independent. He returned to the PLP fold in 1990 and again served in a Pindling cabinet, this time as minister of agriculture, trade, and industry. In 1992 Centerville voters once again returned him to office, but the PLP lost badly in the general election that year, and Pindling was forced to step down as prime minister. At the time, he was the longest-serving elected leader in the Western Hemisphere. Christie's former law colleague Ingraham, by then head of the Free National Movement (FNM) party, became prime minister for the next ten years.

Christie, meanwhile, rose through the ranks of his own party. In 1993 he became the PLP's co-deputy leader and four years later was elected PLP chair, succeeding Pindling. Between 1997 and 2002 he was the official leader of the opposition in the National Assembly, but in the 2002 general elections the PLP fared much better, taking 29 of the 40 National Assembly seats. It was a historic landslide election, and Christie became only the third prime minister in the history of an independent Bahamas. He was sworn into office in September of 2002. His first cabinet included Cynthia "Mother" Pratt, a popular figure in the Bahamas whom he made minister of national security and the also first woman deputy prime minister in the country's history. Christie also established a constitutional review commission to suggest constitutional reforms. This was an important step in the political achievement of women in the Bahamas, who had been shut out of the 1972 convention that drafted the Constitution for an independent Bahamas.

Christie's main political rival is Tommy Turnquest, who leads the FNM. Married to Bernadette, an accountant, Christie is the father of three. The longest-serving member of the National Assembly, Christie is known for his campaign crowd-pleaser, the junkanoo dance. Junkanoo is an annual December 26 event in Nassau, when groups of musicians parade through the streets in colorful costumes and an array of musical instruments that include the cowbell. Christie is a longtime member of the Valley Boys, one of the oldest junkanoo groups.

Sources

Books

Worldmark Encyclopedia of the Nations: World Leaders, Gale, 2003.

Periodicals

Financial Times, December 19, 2001, p. 2.
Miami Herald, May 4, 2002.
Mondaq Business Briefing, September 16, 2002.
Travel Agent, September 9, 2002, p. SS21.
Travel Weekly, September 29, 2003, p. 4.

On-line

"Office of the Prime Minister," *Commonwealth of the Bahamas,* www.opm.gov.bs/pmbio.php (June 22, 2005).
"The Rt. Hon. Perry Gladstone Christie," *Government of the Bahamas,* www.bahamas.gov.bs/bahamasweb2/home.nsf/Lookup/Perry+Christie (June 29, 2005).

—Carol Brennan

Lyn Collins

1948-2005

Singer

As the most commercially successful member of James Brown's Revue, Lyn Collins became a funk diva well before either word had much meaning. Her song "Think (About It)" topped the charts in 1972 and inspired a generation of sample-happy hip-hoppers in the 1990s. Yet, despite her talent and success, her name has barely registered on the country's musical conscious. Hidden behind the wall of fame that is James Brown, Collins and her thundering vocals remained mostly unheard. This did not stop the soulstress from singing her way around the world right until her untimely death. "She was a musical treasure that really didn't get the recognition," her son Bobby Jackson told the *Mercury News*. "But she rose above that anyway."

Leaped from Local Group to Legend's Stage

Gloria Lyn Collins was born on June 12, 1948, and raised in Abilene, Texas. By her early teens she was already flexing her powerful voice with a local group, the Charles Pike Singers. At 14 she recorded her first single, "Unlucky in Love." Around the same time, she married a local man who worked as a promoter for the James Brown Revue. After seeing Brown in concert in 1968 she worked up the nerve to send him a demo tape. The "Godfather of Soul" liked what he heard and gave Collins a call.

The James Brown Revue featured a roster of female singers known for their vocal dexterity, powerful range, and unmitigated funk. In 1969 principal singer Marva Whitney gave word that she would be leaving the group and Brown needed a replacement. Collins's timing was perfect. Before she could join the group, however, former Brown singer Vicki Anderson showed up and signed on for a two year stint. Collins was pushed back to the waiting list.

In February of 1971, while waiting for a place on the Revue roster, Collins went into a Macon, Georgia, studio with Brown and recorded a five-song sampler. Two of those songs, "Wheels of Life" and "Just Won't Do Right," were released as a two-sided single on Brown's label, People Records, an imprint of Polydor. A few months later, Anderson left the Revue and Collins was offered the principal singing spot. She jumped at it. "[Brown] kind of gave you the feeling that you better do it now while you got the chance," Collins later told *Billboard*. "He never said it, but you kind of got that feeling."

Baptized the "Female Preacher" of Funk

Brown was a strict boss who demanded that his singers wear a lot of hats—from background vocalist to songwriter to warm-up act. Though just 23 when she joined the tour, Collins was up to the challenge. Her howling, deep-throated vocals evoked old-school gospel and caused Brown to nickname her the 'Female Preacher.' Under his tutelage she corralled that voice around funk. Characterized by a heavy bass line, complex rhythms, and horn interludes laid over tight, infectious grooves and often screaming vocals, funk was pioneered by

At a Glance . . .

Born on June 12, 1948, in Texas; died on March 13, 2005; children: Bobby, Anthony.

Career: Singer, James Brown Revue, 1972-76; session singer, back-up singer, 1976-2005.

Brown and his crew. "We were funky when the word 'funk' couldn't even be discussed," Collins told *Billboard*.

Another characteristic of Brown's revue was the female empowerment expressed by the women in his entourage. "Singers like [Collins] are among the originators of the feisty, back-talking 'dish it and take like a man can' attitudes that exist in much music made by women today," a *Billboard* reviewer noted. At a time when women's lib and black empowerment were converging, female-sported afros were growing, and the music scene was embracing diversity, Brown's female singers became the music world's original divas.

In 1972 Collins released the single "Think (About It)," a feminist anthem disguised as deep funk. Official records say it was penned by Brown, though many give credit to Collins, especially in light of the song's hard-talking lyrics. In a backlash against men who take advantage of women, Collins sang, "those of you who go out and stay out all night // and expect us to be home when you get there // the sisters are not going for that no more // We got to use what we got to get what we want." The song rushed to number nine on the Billboard R&B charts and made Collins a household name. Its refrain—"It takes two to make a thing go right, // It takes two to make it out of sight"—was catchy and singable and destined to become a classic funk line.

Released Two Albums under Brown

Collins's debut album, also named *Think (About It)*, was propelled up the charts as a result of the single's popularity. Released in 1972 on the People/Polydor label, the album was produced by Brown and five of its nine songs were written by him. However it was Collins's name on the cover and her vocals fueling its success. Her early recordings, "Wheels of Life" and "Just Won't Do Right," made appearances as did "Women's Lib," a slow-tempo feminist ballad. Collins also performed several cover songs including Bill Withers's "Ain't No Sunshine" and an unusual rendering of the Frank Sinatra classic "Fly Me to the Moon."

Like most members of Brown's Revue, Collins was paid a salary in lieu of royalties. As a result she saw very little of the profits from *Think (About It)*. Nonetheless, she continued to tour and record with Brown. In the early 1970s she recorded "Mamma Feelgood" for the soundtrack to *Black Caesar* and "How Long Can I Keep It Up" for the film *Slaughter's Big Rip-Off*. Collins also recorded a popular duet with Brown, "What My Baby Needs Now is a Little More Loving." These songs have made appearances on several compilations over the years.

In 1975 Collins released her second album, *Come Check Me Out If You Don't Know Me By Now*. It featured 18 tracks that spanned the range of Collins's vocals—from smooth, silky soul to impassioned wailing to classic Brown funk. Standouts included the melancholic moan of "Put It On the Line," the emotional sass of "Me and My Baby Got a Good Thing Going On," and a moving rendition of the R&B standard "If You Don't Know Me By Now." The repetitively titled "Rock Me Again & Again & Again & Again & Again & Again" is straight up funk featuring bare instrumentation and in-your-face sexuality.

Found Renewed Fame with New Fan Base

Collins left the James Brown Revue in 1976. She settled in Los Angeles and took a clerical job at Record Plant Recording Studios. However, her life-long love affair with singing could not be filed away and she soon found work as a back-up singer for musical powerhouses such as Dionne Warwick, Rod Stewart, and Al Green. In the 1980s she appeared on soundtracks for the film *Dr. Detroit* and the television show *Fame*. Meanwhile she raised two sons, Bobby and Anthony, and divided her time between California and her hometown of Abilene.

In the mid-1980s, all things funk became hip again and there was renewed interest in Brown's galaxy of stars. Obscure Belgium label ARS lured Collins back into the studio and she recorded a dance club single called "Shout." In 1988 British label Urban Records rereleased her two Polydor albums, making her soul-searing voice accessible to a new generation of listeners. The following year, hip-hop duo Rob Base and DJ E-Z Rock sampled her classic line from "Think (About It)" into their 1989 song "It Takes Two." It became an instant hit, climbing to number 3 on *Billboard's* dance charts. "She was surprised and elated by how it took off," son Bobby told *The Mercury News*. The song also set off a frenzied sampling of her work with artists from Janet Jackson to De La Soul to Public Enemy popping her vocals into their mixes. Soon Collins had earned the nickname, "the most sampled woman in hip-hop."

Collins found additional fame in 1998 when Polydor released *James Brown's Original Funky Divas*, featuring 11 of Collins's best songs. In 2005 Collins embarked on a European tour with Martha High, another Brown alum. Bassist Lars Lehmann recalled the Paris show on the Bass Players web site: "You could tell that [Collins] is a star in France.... Many people would hold up record covers of her albums ready to be signed by her." He continued, "[When she] spoke the introduction of 'If You Don't Know Me By Now,' she was so overwhelmed by the love that came from the audience towards her, she started crying on stage." Sadly it was one of her last performances. On March 13, 2005, Collins died as a result of complications from a seizure she suffered after choking on a piece of food. She was only 56.

Selected discography

Albums

Think (About It) (includes "Just Won't Do Right," "Wheels of Life," and "Women's Lib"), People/Polydor Records, 1972; reissued, Urban Records, 1988.

Check Me Out If You Don't Know Me By Now (includes "If You Don't Know Me By Now," "Me and My Baby Got a Good Thing Going On," "Put It On the Line," and "Rock Me Again & Again & Again & Again & Again & Again"), People/Polydor Records, 1975; reissued, Urban Records, 1988.

Singles

"Unlucky in Love," c. 1962.
"What My Baby Needs Now is a Little More Loving," 1972.
"Mamma Feelgood," 1973.
"How Long Can I Keep It Up," 1973.
"Do Your Thing," 1988.
"Shout," 1988.
"It Takes Two," with Patra, 1993.

Sources

Periodicals

Billboard, April 4, 1998; March 26, 2005.
Independent (London, England), March 18, 2005.
Jet, May 2, 2005.
New York Times, March 16, 2005.

On-line

"Lyn Collins, Singer and James Brown Revue Member, Dead at 56," *The Mercury News*, www.mercurynews.com/mld/mercurynews/news/breaking_news/11136520.htm (June 10, 2005).

"My Most Memorable Gig, La Maroquinerie 21/02/05, by Lars Lehmann," *Bass Players*, www.bassplayers.co.za/memgiglars-l.html (June 10, 2005).

—Candace LaBalle

Afua Cooper

1957—

Poet, historian, educator

Cooper, Afua, photograph. Photo by Ian Gibbons. Courtesy of Afua Cooper.

Jamaican-born Afua Cooper is a pioneer of the Canadian dub poetry and spoken word movement. Her poems reflect what she calls her "historical, global, woman-centered, political, and social consciousness;" they have appeared in many journals and anthologies around the world, and in three books, the first of which was published in 1983. Cooper has also recorded her performances and her CDs sell around the world. One of them, *Worlds of Fire: In Motion* (2002) took the number one spot on CKLN's radio playlist; she has given hundreds of live performances and readings.

Cooper is also an influential historian who has taught history, women's studies, and Caribbean studies at Canada's Ryerson and York universities, and at the University of Toronto, where she teaches African Canadian history and women's history. She sits on the board of the James Johnston Chair in Black studies at Dalhousie University and is considered to be one of the most important scholars working in the area of black Canadian history. Already a leading and influential scholar specializing in the hidden black history of Canada, in 2000 she completed a PhD dissertation about the life of Henry Bibb, a fugitive slave from Kentucky who became an abolitionist in Canada. This led to her being named a "Kentucky Colonel," the highest award made by the commonwealth of Kentucky; the Canadian government used her work to designate Bibb a person of national historic significance. Cooper has written many articles and several books on Canadian history, one of which, *We're Rooted Here and They Can't Pull Us Up* (1994) was awarded the prestigious Joseph Brant Award for history.

Inspired in School

Afua Cooper was born on November 8, 1957, in the Whithorn district of Westmoreland, Jamaica, one of nine children, five sisters and three brothers. Her father's name was Edward Cooper. Her mother, Ruth Campbell Cooper, was descended from a woman known as Alison Parkinson, who was born in Africa and sold into West Indian slavery. The name "Cooper" comes from William Cooper, the Scottish owner of the Whithorn sugar plantation and its slaves before emancipation in 1838. Afua Cooper attended Haddo and

At a Glance . . .

Born Afua Cooper in 1957 in Whithorn, Westmoreland, Jamaica; married Courtney Powell, 1976 (divorced); married Alpha Diallo, 1991; children: Akil (first marriage), Lamarana (second marriage), Habiba (second marriage). *Education:* University of Toronto, BA, African Studies and Women's Studies, 1986; MA, Black Canadian History, 1991; PhD, Black Canadian History, 2000. *Religion:* Muslim.

Career: Began performing and publishing poetry in Toronto, 1983; teacher of history at University of Toronto, 1994–(assistant professor from 2004). historian/consultant with Parks Canada, 1999–; taught sociology at York and Ryerson universities, 2001-04.

Memberships: Dub Poets Collective; Canadian Historical Association; National Advisory Board on Black History; Writers' Union of Canada.

Awards: Casa de Las Americas Poetry Award Finalist, 1992; Joseph Brant Award for History, for *We're Rooted Here and They Can't Pull Us Up: Essays in African Canadian Women's History*, 1994; Marta Danylewycz Award for Historical Research, 1995; Margaret S. McCullough Graduate Scholarship, University of Toronto, 1997-98; Federal Ministry of Heritage grant for historical research; University of Toronto Exceptional Student Award, 1998-99; John Nicholas Brown Center Fellowship, Brown University, 2001; Canada Council Research Grant, 2001; Commonwealth of Kentucky Award for Contribution to Kentucky history, April 2002; Canadian Federal Government Award for Contribution to Black History; Canada Council Writing Grant, 2003; Academic Leadership Award, University of Toronto Black Alumni, 2004; Harry Jerome Award for Professional Excellence, 2005.

Addresses: *Agent*—The Bukowsky Agency, 14 Prince Arthur Avenue, Suite 202, Toronto, Ontario, M5R 1A9, Canada; *Office*—Office: History Dept., University of Toronto, 100 St. George Street, Toronto, ON M5S 3G3, Canada.

Petersfield primary schools, moving to Kingston at the age of eight. She told *Contemporary Black Biography* that it was there in Kingston in the late 1960s that she began to learn about Black Power and the South African apartheid regime from the men who played ludo and dominoes at her uncle's store.

Cooper attended Camperdown High School from the age of 12 and was inspired by her teachers there. She told *CBB* that unlike most other high schools Camperdown allowed its pupils to wear their hair in afros and dreadlocks. Cooper was a founding member of the African Studies club at the school. By the time of her graduation in 1975 Cooper had become a Rastafarian and she spent a year living with the dub poet Mutabaraka and his wife Yvonne Peters before marrying Courtney Powell. In 1976 she trained as a teacher and went to teach at Vauxhall Secondary School, but in 1979-80 the political violence that divided Jamaica made life there intolerable. After witnessing gunmen chasing students in the school yard Cooper decided to move to Canada in December 1980.

Joined Black Cultural Renaissance

After the birth of her son Akil in July 1981, Cooper worked as an instructor at Bickford Park High School in Toronto, but she was already beginning to perform her poetry at Toronto's spoken word venues, such as Fall Out Shelter, Strictly Ital, and Trojan Horse. Later she joined Gayap Rhythm Drummers as resident poet and percussionist, touring Canada with her poetry of pan-Africanism, social commentary, and radical feminism. Her first book of poetry, *Breaking Chains* was published in 1983, the same year that she enrolled at the University of Toronto to major in African Studies. Cooper told *CBB* that the critics described the book as a "feminist call to arms" while she calls it a "love chant." She was also performing with Lillian Allen, Clifton Joseph, and Devon Haughton as part of what she described as a "black cultural renaissance."

Cooper's marriage broke up in 1986, and in 1988 she became a Muslim. The same year she took up a residency fellowship at Banff School of Fine Arts and wrote two books of poetry, *The Red Caterpillar on College Street* (1989), for children, and *Memories Have Tongue* (1992), which was a finalist in the 1992 Casa de las Americas Award. In 1990 she toured Senegal and Gambia before returning to Toronto to begin her MA degree. Her dissertation, which began her career studying black Canadian history, was a study of black teachers in Ontario 1850-1870. In 1991 she married Alpha Diallo, with whom she has two daughters. After graduation Cooper intended to write a PhD thesis on women and Islam in Sierra Leone, but the civil war prevented her from studying there and she switched to studying Canadian history.

Cooper's doctoral dissertation was a biographical study of the fugitive Kentucky slave Henry Bibb, who lived in

Ontario and became a well-known abolitionist. It continued her interest in telling the hidden or forgotten stories of black history and links with her work as a poet, where she often takes on the voices of slaves, migrants, and children. The significance of her work on Henry Bibb has been recognized by the Commonwealth of Kentucky and by the Canadian government. Partly as a result of her work a plaque honoring Bibb as a person of national historic significance will be unveiled in 2005; Cooper received a certificate of recognition for her work from the Canadian government.

By the time she completed her dissertation Cooper was already an established and award-winning scholar in the field of black Canadian history. In the 1990s she worked as a teaching assistant at the University of Toronto, as well as holding posts at Ryerson and York universities. In 2004 she joined the history department at the University of Toronto, where she teaches African Canadian history and women's history.

Brought Black Canadian History to the Mainstream

Cooper's academic career has been as successful, and as pioneering, as her contribution to the poetry scene; she has been at the forefront of bringing the history of black Canada into the mainstream. In particular Cooper's co-authored book *We're Rooted Here and They Can't Pull Us Up: Essays in African Canadian Women's History* (1994) combines her interest in black history with the issue of gender, examining the representation of women's lives; it won the prestigious Joseph Brant Award for history. *The Underground Railroad* (2002) was the first book to make the firm case for Toronto as a terminus for black Americans fleeing the United States. Cooper's third history book, *The Hanging of Angelique* (2006), explores the life of Marie-Joseph Angelique, a slave accused of starting a fire that destroyed a large area of Montreal in 1734. Her "confession," extracted under torture, was taken down by the chief investigator and, Cooper contends, form the first North American "slave narrative," putting a new perspective on the later slave narratives that contributed to the abolition of slavery in the United States and on the role of slavery in the development of Canadian society.

Cooper's work in both her poetry and her academic writing has been well received by audiences around the world. She is a founding member of the Dub Poets' Collective, the only grassroots poetry organization in Canada, she advises Parks Canada on black history, and has curated several exhibits at museums in Toronto; she sits on the board of the James Johnston Chair in Black Studies at Dalhousie University. Through her work in poetry and as an historian she commemorates 400 years of black Canadian history, telling stories that have never been heard before. In 2005 she was honored with the Harry Jerome Award by the Black Business and Professional Association, for her contribution to black Canadian life.

Selected works

Books

We're Rooted Here and They Can't Pull Us Up: Essays in African Canadian Women's History, with Peggy Bristow, Dionne Brand, Linda Carty, Sylvia Hamilton, and Adrienne Shadd, University of Toronto Press, 1994.
Utterances and Incantations: Women, Poetry, and Dub, Sister Vision Press, 1999.
Doing Battle in Freedom's Cause: Henry Bibb, abolitionism, race uplife, and Black Manhood, 1842-1854 (PhD dissertation), University of Toronto, 2000.
The Underground Railroad: Next Stop, Toronto! with Adrienne Shadd, and Carolyn Smardz Frost, Natural Heritage/Natural History Inc., 2002.
The Hanging of Angelique, HarperCollins, 2006.
Phillis Wheatley, America's First Black Poet, (Young Adult novel), Kidscan Press, 2006.

Exhibits Curated

A Glimpse of Black Life in Victorian Toronto: 1850-1860, Museum Division, City of Toronto, February to September 2002.
The Underground Railroad, Next Stop: Freedom! Royal Ontario Museum, Toronto, April 2002-03; Black Creek Pioneer Village, 2003—.

Poetry

Breaking Chains, Weelahs, 1983.
Red Caterpillar On College Street, Sister Vision Press, 1989.
Memories Have Tongue: Poetry, Sister Vision Press, 1994.

Recordings

WomanTalk: Women Dub Poets, Heartbeat Records, 1984.
Sunshine, Maya Music, 1989.
Poetry Is Not a Luxury, Maya Music 1990.

Sources

Books

Dawes, Kwame, *Talk Yuh Talk: Interviews with Anglophone Caribbean Poets,* University Press of Virginia, 2001.

Periodicals

Journal of Women's History, March 1998.

On-line

"Afua Cooper," *Dub Poets Collective*, http://dubpoetscollective.com/afua.html (June 6, 2005).

"Afua Cooper," *James Robinson Johnston Chair in Black Canadian Studies*, http://jamesrjohnstonchair.dal.ca/johnston_6458.html (June 6, 2005).

"Lessons in Dub," *Now magazine Online Edition*, www.nowtoronto.com/issues/2002-08-29/music_feature_p.html (June 6, 2005).

Ryerson University Black History Month Newsletter, www.ryerson.ca/equity/dhps/BHMNEWSLETTER.doc (June 6, 2005).

Other

Additional information for this profile was provided through an interview with Afua Cooper conducted by email in June 2005 and from documents supplied by her.

—Chris Routledge

Garth Crooks

1958—

Athlete

Crooks, Garth, photograph. Ben Radford/Getty Images.

Garth Crooks made English soccer history as the first black player to score a goal in a championship final in England's FA (Football Association) Cup, the oldest organized soccer competition in the world. Crooks' kick that day in 1981 came at a time when black players among the teams of England's most popular sport were still a rarity, and often subject to hostile chants from the stands.

Crooks was born on March 10, 1958, in Stoke-on-Trent, a city in England's Midlands district. His parents were part of large wave of West Indian immigrants to Britain in the 1950s. In his teens, Crooks was a lackluster student but he emerged as a talented soccer player. He won a spot on the junior division of the Stoke City team, and his skills as a forward and striker—key offensive positions—attracted the attention of the Tottenham Hotspur F.C. (football club). This North London organization was one of England's most popular soccer teams, and in July of 1980 its executives signed Crooks to their roster.

At the time, England was becoming a more multicultural nation, but prejudices against Britons of West Indian, African, and Asian descent were still somewhat commonplace. The professional teams of English soccer—or football, as it is known outside of North America—had had the occasional black player dating back as far as the 1880s, but the first genuine black star in the sport in was Lloyd "Lindy" Delapenha, a Jamaican-born athlete who played for the Middlesbrough team in the 1950s. In 1977 the West Bromwich Albion organization signed the trio of Brendon Batson, Laurie Cunningham, and Cyrille Regis, who were known as the "Three Degrees." Their first season in 1977-78 marked the first time in which an upper-tier English soccer team had three black players on its roster.

During Crooks' first season, he was paired with Steve Archibald, and between them the formidable forward duo scored 46 goals in the regular season. Tottenham went on to the finals of the FA Cup championship series and played Manchester City in May of 1981. In that game, Crooks became the first black player to score a goal in an FA Cup final. The Hotspurs won the cup that year and took it again the following. Crooks also helped the team win a prestigious 1984 pan-European team competition known as the UEFA Cup,

At a Glance . . .

Born on March 10, 1958, in Stoke-on-Trent, England. *Education:* Attended College of North East London, 1984-85; earned B.Sc. from North London Polytechnic College.

Career: Stoke City, professional soccer player, 1974-80; Tottenham Hotspur F.C. (football club), professional soccer player, 1980-84; Manchester United, professional soccer player, 1984-85; West Bromwich Albion, professional soccer player, 1985-87; Charlton Athletic, professional soccer player, 1987-90; BBC TV and radio, broadcaster, 1990–; Professional Footballers Association (union), chairman, 1988-90.

Memberships: English Sports Council; Sickle Cell Anaemia Relief (SCAR) Organization, founder and chair; Institute of Professional Sport, chair.

Awards: Order of the British Empire (OBE).

Addresses: *Office*—c/o Institute of Professional Sport, Francis House, Francis Street, London SW1P 1DE, England.

the acronym for the Union of European Football Associations.

Soccer was still largely a working-class sport in Britain in the 1980s, and local team rivalries were strong. During the decade, violence and "hooliganism" blighted the game in England, and some European teams even barred British fans from attending the away games of their favorite teams. During Crooks' career, racist chants and banners were commonplace in the stands, and sometimes fans even threw bananas onto the field or made monkey noises. "Black players didn't complain about racism because it was made clear to us that we had to cope with it, it was seen as a test of character," Crooks was quoted as saying by *Guardian* writer Vivek Chaudhary.

In 1985, Crooks was traded to West Bromwich Albion, but that same year he also began taking advantage of a tuition-reimbursement benefit offered by the Professional Footballers' Association (PFA), the players' union for soccer athletes in the United Kingdom. He started with classes at the College of North East London, and eventually earned a degree in political science from North London Poly. In 1988, now playing for the Charlton Athletic club, he was elected chair of the 4,000-member PFA, which is also the world's oldest professional athletes' association. Crooks was the first black player ever to lead the PFA, and supported a clean-up campaign in British soccer that helped end some of the racism and hooliganism with which it had become associated. A 1991 British law that prohibited chanting of racial slurs at soccer games, and gave law-enforcement officials the power to arrest fans who did so, was a major milestone for all players of color in the sport.

Despite his high profile in British sports, Crooks was unable to avoid an ugly incident of police harassment in 1990, when a plainclothes officer stopped him on a London street and accused him of shoplifting. Crooks had gone out to get some snacks during a board meeting of the Institute for Sickle Cell Anaemia Relief, one of the many charitable causes to which he lent him name and time. He had also helped promote the youth soccer league of the London Metropolitan police force, and when he asserted his innocence and then mentioned the name of a high-ranking officer he knew through his youth-league work, one of officers responded, "'Yes, and I'm a personal friend of the Queen,'" Crooks recounted in a *Sunday Times* interview with Tim Rayment. It was only when a third officer arrived and recognized Crooks that was he released. He filed a formal complaint of "incivility" because, as he told the *Sunday Times,* he hoped to make a point to others, "and I was one of them who think criticism of the police is exaggerated, just a knee-jerk reaction within our community." In the same interview, he reflected, "Everyone I have told has had the same reaction: if I don't have a chance, what chance has anyone else?"

Crooks had retired by then, after an 18-year professional career, but had gone on to become a radio and television announcer for British soccer. By the late 1990s he was even hosting his own show on the BBC2, one of the radio stations of the British Broadcasting Corporation network. Called *Despatch Box,* it dealt with news issues of the day, and Crooks' high profile and interest in politics led to the occasional rumor that he might run for a seat in the House of Commons.

Crooks remained active in his various charitable projects, and also worked with Britain's Commission for Racial Equality (CRE) as well as athletic bodies such as the Institute of Professional Sport. In 2003, he became chair of the racism and equality issues committee of the Independent Football Commission. A year later he delivered a somewhat controversial speech at the "London Schools and the Black Child 2004 Conference," in which he warned against "gangsta" culture in Britain and its negative effects on the younger generation. "We must convey to the next generation that street culture was meant to be a fashion not a lifestyle," the father of two told the audience that day, "a bit of fun not a code of conduct. Our job as parents is not to dismiss it but to put it in its proper perspective. If we don't then 'street culture' will become a deadly virus ripping indiscriminately through yet another generation and robbing millions of their potential." The remarks were widely quoted in the British media, and earned Crooks comparisons to American entertainer Bill Cosby, who had also recently made statements about family values in the African-American community.

Sources

Periodicals

Guardian (London, England), April 22, 2000, p. 7; March 3, 2003, p. 12.

Independent (London, England), September 13, 2004, p. 33.

Independent Sunday (London, England), April 11, 1999, p. 4; April 27, 2003, p. 11.

Sunday Times (London, England), May 20, 1990.

Times (London, England), November 30, 1988.

On-line

"Garth Crooks—London Schools and the Black Child 2004 Conference," *Commission for Racial Equality,* www.cre.gov.uk/Default.aspx.LocID-0hgnew03v.RefLocID-0hg00900c002.Lang-EN.htm (June 23, 2005).

"The Garth Crooks Years: 1988-1990," *givemefootball,* www.givemefootball.com/display.cfm?article=3077&type=1 (July 12, 2005).

—Carol Brennan

Craig David

1981—

Musician

British rhythm-and-blues (R&B) singer Craig David rocketed to success at age 19 with his very first album, *Born to Do It*. His unique blend of soulful lyrics, subtle melodies, and infectious beats have earned him critical admiration and popular fame, prompting Sir Elton John to proclaim him the best singer in England.

David, Craig, photograph. Jens Kalaene/DPA/Landov.

Became Teenage MC

The son of a black father and white mother, Craig Ashley David was born on May 5, 1981, and grew up in Southampton, a city southwest of London. As a young child he absorbed a wide variety of musical influences. His father, a carpenter and bass player in a reggae band, took him to rehearsals and gigs. His mother played Stevie Wonder, Terence Trend D'Arby, and the Osmonds' records. As he later commented to *New York Times* writer James Hunter, "I kind of caught that puppy love thing" from his mother's favorite music. Though his parents divorced when he was eight and he lived thereafter with his mother, David remained close to his father, who encouraged the boy to take guitar lessons. "I loved the guitar," David told *Entertainment Weekly* writer Rob Brunner, "but I wasn't really feeling these classical songs. I wanted to sing."

By age 14, David was spending a lot of time at the dances sponsored by his father's West Indian social club. One night, the DJ there let the boy try his hand as an MC. He proved quite popular, and was soon offered gigs at local clubs and parties. With his earnings—about $150 per week—he built a small studio in his bedroom. He sang on the single "Let's Kick Racism Out of Football" for the English Premier League soccer organization, and won a national song-writing contest with the tune "I'm Ready" for the boy-band Damage.

David's first big career break came in 1997, when he met producer Mark Hill, who recorded dance tracks under the name Artful Dodger. Hill invited David to collaborate on the single "What Ya Gonna Do," which they released on vinyl and which was included on the album *Rewind (When the Crowd Say Bo Selecta)*. The song was an instant hit, helping to popularize the British dance-music genre known as the two-step. "It caused a storm on the underground scene," David said of the record in remarks quoted by Brunner. "We were just amazed. We were these guys from Southampton,

At a Glance . . .

Born on May 5, 1981, in Southampton, England; son of George and Tina David. *Education:* Attended Southampton City College.

Career: Recording artist and touring performer, 1997–. Worked as deejay and MC in Southampton, England; lyricist and performer on dance singles.

Awards: MasterCard Music of Black Origin (MOBO) Awards, Best R&B Act, Best U.K. Single for "Fill Me In," and Best U.K. Newcomer, 2000; *Billboard* Music Video Awards, Best Dance New Artist Clip, Best R&B New Artist Clip, 2001; MTV Europe Music Video Awards, Best R&B Act, Best U.K./Ireland Act, 2001.

Addresses: *Label*—c/o Warner Music International, Ave. de Chillon 70, 1820 Montreaux, Switzerland. *Web*—www.craigdaviduk.com.

and we'd made a record that was getting five-star reviews. It was crazy."

Launched Solo Career

With the huge success of two-step, David was in an ideal position to make his first solo recording. In March 2000 he released the song "Fill Me In," which went straight to the top of the U.K. pop charts. At age 19, David was the youngest British male solo artist ever to enjoy the distinction of a number-one hit song. *Born to Do It,* his debut album featuring the hit single, was released in 2001. Produced by Mark Hill, it sold 7 million copies and reached gold, platinum, or multi-platinum status in more than 20 countries. *Entertainment Weekly* writer Will Hermes described *Born to Do It* as a "brilliantly market-tuned fusion of R&B elegance and all ages pop sugar" that made David a "post-race, post-class poster boy for England's new melting-pot culture."

David's second album, *Slicker Than Your Average*, was released in 2002. It presents "a more assured, intimate sound and lyrics," noted a reviewer on the *Craig David* Web site. "Anyone expecting a sequel to *Born to Do It* is in for a surprise. *Slicker* is the sound of a man who has seen the world, perfected his live sound and is truly comfortable in his own skin. More accomplished and diverse than his debut, it sees Craig merge the influences he grew up on with the experiences he had absorbed." The hit single from the album, "What's Your Flava," was the basis of a music video that David based on his favorite film, *Willie Wonka and the Chocolate Factory*.

Solid hits in England and Europe, both albums also sold well in the United States, where David's celebrity fans include Quincy Jones, Beyonce, Missy Elliot, J-Lo, and Usher. Nevertheless, some American hip-hop fans have accused David of creating music that is too soft. But the singer told James Hunter of the *New York Times* that these critics are just jealous. "I always knew that my music had a lot more pop-R&B influence," he noted, "and I wasn't going to just jump on being the face of two-step garage." The singer makes no apologies for his polite, cheerful image. He does not smoke, rarely drinks, and avoids rough language and topics in his songs. As he commented in *Hello!* magazine, "Growing up with my mum, I think it gave me so much more respect for women in general, and to not be vulgar in the way you go about writing songs."

Remained Loyal to Home-Grown Values

Though David has won numerous awards, including Best R&B Act, Best U.K. Newcomer, and Best U.K. Single in 2000 by the MasterCard Music of Black Origin Awards in 2000, those close to him say that success has not changed the young musician. He still considers Southampton home and is proud of his roots in that city. David has participated in several charity concerts, including the Tsunami Relief Cardiff concert in 2005, in which he joined such other notable artists as Eric Clapton and the Stereophonics. The event raised more than one million pounds for those affected by the tsunami that hit south Asia in December 2004. Another honor was being invited to join the roster of performers at the Live 8 concert at Hyde Park in London on July 2, 2005. The concert, one of several staged worldwide, was organized to raise awareness of world poverty, especially in Africa.

Not merely seeking fame, David has aspirations to achieve something deeper with his music. "I just felt that deep inside I was part of something unique and British but yet that was very exportable," he told Hunter. "Coming from a mixed-race family...I was always very open-minded about music.... I love to ask questions and find out what it is that makes things tick." David released his third album, *The Story Goes*, in August 2005. He described the project to interviewer Noel Davies as "another chapter in my life [that] brings me back to things how they used to be when I was starting off. There's a lot of good memories there for me." Noting that the lyrics on this new record differ from his previous work, he said that he thinks it is his best work to date. "Craig's a true gentleman," said Ron Shapiro, co-president of the singer's record label, to Hunter. "Craig's about joyousness."

Selected discography

Albums

Born to Do It, Atlantic, 2001.
Slicker Than Your Average, Atlantic, 2002.
The Story Goes, Warner Music International, 2005.

Singles

"What Ya Gonna Do," 1997.
"Fill Me In," 2000.

Sources

Books

Contemporary Musicians, Vol. 42, Gale Group, 2003.

Periodicals

Entertainment Weekly, July 20 , 2001, p. 64; August 3, 2001, p. 30.
Jet, August 6, 2001.
New York Times, January 19, 2003.
People Weekly, December 9, 2002, p. 109.

On-line

Craig David, www.craigdaviduk.com (August 30, 2005).
"Craig David," *Hello!*, www.hellomagazine.com (June 14, 2005).
Davies, Noel, "Q & A with Craig," *Southern Daily Echo*, www.thisissouthampton.co.uk (June 7, 2005).

—E. M. Shostak

Deezer D

1965—

Actor, musician

Deezer D, photograph. Amanda Edwards/Getty Images.

Best known for his role as nurse Malik McGrath on the popular television show *ER,* Deezer D transformed himself almost overnight from a gang member and alcoholic to a dedicated, clean-living Christian. His conversion included a movement towards the Christian rap music industry that culminated in an album with a strong message about the artist's own life and fame. Having listened to rap music most of his life, Deezer D wanted to send out a positive message to kids as opposed to the negative messages from the rap music he had grown up with. As an actor and a Christian rap artist, Deezer D has proven that success is possible in spite of the roots from which a person comes. His music and changed lifestyle have inspired and given hope to those he grew up with, as well as to the world that knows him as a rebel turned Christian.

Deezer D was born Dearon Thompson in 1965 into a family that drank heavily. He grew up in South Central Los Angeles, California, where he eventually became the member of a gang. "My house was like the Jerry Springer Show," claimed Deezer D on the *Connection Magazine* Web site. Although he harbored a dream of becoming a professional basketball player, he was thrown off his high school team and soon after left high school without graduating. Being forced to leave his high school basketball team changed Deezer D's life. Sports had served as a slight buffer from bad influences. Without a spot on the basketball team, Deezer D soon began drinking heavily. Deezer D recalled his parents' early discouragement from drinking and drugs, but he noted in an interview with *Connection Magazine* that "When I started doing it, it wasn't really a big deal." Drinking and rap music became a big part of Deezer D's life—a lifestyle he shared with his family and friends.

Encouraged by friends, Deezer D followed his interest in music by writing and singing rap songs. Music was in his blood and it came naturally to him, even though breaking into the music industry required hard work and persistence. His real break came with a rap song he had written about the dangers of smoking, which led to a television spot and an agent. Using the name "Deezer D," he was soon playing small television roles, and in time decided to pursue acting as a career. He attained two roles in the early 1990s in John Wells' series *China Beach* and *Angel Street,* which

At a Glance . . .

Born Dearon Thompson in 1965, in Los Angeles, CA; married Samantha Enson (2004). *Religion:* Christian.

Career: Actor, 1994–; musician, 2000–.

Addresses: *Office*—Crichton TV, 4000 Warner Brothers Blvd., Production Building #1, Burbank, CA 91505; *Record Label*—N*Soul Records Inc., 11455 Burbank Blvd., North Hollywood, CA 91601-2303.

introduced him to the entertainment world and set him on the path to becoming a well-known actor. His first feature films included the 1991 rap-oriented remake of *Rebel without a Cause, Cool as Ice,* starring rapper Vanilla Ice, and in the 1993 comedy *CB4,* playing a member of an up-and-coming rap group, followed by bit parts in *The Great White Hype* in 1996 and *Romy and Michelle's High School Reunion* in 1997.

But it was on television that Deezer D first found great success. John Wells remembered Deezer D and offered him the opportunity to play the role of nurse Malik McGrath on NBC's popular television drama, *ER,* in 1994. Deezer D eagerly took to the part, and has appeared in the show's 12 seasons.

During his tenure as Malik on *ER*, Deezer D grew close to his fellow cast members. When he wed makeup artist Samantha Enson on November 14, 2004, Deezer D celebrated the occasion with cast members from eleven season of *ER*; Noah Wyle and Abraham Benrubi served as groomsmen. About his feelings for his *ER* coworkers, Deezer D told *People Weekly* that "They're much more than co-workers. They're part of my extended family."

Although Deezer D had achieved steady work in Hollywood, his life was tumultuous because of his drinking and carousing. But one Saturday night at a down time in his life that all changed when Deezer D's roommate invited him to attend church. With nothing else to do that night, Deezer D agreed. Minister Tim Storey began preaching, and "He was backing stuff up with scripture, and I'd never heard that before. He was applying scripture to your everyday life," Deezer D noted on the *Crosswalk* Web site. After hearing the pastor's inspirational message, Deezer D decided to become a Christian. He "quit his old sinful ways cold turkey," according to *Crosswalk,* and completely committed his life to the Lord. Deezer D has since taken care to incorporate his religious values into every aspect of his life and work. He is an active member of his West Covina, California, church and has maintained a strong relationship with Minister Tim Storey.

After his conversion, he felt responsible to improve the standard of Christian rap music, and to send a positive and hopeful message to youth. "My acting career has allowed me to do Christian rap music and speak to kids.... I believe I have a responsibility to make some good, positive hip-hop that's not cheesy," Deezer D explained to *Connection Magazine.* His disappointment in Christian rap music prompted him to self-fund a Christian rap album in 2000 called *Livin Up In A Down World.* The hip-hop album has 19 tracks that celebrate and was produced by D. Black & Chris Gunn for Black Gunn productions. At the release of his new album, Deezer D vowed to his audience to produce authentic rap music that people could relate to. Referring to the quality, content, and funding of his album, Deezer D told the *Crosswalk* Web site, "If we're going to be doing it for God, let's do it on God's level." The N*Soul Web site promoted Deezer D as a "pioneer of an intrinsic craving within rap music: a beat you can listen to and the lyrics worth living for." Deezer D's further involved himself in the Christian music community by acting in Christian singer Carman's 2005 video and hosting a Christian rap radio show on Los Angeles station KFSG for a short time.

Deezer D 's success in the film and music industries is evidence of his ambition and will to overcome tremendous odds. Having grown up in an environment where drinking and gangs were conventional, Deezer D strove to become more, and his life serves as a testimonial of the power of commitment, willpower, and dedication to a higher standard. He shares his new values and life experiences with audiences as a motivational speaker, and serves as a counselor to Alcoholics Anonymous.

Selected works

Albums

Livin Up In A Down World, N*Soul, 2000.

Films

Cool as Ice, Universal Studios, 1991.
CB-4, Universal Studios, 1993.
Fear of a Black Hat, Columbia Tristar, 1994.
The Great White Hype, Fox Home Entertainment, 1996.
Romy and Michele's High School Reunion, Touchstone Pictures, 1997

Television

ER, 1994—.

Sources

Periodicals

"Two Hearts," *People Weekly*, November 29, 2004, p. 190.

On-line

"Deezer D," *N*Soul*, www.nsoul.com/artdisp.cfm?artistnum=61 (June 4, 2005).
"Deezer D Acts Up," *Crosswalk,* www.Crosswalk.com/fun/music/540224.html (June 4, 2005).
"Hollywood Hip-Hop & Heaven: On the Set with Actor Deezer D," *Connection Magazine*, http://ftp.connectionmagazine.org (June 4, 2005).

—Cheryl Dudley

Birago Diop

1906-1989

Writer

At the time of his death in 1989, Birago Diop was one of Senegal's most prominent writers, and had been since he first rose to fame in the 1950s. Though he wrote in the French language, Diop's works drew upon the folktales of his West African nation's indigenous Wolof culture. An obituary in the *Times* of London praised his "deceptively simple stories" with their "many memorable animal-people and master-tricksters."

Born on December 11, 1906, Diop came from the Ouakam area just outside of Dakar, Senegal's largest city and later its capital. At the time, Senegal was part of French West Africa. The country was situated on the African bulge on the Atlantic Ocean coast, and it had once been a major slave-trading center in centuries past. Slaves were captured from the Wolof, its largest ethnic group, and from the Fula, Serer, Jola, and Mandinka ethnic groups. Though animist beliefs were still strong, Islam had dominated Senegal's culture since the eleventh century.

Diop's father was a mason, but left the family when the mother, Sokhna, was pregnant with Diop. He grew up with two older brothers, and by the age of fifteen was living in Saint-Louis, then Senegal's capital, where he was a scholarship student at the Lycée Faidherbe, a French-language school. As a young man he served a stint in the military as a nurse in a military hospital in the city in the late 1920s, and from there went on to France to attend veterinary college.

In France, Diop studied at the École Nationale Vétérinaire in the city of Toulouse, and completed further studies in exotic veterinary medicine in Paris. While living in the culturally flourishing capital in 1933, he met other black writers from French colonies in Africa and the Caribbean. These included Léopold Sédar Senghor, also from Senegal, and Martinique's Aimé Césaire. Encouraged by Senghor, Diop began writing during this period, and his earliest poems were published in *L'Etudiant noir* (The Black Student), edited by Césaire. *L'Etudiant noir* was the leading voice of the exciting new Négritude literary movement. Négritude opposed the assimilation of black writers into European culture, arguing instead for a unique black voice within French culture.

When Diop returned to Senegal, he took a job as head of the government cattle-inspection service in Senegal and the French Sudan (now Mali). But he had long been fascinated by the folktales of Senegal's tribes, the first of which he had heard as a child from his grandmother. His veterinary work took him to remote regions of the interior, where he learned other stories from tribal elders. These he sometimes shared with other Négritude writers when he found himself stranded in France once again during World War II. They urged him to commit these oral folktales to paper, and his homesickness spurred him to write them down.

When Diop finally returned to Africa, he served as director of zoological technical services in Ivory Coast and Upper Volta after 1946, but his literary debut came in 1947 with *Les Contes d'Amadou Koumba,* a collection of short stories based on Senegalese folk takes. Diop claimed that Amadou Koumba was a griot, or traditional West African storyteller, that Diop had

At a Glance . . .

Born on December 11, 1906, in Ouakam (some sources say Dakar), Senegal; died on November 25, 1989, in Dakar, Senegal; son of Ismael (a master mason) and Sokhna (Diawara) Diop; married Marie-Louise Pradére, 1934 (deceased); children: Renee, Andree. *Education:* École Nationale Vétérinaire de Toulouse, doctorate, 1933; attended Institut de Médecine Vétérinaire Exotique, c. 1934, and École Francaise des Cuirs et Peaux. *Military Service:* Nurse in military hospital in St.-Louis, Senegal, 1928-29.

Career: Short-story writer and poet. Head of government cattle inspection service in Senegal and French Sudan (now Mali), c. 1934-42; Institut de Médecine Vétérinaire Exotique, Paris, France, veterinarian, 1942-44; Ivory Coast, interim head of zoological technical services, 1946; head of zoological technical services, Upper Volta (now Burkina Faso), 1947-50, in Mauritania, 1950- 54, and in Senegal, 1955; Société de la Radio-Diffusion d'Outre-Mer, administrator, 1960s; Dakar, Senegal, veterinarian in private practice, beginning c. 1964.

Memberships: Association des Écrivains du Sénégal, president; Bureau Sénégalais des Droits d'Auteur , president of administrative council; Société des Gens de Lettres de France; PEN.

Awards: Grand Prix Littéraire de l'Afrique-Occidentale Francaise, for *Les Contes d'Amadou Koumba*; Association des Ecrivains d'Expression Francaise de la Mer et de l'Outre Mer, Grand Prix Littéraire de l'Afrique Noire, for *Contes et lavanes;* Officier de la Légion d'Honneur; chevalier de l'Étoile Noire; chevalier du Mérite Agricole.

met on his travels, but he later said that Koumba was a composite of many such griots he had come to know.

The animal-centered tales in *Les Contes d'Amadou Koumba* usually featured a rivalry between hyena and a clever rabbit known as Leuk the Hare. In one, Leuk urges the other animals to burrow with him one night to a nearby village called N'Doum, where he knows of an immense storehouse of food in a doorless hut surrounded by seven tall reed fences. The food has been stored there by King Bour, who also put his daughter there to see if she would become pregnant. "So Rat, Palm-squirrel, Civet-cat, Skunk, and the others burrowed all night till they emerged into the doorless hut, but as soon as they saw that the riches Leuk had promised them were guarded by a girl, they turned tail and fled," wrote Diop. "The memory of the misfortunes that had befallen their forebears came back to them. They remembered in time that in N'Doum girls were as skilful as boys in handling cudgels and hunting-spears. So they all fled back to the bush, vowing to get their own back on Hare, who watched them scamper away."

Left with the lonely princess Anta, Leuk offered to serve as her husband. When she asked his name, he replied "Mana" ("It's me"). In time, she became pregnant, and her father, King Bour, grew angry when reports reach him that a child's cries have been overheard from the doorless hut. When Bour asks Anta who the father of the child is, she replies, "Mana." Bour then asks the child who is father is, and the child answers "Mana," too. Confused, the king assembles all the animals in a circle, gives the child a treat, and tells the boy to give them to his father. Despite his attempts to evade detection, Leuk is caught and Bour threatens to kill him. But Leuk skillfully pleads for his life, and so Bour demands that he venture forth and bring back a panther skin and one from a lion as well, a set of elephant tusks, and also the hair of Kouss, a bearded goblin. The story continues in the next tale in Diop's volume.

Diop's work proved so popular in Senegal that he published a second volume, *Les Nouveaux Contes d'Amadou Koumba* ("The New Tales of Amadou Koumba"), for which Senghor authored the preface. In 1960 Diop's first volume of poetry, *Leurres et lueurs,* appeared, and that was the same year that the Senghor-led independence movement gave Senegal its first elected black government, with Senghor as president. Senghor sent Diop to Tunisia as Senegal's ambassador to the North African nation.

Diop established his own veterinary practice in Dakar after 1964, and continued to write folktales and dramas. Widely celebrated for his writing, he won many awards and spent years writing a five-volume autobiography. His last work was *Mother Crocodile: Maman-Caiman,* a volume of short stories, which appeared in 1981. Only this and *Contes et lavanes,* a 1963 collection of folk tales, have been translated into English. He died at the age of 83 in Dakar. Married to accountant Marie-Louise Pradére for many years, he was the father of two children, Renee and Andree.

Selected writings

Les Contes d'Amadou Koumba (short stories), Fasquelle, 1947; translated as *Tales of Amadou Koumba* by Dorothy S. Blair, Oxford University Press, 1966.

Sarzan (play), performed in Dakar, Senegal, 1955.

Les Nouveaux Contes d'Amadou Koumba (short stories; includes "L'Os de Mor Lam"), preface by Léopold Sédar Senghor, Présence Africaine, 1958.

Leurres et lueurs (poems; title means "Lures and Lights"), Présence Africaine, 1960.

Contes et lavanes (short stories), Présence Africaine, 1963.

Contes choisis (short stories), edited with an introduction by Joyce A. Hutchinson, Cambridge University Press, 1967.

L'Os de Mor Lam (play), performed at Theatre National Daniel Sorano, Senegal, 1967-68; published by Nouvelles Editions Africaines, 1977.

Contes d'Awa (short stories), Nouvelles Editions Africaines, 1977.

Memoires (autobiography), Vol. 1: *La Plume raboutée,* Présence Africaine, 1978; Vol. 2: *Á Rebrousse-temps,* Présence Africaine, 1982; Vol. 3: *A Rebrousse-gens: Epissures, entrelacs, et reliefs,* Présence Africaine, 1985, Vol. 4: *Sénégal du temps de,* L'Harmattan, 1989; Vol. 5: *Et les yeux pour me dire,* L'Harmattan, 1989.

Mother Crocodile: Maman-Caiman (short stories), translated and adaptated by Rosa Guy, illustrated by John Steptoe, Delacorte Press, 1981.

Sources

Periodicals

Research in African Literatures, Winter 2002, p. 101.

Times (London, England), November 27, 1989.

On-line

Birago Diop, http://neveu01.chez.tiscali.fr (July 7, 2005).

"Birago Diop," *Books and Writers,* www.kirjasto.sci.fi/bdiop.htm (July 7, 2005).

"Birago (Ismail) Diop," *Biography Resource Center,* www.galenet.com/servlet/BioRC (June 7, 2005).

—Carol Brennan

Denzil Douglas

1953—

Prime Minister of St. Kitts and Nevis

Douglas, Dr. Denzil, photograph. AP/Wide World Photos. Reproduced by permission.

With his election to Prime Minister of St. Kitts and Nevis on July 3, 1995, Dr. Denzil Llewellyn Douglas, leader of the country's Labour Party (SKNLP), ended a twelve-year period in which the People's Action Movement (PAM) dominated the country's assembly. Douglas's arrival in high office followed the resignation of Kennedy Alphonse Simmonds, whose government had been tarnished by a series of scandals involving drug smuggling and organized crime. For several years SKNLP supporters had protested against Simmonds's seemingly unbreakable grip on power and the suspicion that government officials and their families were benefiting from special treatment by the police and security services. Among Douglas's first actions as prime minister was to begin reform of the police force in the hope that the country could shed its reputation as a haven for drug gangs and money launderers. He also faced the difficult task of solving the longstanding problem of violent crime, unrest, and increasing lawlessness, some of which had involved his own party's supporters. He even enlisted help from the British government to achieve this goal.

Progress on law and order was slow, but by 2004 Douglas had succeeded in re-establishing St. Kitts and Nevis as a tourist destination, giving as evidence for this a new 600-room Marriott hotel. In 1998 he successfully fought for the "No" campaign in Nevis's referendum over independence from St. Kitts, arguing that the smaller island could not sustain itself. Despite criticism of his record on crime, rising national debt, rising taxes, high unemployment, and the faltering banana and sugar markets, Douglas held on to power in elections in 2000 and 2004. He has consistently fought for social justice in domestic policy and for the place of St. Kitts and Nevis in the international community.

Began Political Career Early

Born on January 14, 1953, in the village of St. Pauls in St. Kitts and Nevis, Denzil Llewellyn Douglas was educated in local schools before attending the University of the West Indies in Trinidad and Tobago, where he graduated with a BSc in surgery in 1977 and a degree in medicine in 1984. After a two-year internship in Trinidad, Douglas returned to St. Kitts and Nevis and opened his own private medical practice where he became a popular family doctor.

At a Glance . . .

Born Denzil Llewellyn Douglas on January 14, 1953, in St. Kitts and Nevis. *Education:* University of the West Indies, BSc, Surgery, 1977; BSc, Medicine, 1984.

Career: Medical practitioner, 1986–; St. Kitts and Nevis, prime minister, elected 1995, 2000, and 2004; minister of finance, development, planning, and national security, St. Kitts and Nevis, 1995–.

Memberships: SKNLP National Executive, Young Labour representative 1979; St. Kitts Amateur Football Association, secretary, 1979; St. Kitts and Nevis Medical Association, president, late 1980s; St. Kitts and Nevis Labour Party, chairman, 1989.

Addresses: *Office*—Office of the Prime Minister, Church St., P.O. Box 186, Government Headquarters, Basseterre, Saint Kitts and Nevis.

Douglas began his career in the St. Kitts and Nevis Labour Party (SKNLP) as a student and by 1979 he had become the first Young Labour representative to sit on the National Executive Committee. His political ambition and commitment to public service also saw him become the secretary of the St. Kitts Amateur Football Association and, in the late 1980s, president of the St. Kitts and Nevis Medical Association. In 1987 he took on a more significant role in the SKNLP when he was made deputy chairman; he sought election to the Parliament of the National Assembly in the general election of 1989.

Douglas stood for election in the constituency of Newton Ground/Harris and, though he won one of the 11 available elected seats, the election was disastrous for the SKNLP which lost to Prime Minister Kennedy Alphonse Simmonds and his conservative PAM. PAM had held power since St. Kitts and Nevis, with its population of 39 thousand, became independent in 1983. In the aftermath of the defeat Douglas took over the leadership of the party and became the official leader of the opposition in the assembly. He faced a difficult task restructuring and modernizing the party and was over five years before the SKNLP was ready to take power.

Experienced Troubled Political Times

Between 1989 and 1993 PAM fell out of favour with the St. Kitts and Nevis voters, partly because Simmonds and his government were tarnished by political scandal, but also because after ten years in power they seemed to have achieved very little. In the election of 1993 PAM won only four seats, forcing Simmonds to make alliances with the Nevis Reformation Party (NRP), which held one seat. By doing so he held on to power with 41 percent of the popular vote, to SKNLP's 54 percent. But by then PAM's collapse as a political force was imminent. Rioting broke out in the capital Basseterre in protest at the way the popular vote had been ignored, with SKNLP supporters claiming not only that the government was illegitimate, but that Simmonds and his party was responsible for the general breakdown in law and order, St. Kitts and Nevis' growing role in the drug trade, and problems in the tourism industry.

In 1994 the political tension erupted into scandal when a fisherman discovered cocaine valued at millions of dollars buried on a beach. Two sons of the deputy prime minister, Sydney Morris, were implicated in drug smuggling and a third disappeared but they were bailed and seemed beyond the law; Morris, who resigned his post, soon returned to the government. Rioting broke out again, eventually triggering the formation of a multi-party national unity forum, and in 1995-three years early-an election.

Won a Landslide Victory

The election in 1995 marked a dramatic change in the country's political fortunes. The SKNLP won seven of the 11 elected seats, including Simmonds's own, and Douglas was sworn in as prime minister on July 4 with a mandate to reform the police, resolve the country's problems with money laundering and drug smuggling, improve the agricultural economy, and boost tourism. He also had to act on commitments to improve housing, education, healthcare, and other central issues. His first term, in which he also served as finance minister, was followed by an even more significant victory in the election of 2000, when the SKNLP won all eight of the St. Kitts seats in the assembly.

Many of the reforms Douglas established in his first term began to show signs of working in the second. For example, he had requested help from the British government over reforming the police force and by 2000 levels of crime had fallen significantly; in 2002 St. Kitts and Nevis was removed from the Organisation for Economic Cooperation and Development (OECD) list of countries involved in money laundering. Tourism and foreign investment also improved and while the economy continued to struggle, in the run-up to the 2004 election Douglas was able to to point to a brand-new 600-room Marriott hotel as evidence that foreign investors and tourists were returning to the islands after a series of setbacks, including hurricanes, drought, and the World Trade Center attacks of 2001. Perhaps most importantly one of Douglas's first acts as premier in 1995 was to attend a conference of Caribbean leaders in Guyana, where he helped negotiate further integration of the Caribbean economies within the Caribbean Community and Common Market (CARICOM). Improved free trade with other Caribbean countries made Douglas popular with businesses in St. Kitts and Nevis. Douglas has also shown considerable political skill in negotiating with countries outside the region to garner assistance and investment, including the United States, the United Kingdom, Norway, and Japan. His success has allowed the country to become a fully-fledged member of the international community.

Won a Third Term

After the victory in 2000 Douglas's government pushed forward with reforms to the welfare, education, and health systems, managing to retain his government's popularity despite the opposition's criticism of his management of the economy, in particular the decline of the banana and sugar growing industries. When Douglas called the early election in October 2004 there was certainly room for improvement. PAM leader Lindsey Grant attacked Douglas on unemployment, which stood at 10 percent in 2004, and the Eastern Caribbean $2 billion (US$742 million) deficit, but PAM managed to claw back only one seat on St. Kitts, giving the SKNLP seven to PAM's four elected seats.

But challenges facing Douglas and his government in his third term of office are significant. In particular Douglas has campaigned strongly to address the threat of HIV/AIDS in the Caribbean region, leading the effort to develop locally-produced generic anti-retroviral drugs, to provide benefits for those affected by the disease, and to promote public health campaigns. He told the *Stabroek News* that besides its human cost, HIV/AIDS could undermine social cohesion and damage the region's developing economies. In domestic politics Douglas also faces the challenge of the possible break up of St. Kitts and Nevis if the smaller island goes ahead with its claim to independence and holds a second referendum (the first was held in 1998). Douglas has said that he does not believe Nevis's economy is self-sustaining, but many Nevisians disagree.

After over a decade in power, in 2004 Douglas remained a popular and respected leader both at home and in the many regional and international organizations in which he has represented his country. These include the Organisation of Eastern Caribbean States (OECS), the Eastern Caribbean Central Bank (ECCB), the Caribbean Community and Common Market, (CARICOM), the Caribbean Development Bank (CDB), the Association of Caribbean States (ACS), the Organisation of American States (OAS), the International Monetary Fund (IMF), the World Bank, the British Commonwealth, and the United Nations.

Sources

Periodicals

Asia Africa Intelligence Wire, October 29, 2004.
Jamaica Observer, October 27, 2004.
Presidents and Prime Ministers, November 2000, p. 36.
Stabroek News, May 23, 2005.

On-line

"Biography of the Prime Minister," *St. Kitts & Nevis*, www.stkittsnevis.net/pm/index.html (June 2, 2005).
"St. Kitts and Nevis," *Caribbean Net News*, www.caribbeannetnews.com/stkitts/stkitts-nevis.htm (May 26, 2005).
St.Kitts-Nevis Labour Party, www.sknlabourparty.org/main.html (June 2, 2005).
"Denzil Douglas," *Biography Resource Center*, www.galenet.com/servlet/BioRC (May 26, 2005).

—Chris Routledge

Vivica A. Fox

1964—

Actor

In 1997 *Essence* magazine asserted Vivica A. Fox was "the Hollywood homegirl of the moment." Nearly a decade later, Fox had parlayed her screen appeal into a successful acting career with more than a dozen films and nearly as many television appearances to her name. In the early 2000s, Fox had her sights set on a long, powerful career in Hollywood, and had begun to develop a behind-the-scenes career as a producer.

Fox was born in South Bend, Indiana, on July 30, 1964, the youngest of four children. Her parents—Fox's father is an administrator at a private school, and her mother a pharmaceutical technician—divorced when she was just four. Fox's teenage years were active ones as she grew up in Indianapolis; she worked at a fast-food restaurant while also playing school sports and singing in the choir, but confessed to being star struck from an early age. "I always knew I was going to perform. As soon as I finished my homework, I would dig into a magazine and read about show business," she recalled in *People*. After graduation, she moved to Los Angeles to pursue that performing career, but wisely enrolled in school part-time at Golden West College in Huntington Beach as well. She also worked in a restaurant on Sunset Boulevard, and one day a customer—who turned out to be a film producer—recommended that she give his agent-friend a call.

Fox called the woman, and was soon auditioning for and winning small roles on television shows such as ABC's *Matlock*, *Days of Our Lives*, and *Generations*, another 1989 NBC daytime soap, but aimed at an African American audience. She also won a small part in *Born on the Fourth of July*, the 1989 Tom Cruise movie about a Vietnam veteran; Fox played a hooker in her big-screen debut. A role in an 1991 episode of NBC's *The Fresh Prince of Bel-Air* led to a recurring one on *Out All Night*, also on NBC, in which she played Patti LaBelle's fashion-stylist daughter; however, unlike the popular *Fresh Prince*, *Out All Night* failed to reach an audience and was cancelled.

Nevertheless, the occasional parts and the uncertainty of sitcom work left Fox in worrisome financial straits. She considered moving back to the Midwest, but her parents loaned her money at one point to keep her in California, "thank God, because they believed in me," Fox told writer Deborah Gregory in an *Essence* interview. For guidance, her mother suggested prayer, and Fox began attending church. After being out of work for a year, in 1994 she took a recurring part as Dr. Stephanie Simmons on another daytime soap, *The Young and the Restless*. Fox was noticed by a fan of the CBS show who was also married to a film producer. That viewer told her husband about the actress, and Fox was called in for an audition for a supporting role in the action thriller *Independence Day*; she would play lead actor Will Smith's love interest.

"When I heard I got the part, I ran about the house screaming!" Fox told *People* magazine. Yet as she confessed to *Essence*'s Gregory, she did have reservations about the role—as go-go dancer Jasmine DuBrow, Fox would wear little but a G-string in some scenes. "I'm not gonna lie. I was scared to death to play a stripper," she told Gregory. "There were many days when I left that set crying. I was like, 'What if people think I'm a slut?' You know we're never allowed to be

At a Glance . . .

Born on July 30, 1964, in South Bend, IN; daughter of William (a dean at a private school) and Everlyena (a pharmaceutical technician) Fox; married Christopher Harvest 1998 (divorced 2002). *Education:* Attended Golden West College.

Career: Actress, 1989–.

Addresses: *Office*—Foxy Brown Productions, P.O. Box 3538, Granada Hills, CA 91394.

sexy on-screen." Yet in the end, Fox's character wins Smith's heart and remains a good mom to her son, even while aliens are invading the planet; Smith's character helps save the world. *Independence Day* was one of the box-office smashes of the year. "That success," Fox told *People*, "changed my life. I don't have auditions anymore. I have meetings."

With her newfound good fortune, Fox allowed herself a few well-earned luxuries after years of struggling, including a white Mercedes. Her next screen role came in *Set It Off*, released later in 1996. Fox played a fired bank teller who joins three other women in a series of daring bank robberies; her co-stars were Queen Latifah, Jada Pinkett, and Kimberly Elise. For this action film that showcased its characters' smarts as well as looks, there had been no shortage of African American professionals auditioning for the coveted roles. Fox had been cast against the role of Frankie, and for that she was pleased. "I was so grateful for the chance to shed my 'nice-girl' Hollywood image," Fox told *Essence* shortly before its premiere. Until that point, she added, she "couldn't get an audition for anything other than cute Buppies!"

Shortly after *Independence Day* hit the screens, no less than former late-night host Arsenio Hall came calling for Fox after seeing her performance. To entice her to join the cast of his scheduled new sitcom, Hall set up a meeting with Fox that happened to fall on her birthday, brought her a cake, and sang "Happy Birthday." Fox accepted the role of Vivian, the lead character's sharp wife, and the show debuted in March of 1997. It was another coveted role, since Fox played a smart, newlywed attorney. "I'm so proud of our project," Fox told *Essence*'s Gregory around the time of its debut. "We get to act like a real Black couple." Unfortunately, critics found it lacking, and it was cancelled after only a few weeks.

Fortunately, Fox had won meaty parts in several other projects that would debut in 1997. Fox's next role brought a bit of controversy, but her role and performance were not the problem. *Booty Call*, released in early 1997, was called a "safe-sex" comedy by its makers, but many objected to a marketing campaign seen by some as degrading to women. In the film, Fox played Lysterine, a banker with a healthy appetite for life and love. Later in 1997 Fox appeared as Ms. B. Haven, clad as a twenty-first century snow bunny. She would also tackle a more serious role in *Soul Food*, which starred both Vanessa Williams and Nia Long as well; the threesome play sisters on-screen.

Although Fox enjoyed her success on screen, she was keenly aware of the prejudice toward youth in Hollywood. She kept her physique in top form, dropping 30 pounds to play an ex-assassin in *Kill Bill* in 2003. Though she was hailed as a Hollywood beauty in her forties, Fox actively planned for a future off-screen. "In Hollywood when your time is up, they spit you out like chewing gum," she told *Essence,* adding that someday she hoped to "step behind the camera and write, direct or produce so that I can help make someone else's dreams come true."

By the early 2000s, Fox had begun her work in production, partnering with her manager, lawyer Lita Richardson. In 2004 Fox took on the executive production as well as the lead role in the television series, *Missing,* a drama about FBI investigations. She also produced the 2005 film *The Salon,* a comedy about a beauty shop owner, and had another film, called *Getting Played*, in the works. About her plans for the future, Fox told *Jet* that "I've made studios a whole bunch of money. I'm just learning that I green-light projects. I get fundings for projects that I should reap the benefits of what my name does...There's a business behind the show. Once you learn more about the business going on behind the show, the longer you'll be able to stay in show business. Get very involved."

Selected works

Films

Born on the Fourth of July, 1989.
Independence Day, 1996.
Batman, 1997.
Booty Call, 1997.
Set It Off, 1997.
Soul Food, 1997.
Why Do Fools Fall in Love? 1998.
Two Can Play that Game, 2001.
Kill Bill, 2003.
Ella Enchanted, 2004.
The Salon, 2005.

Television

Days of Our Lives, 1988.
The Young and the Restless, 1994-95.
Arsenio, 1997.
Walking after Midnight, 1999.
Missing, 2004–.
The Starlet, 2005.

Sources

Periodicals

Ebony, June 1990, pp. 118-123.
Essence, October 1996, p. 56; June 1997, p. 69; January 2005, p. 106.
Jet, December 20, 2004, p. 14.
People, November 11, 1995, pp. 113-114; March 3, 1997, p. 114.
Rolling Stone, November 28, 1996, p. 143.
Variety, February 28, 2005, p. 41.

On-line

Vivica Fox, www.vivicafox.com (August 3, 2005).

—Carol Brennan and Sara Pendergast

Gilberto Gil

1942—

Musician

Gil, Gilberto, photograph. Evan Agostini/Getty Images.

Brazilian legend Gilberto Gil is sometimes described as his country's version of Sting or Bono. Like the British musical stars who have become active in environmental and social-reform causes, Gil has long been a crusader for protection of the Brazilian environment and for help for those who live in the overcrowded urban slums known as *favelas* that ring cities like Rio de Janeiro. Many of Brazil's poorest are of African heritage, like Gil himself. Gil is a celebrated and respected figure in the South American country solely for the achievements of his musical career alone, but his activism has made him a hero to many.

Gil's rise as an artist began in the 1960s, and within a decade he was an important pioneer in Afro-Brazilian musical styles. He has spent much of his subsequent career promoting the links between African musical styles and the new genres they created when transplanted to the Western Hemisphere. His albums blend the two worlds to create a new, distinctive voice and sound respected around the world by a long list of outstanding musicians. In Brazil, his concerts are usually sold out—unless they are staged for free, which he regularly does for the poor. A Grammy recipient and winner of the prestigious Polar Music Prize in 2005, Gil was hailed by *Billboard* writer Gerald Seligman for his "exemplary and extraordinary career. Imprisoned by one government, he came to be appointed minister by another. It is a sign of how far Brazil has come, certainly, but also of the integrity, consistency and accomplishment of one remarkable citizen."

Immersed in Rich Cultural Heritage

Gil was born on June 29, 1942, in Salvador, Brazil, the capital of the state of Bahia in northeast Brazil. In previous centuries, Bahia served as one vast sugar plantation, and over a third of the Africans brought to Brazil as slaves settled there. Unlike slavemasters in North America, however, the Portuguese colonists generally did not separate slave families, and even those brought over from same tribe generally stayed in same area. Because of this, African culture took root more firmly in Brazil than elsewhere in the New World, and especially in Bahia. There, the local cuisine is heavily influenced by African styles, while a religion known as Candomblé is an amalgam of Roman Catholic and Yoruba practices. Furthermore, new musical styles flourished in Bahia that drew upon

At a Glance . . .

Born Gilberto Gil Moreira on June 29, 1942, in Salvador, Brazil; son of a physician and a teacher; married three times; seven children. *Education:* Studied business at the University of Bahia, early 1960s; studied music with Antonio Carlos "Tom" Jobim at the Goethe Institute. *Politics:* Green Party (Partido Verde) of Brazil. *Religion:* Candomblé.

Career: Guitar player, percussionist, singer, songwriter, and record producer; joined group Os Desfinados as a teenager; worked briefly for Gessy-Lever, a consumer-products conglomerate in São Paulo, Brazil, c. 1965-66; began collaborating with Caetano Veloso, late 1960s; pioneered a new musical style called Tropicalismo; spent 1969 to 1972 as a political exile in Britain; Salvador, Bahia, elected to city council, 1988; named Bahia's minister for culture; Government of Brazil, Minister of Culture, 2003–.

Awards: Grammy Award for Best World Music Album, for *Quanta Live,* 1998; Latin Academy of Recording Arts and Sciences (LARAS), Person of the Year, 2003; Polar Music Prize, Royal Swedish Academy of Music, 2005.

Addresses: *Office*—c/o Blue Jackel Entertainment, P.O. Box 87, Huntington, NY 11743. *Web*—www.gilbertogil.com.br.

African rhythms, the songs of the indigenous Indian tribes, and European influences and instruments.

Gil was a product of this rich Afro-Brazilian heritage in Bahia. His father was a physician and his mother a teacher, and he has described his background as one that was middle class, but tenuously so. Fascinated by music at an early age, he was playing the drums at the age of three; by the time he turned seven, he was teaching himself the trumpet by playing along with the radio. In his teen years, he took up the accordion. By then his family had moved to Salvador, and it was there he joined his first musical group, Os Desfinados (The Out-of-Tunes). He played the accordion and vibraphone, but soon switched to guitar after he heard another musical talent from Bahia, João Gilberto, and the new style called bossa nova for which Gilberto was gaining fame in the late 1950s.

Bossa nova soon replaced samba as the dominant popular music in Brazil. Gil with his guitar teamed with Caetano Veloso, whom he first met while a student at the University of Bahia in 1963. Introduced by Veloso's sister and fellow musician, Maria Bethania, they two musical collaborators would go on to a long career together, first in bossa nova and then as they created their own sound. Within a few years they had pioneered a new musical form called Tropicalismo, which drew upon Western rock 'n' roll and became the soundtrack for the counterculture protest movement in Brazil in the late 1960s.

Arrested, Jailed, and Sent into Exile

Gil himself had dropped out of his own middle-class life after finishing his business degree from the University of Bahia in 1965. He had taken a job as a management trainee with Gessy-Lever, a consumer-products conglomerate, in São Paulo, but quit in 1966 to concentrate on his music career. He had a hit as a songwriter that same year in "Louvaçáo," recorded by Ellis Regina, and a music-festival entry done with Veloso, "Domingo no Parque," was another early hit. *Louvaçáo* was also the title of his first full-length LP, released in 1967 on the Philips label.

Despite his growing popularity, Gil and the other Tropicalismo pioneers soon ran afoul of government authorities. Brazil had been under a military dictatorship since 1964, and a new crackdown on free speech and the arts came in 1968 with Institutional Act V. The harsh new laws meant tough censorship guidelines for musical recordings and live performances, and when Gil and Veloso appeared on a television program and appeared to poke fun at the government, they were arrested and charged with degrading the national flag and Brazil's anthem. Their heads were shaved and they were jailed in a solitary confinement wing, where they could hear the screams of other prisoners being tortured. After two months, both were released, but Gil was placed under house arrest for several months before he and Veloso were strongly encouraged to leave the country.

Gil settled in London, England, for the next three years. It was not an altogether terrible time, he recalled in an interview with the *Independent Sunday*'s Garth Cartwright. "We arrived the week The Beatles released Abbey Road, saw the Rolling Stones at the Roundhouse, jammed with Weather Report, heard reggae. A great experience. The fact you could walk up to a policeman and ask directions—in Brazil that just doesn't happen." Gil became particularly intrigued by reggae, the indigenous Jamaican musical form. As he explained in a *Nation* interview with Gene Santoro, he quickly grasped the political message in this kind of music. "The whole Rasta cultural thing, the hair and the colors and the communal life, the message and the fight for freedom, the need for ending problems of decolonization in Africa—it was quite something, the way that it followed up on the '60s black power movement in the United States," he told Santoro. "I made the links between Stevie Wonder and Miles Davis and Jimmy Cliff and Bob Marley: people speaking out, being proud of being black, understanding the difficulties of getting black culture into Western civilization."

To witness that black culture himself from its source, Gil began visiting Africa in the 1970s. He spent time in the Ivory Coast and in Senegal, and went to Nigeria in 1977, where he met American singer-songwriter Stevie Wonder, Nigerian musical superstar Fela Kuti—a pioneer of Afropop—and King Sunny Ade, another Nigerian musician and one who helped popularize African *juju* music, based on traditional Yoruba percussion styles. "That trip really gave me the push toward blackness, toward really trying to understand the roots and spirit of the culture," Gil recalled to Santoro. "Being able to spot the original sources of things we cultivate in Bahia shook me; it was a really emotional experience.... So when I got back to Brazil, I started doing music in a more black-oriented vein."

Gil returned to Brazil in 1972, after a less repressive political regime came to power, and his music began to incorporate Yoruba words and juju forms. He also continued to collaborate musically with Veloso. Together they pioneered another new musical style in the 1970s, which became known as Música Popular Brasileria, or Brazilian Popular Music, and known by its acronym, MPB. Their work began to attract the attention of respected musicians elsewhere, foremost among them David Byrne, founder of the seminal punk-new wave outfit the Talking Heads. In the 1980s and 1990s, Gil would release records on Byrne's Luaka Bop label.

Entered Politics with Green Party

Gil was also drawn into politics. In 1988, he ran for a seat on Salvador's city council on the Green Party (Partido Verde) ticket, and won by a record number of votes. He was sworn into office at a time when it was still relatively rare for a black to be elected to public office in Brazil. He went on to hold a seat on the executive committee of the Green Party in Brazil, and was made Bahia's minister of culture. He was increasingly active in environmental issues as well and founded an organization called Onda Azul (Blue Wave), which worked to protect Brazil's Atlantic shoreline and coastal waters from pollution. He used his high profile to draw attention to rainforest conservation. As always, he also focused his attention on Brazil's poor and the dispossessed, particularly those who lived in the ramshackle *favelas,* the shanty towns originally established by freed slaves.

In 2003, a newly elected Brazilian president, Luiz Inácio da Silva of the leftist Workers' Party, made Gil the country's newest Minister of Culture. Along with another cabinet appointee, Benedita da Silva, Gil was the first black to be appointed to a cabinet post in Brazil since the appointment of Pelé, the internationally famous soccer star. The appointment was somewhat controversial, for some of the more Marxist-centered members of Brazil's left had long been suspicious of Gil for using what were viewed as "decadent" Western musical influences like the electric guitar in his music. Cultural mavens, on the other hand, argued that Gil was perhaps not the best qualified candidate for the job of Culture Minister. But *New York Times* correspondent Larry Rohter framed the debate in another light, writing that because the musical legend was "a native of the state of Bahia and a black man, Mr. Gil may also be the victim of a regional prejudice with a certain racial subtext. Other Brazilians tend to regard people from that northeastern state as disorganized and indolent, to the point that one slang term for a midafternoon siesta is 'bahiano.'"

Gil became perhaps the first cabinet minister of one of the world's leading economic powers to sport dreadlocks. He took an office in the modernist federal capital of Brasilia, and went to work championing Brazilian culture at home and abroad. His new job was not that different from his previous career as a musician, he said in an *Americas* interview with Marcia Cunha and Mark Holston. "Politics is an art form," he declared. "I came here to practice the art of politics in a ministry dedicated to art. This is a change of place, not of substance." He was also determined to promote all forms of Brazilian culture, not just more popular forms that translated well on the international stage. "Brazil's image abroad is associated with popular culture: samba, the way we play football," he told *Newsweek International* writer Mac Margolis. "But what we need to do is break the prejudice that popular culture is a lesser product. Blacks and Afro-Indians are the soul of the country. Brazil needs to come to terms with itself, different from the Brazilian elite, who want to be a copy of Europe or the United States."

Gil is a major celebrity in Brazil. Once, his car was stolen in Salvador, and the crime story appeared on the local news outlets; the next day, his car was returned with a note of apology. Married three times, he has seven children and runs a recording studio and impressive musical mini-empire. In 2005 he was a co-recipient of the Polar Music Prize, a generous award bestowed by the Royal Swedish Academy of Music from an endowment given by Stig Anderson, who earned a fortune as manager of the Swedish pop group Abba in the 1970s. But it is his political career that he hopes will have a more lasting impact on Brazilians, he told Seligman in the *Billboard* interview. "My goal is to help my country and to help my planet establish a more civilized and acceptable process of social change and understanding. I'm looking for a better human society."

Selected discography

Louvaçáo, Philips, 1967.
Gilberto Gil, Philips, 1968.
(With Caetano Veloso) *Barra 69* (live), Philips, 1972.
Gilberto Gil Ao Vivo (live), Philips, 1974.
(With Jorge Ben) *Gil e Jorge,* Verve, 1975.
Refavela, Warner Music Brazil, 1977.
Nightingale, Elektra, 1979.
Brasil, Polydor, 1981.
Luar (A Gente Precisa Ver o Luar), WEA Latina, 1981.
Quilombo (Trilha Sonora), WEA, 1984.
Gilberto Gil em Concerto, Westwind, 1987.
O Eterno Deus Mu Dança, WEA Latina, 1989.
Parabolic, WEA Latina, 1991.
(With Caetano Veloso) *Caetano y Gil: Tropicalia 2,* Nonesuch, 1994.
Quanta Live, Atlanta/Mesa, 1998.
O Sol de Oslo, Blue Jackel, 1998.
Kaya N'Gan Daya, WEA International, 2002.
Eletrácustico (Unplugged), WEA International, 2004.
As Cancoes de Eu Tu Eles, WEA International, 2005.

Sources

Books

Contemporary Musicians, Vol. 26, Gale Group, 1999.

Periodicals

America's Intelligence Wire, October 25, 2004.
Americas, September-October 1993, p. 14; November-December 2003, p. 14.
Billboard, August 23, 2003, p. LM3.
Daily Telegraph (London), July 1, 2003.
Independent Sunday (London), June 10, 2002, p. 7.
Investor's Business Daily, October 7, 2003, p. A4.
Knight-Ridder/Tribune News Service, August 12, 1993.
Latin Trade, December 2003, p. 19.
Nation, May 20, 1991, p. 676.
Newsweek International, February 3, 2003, p. 54.
New York Times, December 31, 2002, p. E1.
Time International, January 27, 2003, p. 67.

—Carol Brennan

Bruce S. Gordon

1946—

Business executive, NAACP executive

Bruce S. Gordon's appointment in 2005 as president and CEO of the National Association for the Advancement of Colored People (NAACP), the oldest civil rights organization in the United States, caught many by surprise. Though Gordon had long been involved in civil rights issues, including the Urban League and the United Negro College Fund, he had built his reputation in the world of business. Gordon had enjoyed a long career in the telephone business and his expertise helped make his longtime employer, Verizon Communications, one of the most successful companies in the communications industry. As president of the retail markets group for the largest phone company in the United States, Gordon worked to keep Verizon's customers from straying in a highly competitive field. In 2002 he was named one of *Fortune* magazine's "50 Most Powerful Black Executives." Verizon's chief executive officer, Ivan Seidenberg, told *Black Enterprise* that Gordon was "an extraordinary executive whose marketing instincts and skills are unsurpassed." Gordon retired from Verizon in 2003. In a news release on the NAACP Web site announcing his appointment, Gordon said: "My goal as president will be to build on the legacy of this organization, to help it continue adapting to this new reality, and to extend its reach and influence to more of our youth, to more people of color, and to more leaders in the academic, business and political worlds."

Born on February 15, 1946, Gordon grew up in Camden, New Jersey, in a strict household headed by two educators. He studied at Gettysburg College in Pennsylvania, where he also played wide receiver on its football team. Gordon wanted to live in the city, and after his graduation in 1968 he applied for a management trainee post with the local phone company in Philadelphia. He accepted an offer from Bell of Pennsylvania—though he had no desire to make a career there, he told Nadirah Sabir, another writer for *Black Enterprise*. He explained, "I had this fear that if I stayed, I would be doing the same job my entire life."

At the time, Bell of Pennsylvania was part of the government-supervised telephone industry, which operated much like a public utility; there was one company providing the service to consumers, and its rates were regulated. But Gordon told Hayes, "Soon after I came into the Bell system, there were talks to convert the monopoly into a competitive business. The whole energy level picked up." Gordon ended his management training by accepting a job as a business office manager in 1970. He also fulfilled his political interests by writing a weekly column for a suburban Philadelphia paper, on subjects that often touched on some of the more contentious race issues of the day. At one point, he even considered leaving Bell in order to run an alternative urban school in Philadelphia, although he changed his mind just before handing in his resignation. "I wasn't a traditional person," he described himself at the time to Hayes. "Being a child of the '60s, I had a natural resistance to the status quo."

Gordon's determined personality almost ended his career in its infancy. There was a rumor that he was going to be fired, but a sales general manager and friend of Gordon's at Bell stepped in and requested that he be transferred to the sales department. Gordon told

At a Glance . . .

Born on February 15, 1946, in Camden, NJ; son of Walter (a teacher) and Violet (a teacher) Gordon; married Genie Alston, February 20, 1970 (divorced); married Tawana Tibbs; children: Taurin (from first marriage). *Education*: Gettysburg College, BA, 1968; Bell Advance Management program, University of Illinois, 1981; Wharton Executive Management program, University of Pennsylvania; Massachusetts Institute of Technology, Sloan School of Management, MS, 1988.

Career: Bell of Pennsylvania, Philadelphia, PA, held various positions, 1968-85, including general manager for marketing and sales, 1985, vice president for marketing, 1988-93; Bell Atlantic Network Services, group president for retail, 1993-2000; retail markets group president for Verizon Communications, New York, NY, 2000-2003; National Association for the Advancement of Colored People (NAACP), president and CEO, 2005–.

Memberships: Alliance of Black Managers; Toastmasters International; Urban League, director, 1984-86; Inroads of Philadelphia, United Negro College Fund Telethon, 1985-86; NAACP.

Awards: Massachusetts Institute of Technology, Alfred P. Sloan fellow, 1987; *Black Enterprise* magazine, Executive of the Year, 1998; *Fortune* magazine, named one of the "50 Most Powerful Black Executives," 2002
.

Addresses: *Office*—NAACP Headquarters, 4805 Mt. Hope Drive, Baltimore, MD 21215.

Hayes in *Black Enterprise* that his mentor "was Jewish and felt that he had also been a victim of discrimination. He liked that I was a black guy who had a lot to say about the business, and we connected on those terms." Gordon spent two years as a marketing sales manager before becoming a personnel supervisor in 1974. His career advanced quickly, and he held various management positions over the next decade, eventually becoming general manager for marketing and sales in 1985. In the interim, Bell of Pennsylvania was undergoing a transformation. Under existing antitrust laws, its parent company, AT&T, had been ordered to dissolve its local and long-distance phone companies, and in 1985 the deregulation resulted in the creation of seven regional "Bell" phone companies. The former Bell of Pennsylvania became the Bell Atlantic Corporation.

Bell Atlantic provided phone service for some 12 million customers from New Jersey to Maryland, and Gordon's keen business sense fit well with the new era. The phone company was suddenly forced to compete for customers, and Gordon worked with those under him in order to set and meet goals. After he became vice president for marketing in 1988, he was able to bring about even greater changes. He initiated retail kiosks and greatly improved customer service—once a thorny problem for AT&T/Bell. For example, research showed that the employees in Bell Atlantic's call center who were picking up only 70 percent of customer service or repair calls in the first 20 seconds. Gordon set a goal of 90 percent within that time frame, and looked for ways to meet the goal without simply adding more employees. He found that call center employees were often away at seminars, or just not at their desks. Within two months, Bell Atlantic hit the Gordon's mark.

But Gordon soon realized that the root of the problem might go even deeper. "I had to decide whether the people who got us to this point in history could take us forward," he told Sabir in the *Black Enterprise* interview. Gordon won approval to restructure the way in which employees could advance within the company. He announced that all positions were open to every employee, and that all had to compete for such jobs, which resulted in a 20 percent turnover of staff. Gordon also worked hard to ensure that he was personally as accessible as everyone else. He turned down a private manager's office, preferring to work on the same floor as many of his employees, because "information gets filtered when you're up there, and you cut yourself off," he told *Black Enterprise*.

Gordon was named group president for retail markets in 1993, and four years later was put in charge of a historic changeover, when Bell Atlantic and NYNEX, the New York and New England phone system, merged. The $26-billion deal gave Bell Atlantic millions of new customers from New York to Maine, and made it the number two telecommunications company in the United States. Gordon headed up the all-important integration team for the new merger, which entailed changing the logos on phone booths, buildings, directories, and even some 28 million monthly statements mailed to customers. It was a swift, successful changeover, according to focus-group studies, and helped earn Gordon *Black Enterprise's* Executive of the Year honor in 1998.

In June of 2000, Bell Atlantic merged with GTE, and both names were jettisoned in favor of "Verizon." Gordon remained as president of the retail markets group as the company grew, and continued to work within the company to help others. He founded a mentoring and networking group for African Americans at Verizon before retiring from the company in December of 2003.

His retirement, however, was short-lived, for in 2005 Gordon was tapped to head the NAACP. Once a strong force for civil rights in American, the organization that had been steadily diminishing in size and influence for years. Gordon's appointment signified to many observers that the organization's board was looking for someone to lead the group in a new direction. In an interview published on the PBS *Online NewsHour* Web site, Gordon explained that he was selected because of his business acumen and his proven record at solving tough problems. Describing his goals, the tough-talking Gordon proclaimed, "I intend to go where the trouble is. That says to me once we identify a problem, we will find its solution. If its solution is embedded in political intervention, so be it. If its solution is embedded in building relationships with Wall Street and corporate America, so be it. I'll find the trouble, I'll go to the trouble, we'll find the solution, and utilize any and every mechanism necessary to solve those problems." With his firm leadership and his proven record of business success, Gordon is certain to bring major changes to the NAACP.

Sources

Periodicals

Advertising Age, October 8, 2001, p. S27.
Black Enterprise, May 1995, p. 55; September 1998, p. 84.
Star-Ledger (Newark, NJ), July 11, 2002, p. 38.
USA Today, June 25, 2005.

On-line

"Conversation: Bruce Gordon," *Online NewsHour,* www.pbs.org/newshour/bb/race_relations/july-dec05/gordon_7-4.html (August 15, 2005).
"Key Executives," *Verizon*, http://newscenter.verizon.com/speeches/bio_gordon.vtml (August 15, 2005).
"NAACP Board Overwhelmingly Selects Bruce S. Gordon Next President, CEO," *NAACP,* www.naacp.org/news/2005/2005-06-25.html (August 15, 2005).

—Ashyia Henderson and Tom Pendergast

Ed Gordon

1960—

Television and radio news personality

Ed Gordon emerged in the late 1990s as one of the hottest news personalities in the highly competitive business. For many years, Gordon was a leading news anchor for the Black Entertainment Television (BET) network. During his early years with BET, Gordon made his name as a jack-of-all-trades: he could be seen reporting the news, undertaking investigative pieces, and conducting interviews with important black Americans. His network's small budget and staff notwithstanding, Gordon became a significant force in television news reporting after joining BET in 1988. He interviewed presidents and presidential candidates, important world figures such as South African leaders Nelson Mandela and Desmond Tutu, and figures as diverse as Nation of Islam minister Louis Farrakhan and singer Whitney Houston. "With an impressive and eclectic interview roster," noted *People* magazine, "the personable Gordon is rapidly taking his place among Washington media heavies." Gordon joined NBC's news division for three years in the late 1990s before returning to BET. In 2004 he joined the CBS news magazine *60 Minutes* as a correspondent, and in 2005 he began hosting his own daily public affairs program on NPR Radio.

Edward Lansing Gordon, III, was born in 1960 and raised in Detroit, Michigan. Both of his parents were schoolteachers. His father was also an athlete—he won a gold medal in the long jump in the 1932 Summer Olympic Games. Even as a schoolboy, Gordon liked to pretend that he was a television journalist. He would regale his classmates with the news at the lunch table and after school, and he especially admired anchorman Dan Rather. Gordon's father died when the boy was only 11, but Ed remembers him as a warm and caring man. Gordon inherited from his parents a seriousness of purpose that has helped him to succeed in the highly competitive world of broadcast journalism.

After graduating from Western Michigan University in 1982 with a degree in communications and political science, Gordon briefly considered law school. He knew he wanted to be a television journalist, however, so instead he accepted an unpaid internship at Detroit's public television station WTVS. His hard work there eventually landed him a paying job—with a grand salary of $11,000 per year—as host of *Detroit Black Journal*, a weekly talk show. To supplement his income, Gordon worked as a free-lance reporter for the fledgling cable network BET, headquartered in Washington, D.C.

Gordon recalls his years in Detroit as good training for the position he holds today. "It used to be that on a good day in Detroit, I'd be doing the mayor. But most days it was the dog catcher," he joked in the *Detroit Free Press*. Those "good days" could be tough as well, since the mayor in question was the cantankerous and outspoken Coleman Young. Gordon admitted in the *Washington Post* that his experiences with Young helped to hone his interview skills and make him comfortable with a wide variety of people. "If you can interview Coleman Young, you can interview anybody in the world," he said.

In 1988 Gordon joined BET as anchor of the weekly news show BET News. The small but increasingly

At a Glance . . .

Born Edward Lansing Gordon III in 1960 in Detroit, MI; son of Ed (a teacher) and Jimmie (a teacher) Gordon; married Karen Haney (a computer specialist); children: one daughter, Taylor. *Education*: Western Michigan University, BA in communications and political science, 1982.

Career: WTVS-TV, Detroit, MI, production assistant, 1983-85, host of *Detroit Black Journal*, 1985-88; Black Entertainment Television (BET), Washington, D.C., news anchor, 1988-96, 1999-2005, and host of *Lead Story, Conversations with Ed Gordon*, and *BET Tonight with Ed Gordon*; NBC-TV, commentator for *Today Show* and *Dateline NBC*, 1996-99(?); CBS-TV, *60 Minutes* contributor, 2004–; National Public Radio, host, *News and Notes with Ed Gordon*, 2005–. Gordon Media Group (production company), owner and chief executive officer.

Awards: *People*, named to 50 Most Beautiful People in the World list, 1996; Emmy Award; NAACP Image Award; National Association of Black Journalists, Journalist of the Year Award; Communication Excellence to Black Audiences (CEBA), Award for Merit, Distinction, and Excellence.

Addresses: *Office*—c/o NPR, 635 Massachusetts Ave., NW, Washington, DC 20001.

significant network provides a forum for black entertainment and highlights black issues in its information programming. Due to budget constraints, however, the BET news staff numbers fewer than 20 people—Gordon often finds himself producing his interview shows and other specials with the help of only one or two assistants. "In terms of resources or facilities, we can't compete," he stated in the *Detroit Free Press*. "And we don't want to compete with CNN [the Cable News Network, which broadcasts news around the clock]. We're a supplement."

Gordon has always been frank about the shortcomings of network television news. "Walk into any other newsroom," he told the *Free Press*. "Part of what they're missing is the diversity. It's still a white-male-oriented world." BET's mission is to provide another perspective on national and international events—one that reflects the black American point of view. Thus, when African Americans rioted in Los Angeles in 1991, BET aired a special—with Gordon as its host—entitled "Black Men Speak Out: The Aftermath," which featured blunt opinions on the social conditions that led to the uprising. Gordon also interviewed President George Bush about the situation in Los Angeles. On that story, Gordon noted in the *Detroit Free Press*, "we tried to go a little deeper than what the mainstream media did." BET also allots more air time to news stories about Africa and the Caribbean, providing in-depth pieces, for instance, on Haiti, South Africa, and Rwanda.

"Sometimes I would like to reach a larger audience," Gordon conceded in the *Washington Post*. "Not necessarily a more diverse audience, because I think that is something that the wider community—whites especially—have to aspire to. If they see 'black' attached to something, they have a tendency to turn it off automatically and feel that it does not affect or is not germane to them. And I think that BET is germane to everyone."

Despite its relatively small audience, BET has established a reputation for fairness and objectivity that has enabled Gordon to conduct interviews with a number of prominent blacks from all walks of life, including the colorful Reverend Al Sharpton and Farrakhan, who have generally been accorded one-dimensional coverage in the mainstream media. On his occasional hour-long interview show, *Conversations with Ed Gordon*, the enterprising newsman has sat down with such subjects as President Bill Clinton, actor/director Sidney Poitier, former talk show host Arsenio Hall, Washington, D.C., mayor Marion Barry, and Whitney Houston, who has twice used Gordon's forum to correct misconceptions about her career and her marriage.

The sheer volume of work Gordon does for BET as a news anchor and host of several information shows has led some observers to call the cable channel "the Ed Gordon network." A married father of one who lives in a Virginia suburb of the nation's capital, Gordon is glad for the opportunity to bring the news to people who are not necessarily represented on the major networks. "A lot of young black males tell me, 'I never watched the news before you were on,'" he noted in *People*.

Gordon explained in the *Washington Post* that while he asks hard questions, he also allows his interview subjects as much time as they need to formulate an answer—and he does not edit those answers into meaningless sound bites. "You'll know that your response...will be portrayed on the tube the same way that you delivered it," he insisted. "I'm not going to twist it or turn it or take half of it away and change it."

Gordon proved his toughness as an interviewer early in 1996 when he became the first person to gain a live interview with football star O. J. Simpson after his acquittal for the murder of his ex-wife and her boyfriend. Gordon opened the interview by asking "Did you commit those murders?" The interview won Gordon attention from the major networks, and he was soon wooed by NBC-TV to offer interview and commentary for their programs *Dateline NBC* and the *Today Show*. Gordon returned to BET when his three-year contract with NBC ended, and he continued to win accolades for his interviewing skills with the network. In 2004 he was hired by CBS to be a correspondent with the long-running news magazine *60 Minutes,* an honor granted to few outsiders. Gordon told *Jet* that he was honored by the chance to join the program: "Very few journalists get invited to this party," Gordon said. "So it's very nice to be invited."

Gordon left BET in 2005 to take on a new challenge with National Public Radio. His program, called *News and Notes with Ed Gordon,* is focused on news of interest to the black community. Gordon told *Jet:* "The format of the show allows us to talk about anything from politics to pop culture, and that prospect is exciting. But most importantly we'll be able to shine the light on topics and people of importance to African-Americans. This kind of program is imperative because often these issues and voices are still, unfortunately, under-reported, under-represented or overlooked altogether by most media outlets." With his own program on a mainstream media source and his spot reports for *60 Minutes,* Gordon has become one of the most important African-American news personalities in the United States.

Sources

Periodicals

Detroit Free Press, July 18, 1991, p. 6F; May 31, 1992, p. 1G.

Entertainment Weekly, October 25, 1996.

Jet, December 13, 2004, p. 55; January 17, 2005, p. 62.

Lexington Herald-Leader (KY), May 26, 1993, p. 7D.

People, November 29, 1993, p. 76; May 6, 1996, p. 135.

USA Today, December 15, 1992, p. 3D.

Washington Post, May 20, 1993, p. 1D.

On-line

"Ed Gordon, NPR Biography," *NPR,* www.npr.org/templates/story/story.php?storyId=2101696 (August 11, 2005).

—Anne Janette Johnson and Tom Pendergast

David Henderson

1942—

Poet, author

A well-respected though perhaps under-recognized poet, David Henderson was a founder of the Black Arts Movement in the 1960s. He has been an active member of New York's Lower East Side art community for more than four decades. Henderson has published four volumes of poetry, and his work has appeared in numerous literary publications and anthologies. A revised and expanded edition of his highly-acclaimed biography of rock guitarist Jimi Hendrix was scheduled for publication in 2006.

Co-founded Umbra

Born in 1942 and raised in Harlem, David Henderson later studied writing, communications, and Eastern cultures at various colleges and universities without ever finishing a degree. His first published poem appeared in the New York newsweekly *Black American* in 1960. Upon moving to the Lower East Side of New York, Henderson became an active participant in the various black nationalist, arts, and anti-war movements.

In 1962 Henderson, along with other black writers, founded the Society of Umbra. They held weekly writing and criticism sessions and gave popular public readings. In 1963 the group began publishing the magazine *Umbra* as an outlet for black writers, with Henderson serving as co-editor and later editor. The first issue included poems by Julian Bond and Alice Walker, as well as three of Henderson's poems. *Umbra* introduced the work of Nikki Giovanni, Ishmael Reed, and Quincy Troupe, among others. Henderson also was involved with one of the country's first—and most-admired—counterculture newspapers, the *East Village Other*, which gave rise to the Underground Press Service.

Henderson's first poetry collection, *Felix of the Silent Forest*, appeared in 1967. In the title poem, the cartoon character Felix the Cat "walks the City hungry in every sense," representing disenfranchised blacks and others spurned by American society. These poems introduced many of Henderson's recurrent images and themes, such as the forest in the city and the assassination of Malcolm X. "They Are Killing All the Young Men" was dedicated "to the memory and eternal spirit of Malcolm X." In his introduction to the collection, Amiri Baraka (LeRoi Jones) wrote that the poems were "local epics with the breadth that the emotional consciousness of a culture can make."

Infused his Poems with Jazz

In his article on Henderson in the *Dictionary of Literary Biography*, Terry Joseph Cole described the poet as "the literary heir of Langston Hughes." Cole wrote: "His poetry makes use of personal experience, popular culture, and European and American mythologies to create a new mythology for the people of Harlem and the castaways on Manhattan Island." He clothed himself in "the mantle of the traditional African storyteller and chronicler."

In his introduction to *De Mayor of Harlem*, Henderson described his second collection as "poems, documentaries, tales, and lies" written between 1962 and 1970.

At a Glance . . .

Born David Henderson in 1942, in Harlem, NY. *Education:* Bronx Community College, 1960; Hunter College, 1961; New School for Social Research, 1962; East-West Institute, Cambridge, MA, 1964-65; University Without Walls, Berkeley, CA, 1972.

Career: *Umbra*, co-editor, 1963-68, editor, 1968-74; National Endowment for the Arts, consultant, 1967-68, 1980; City College of New York, lecturer, 1967-69, poet-in-residence, 1969-70; Berkeley Public Schools, artistic consultant, 1968; New York Public Schools, consultant, 1969; University of California, Berkeley, lecturer, 1970-72; University of California, San Diego, lecturer, 1979-80; Naropa University, visiting professor, 1981, 1995, 2004; State University of New York, Stony Brook, visiting professor, 1988-89; New School, visiting professor, 2000; St. Mark's Poetry Project, workshop leader, 1995, 2003.

Awards: Great Lakes College Association of New Writers Award, 1971; California Arts Council, New Genre Poetry Grant, 1992; Foundation for Contemporary Performance Arts, Artist Grant, 1999; New York Foundation for the Arts, Artist Fellowship, 1999.

Addresses: *Home*—PO Box 1018, Cooper Station, New York, NY 10276-1018.

The documentaries described events such as the 1964 Harlem riots: "I see police eight to one // in its entirety Harlem's 2nd Law of Thermodynamics // Helmet // nightsticks bullets to barehead // black reinforced shoes to sneaker // Am I in Korea?" Later poems signaled Henderson's move toward jazz poetry, which he described in the introduction as "the language of the man of the moment; it's improvised; it's street language...African 'talking drums'—the basis of jazz—were one of the world's first mass communications systems. People related to those rhythms in a unified way."

Henderson's poems frequently portrayed jazz musicians, such as Thelonious Monk and John Coltrane, and he began performing on jazz recordings. In 1971 he recorded with the avant-garde saxophonist Ornette Coleman. Henderson wrote the lyrics to composer and pianist Sun Ra's "Love in Outer Space" and recorded with Sun Ra as well with saxophonist David Murray and "Butch" Morris.

Known for His Lush Voice

Henderson worked with the National Endowment for the Humanities, the Free Southern Theatre in New Orleans, and the Teachers and Writers Collaborative at Columbia University. For a time he taught and was poet-in-residence at City College of New York. In the late 1960s and 1970s, Henderson lived in California, serving on the board of directors of the University Without Walls in Berkeley and as artistic consultant to the Berkeley Public Schools. He taught English and Afro-American literature at the University of California at Berkeley and San Diego. Later he taught courses, seminars, and workshops at Long Island University, New York's New School, and the St. Mark's Poetry Project. His 2004 writing workshop at Naropa University in Colorado was entitled "Geography of War."

Henderson has performed at various venues over the past four decades. He interviewed and hosted readings by black poets for Pacifica Radio in San Francisco and wrote, produced, and directed the radio documentary *Bob Kaufman, Poet*. Henderson's funk opera *Ghetto Follies* was first produced in San Francisco in 1978. That same year the Library of Congress began taping his readings for its permanent archives. Henderson's 1980 collection *The Low East* celebrated his return to New York's Lower East Side.

Henderson's poetry has been published in numerous anthologies, including two that were edited by Langston Hughes. The many periodicals that have published his work include *Black American Literature Forum, Black Scholar, Essence, Paris Review, New American Review, Evergreen Review, Saturday Review*, and the *New York Times*.

Wrote Biography of Jimi Hendrix

Henderson spent more than five years researching, conducting interviews, and writing *Jimi Hendrix: Voodoo Child of the Aquarian Age*. Originally published in 1978, it was condensed and revised as *'Scuse Me While I Kiss the Sky* in 1981. A new expanded edition was published in Britain in 2003 and scheduled for American publication in 2006 as *'Scuse Me While I Kiss the Sky—Jimi Hendrix, Voodoo Child*.

Jimi Hendrix included transcripts of recorded conversations and first-person accounts. It was an innovative biography, detailing Hendrix's musical influences, especially blues and jazz, his lyrics, and the development of his groundbreaking electric guitar style and the technology that made it possible. Greil Marcus of *Rolling Stone* called it "the strongest and most ambitious biography yet written about any rock and roll performer."

Henderson described a Hendrix performance at the Fillmore East: "Hendrix assaults the mind, sublimating horrible noises of the city. Subways busting through violent tunnels, exploding Mack trucks, jet exhaust fumes, buses; he turns the fascist sounds of energy exploitation into a beautiful music with a pyramid base of urban blues guitar. B. B. King's looney obbligato screams, Blind Lemon Jefferson's beautiful justice of country space, and Jimmy Reed's diddy-bop beats; Jimi exalts them all into a personal mastery of primordial sound itself, beyond ken and imagination. We hear spaceships landing in the heavy atmospheric gases of fantastic planets, we hear giant engines changing gears, we hear massive turbines that run cities, Frankenstein life-giving electric-shock blasts, jets taking off and exploding into melody."

Henderson described his most recent poetry collection, *Neo-California*, as "meditations on his Third World America." As of 2005 Henderson continued to write and compose poetry criticizing the U.S. invasion and occupation of Iraq. He was also involved in the PoetsConsensus, a group devoted to post-9/11 issues.

Selected works

Books

Felix of the Silent Forest (poetry), Poets Press, 1967.
(Editor) *Umbra Anthology 1967-1968*, Society of Umbra, 1968.
De Mayor of Harlem (poetry), Dutton, 1970; North Atlantic Books, 1985.
(Editor) *Umbra/Latin Soul 1974-1975*, Society of Umbra, 1975.
Jimi Hendrix: Voodoo Child of the Aquarian Age, Doubleday, 1978; condensed and revised as *'Scuse Me While I Kiss the Sky: The Life of Jimi Hendrix*, Bantam, 1981; revised and reissued, Omnibus, 2003.
The Low East, North Atlantic Books, 1980.
Neo-California, North Atlantic Books, 1998.

Anthologies

New Negro Poets: USA, Indiana University Press, 1964.
Where Is Vietnam? American Poets Respond, Anchor/Doubleday, 1967.
Black Fire: An Anthology of Afro-American Writing, Morrow, 1968.
The World Anthology: Poems from the Saint Mark's Poetry Project, Bobbs-Merrill, 1969.
Poetry of the Negro, 1746-1970, Doubleday, 1970.
Open Poetry: Four Anthologies of Expanded Poems. Simon & Schuster, 1973.
Moment's Notice: Jazz in Poetry & Prose (includes "Sonny Rollins," "A Coltrane Memorial," "Thelonious Sphere Monk"), Coffee House Press, 1993.
Trouble the Water: 250 Years of African American Poetry, Signet, 1997.

Recordings

New Jazz Poets, Broadside, 1967.
Black Poets IV, Pacifica Tape Library, 1973.
Poems: Selections, Library of Congress, 1978.
(With Sun Ra) "Love in Outer Space," *The Singles*, Evidence, 1996.
(With Ornette Coleman) *The Complete Science Fiction Sessions*, Columbia/Legacy, 2000.

Other

Color: A Sampling of Contemporary African American Writers (videorecording), The Poetry Center and American Poetry Archives, San Francisco State University, 1994.
"Seven Poems from *Neo-California*," *Poetry.About.com*, www.poetry.about.com/gi/dynamic/offsite.htm?site=http://www.cyberpoems.com/henderson.html.

Sources

Books

Cole, Terry Joseph, "David Henderson," *Dictionary of Literary Biography*, vol. 41, Gale Group, 1985, pp. 166-71.

Periodicals

African American Review, Winter 1993, pp. 579-84.

On-line

"David Henderson," *Biography Resource Center*, www.galenet.galegroup.com/servlet.BioRC (May 12, 2005).
"A Poets Consensus," *Public Art Forum: zumThema!* www.public–art.de/forum/poetcons.html (June 23, 2005).

Other

Additional information for this profile was obtained through an interview with David Henderson on June 21, 2005.

—Margaret Alic

Lauryn Hill

1975—

Singer, songwriter, producer

The adoration and respect accorded Lauryn Hill seems unparalleled. "The most versatile vocalist of her generation," wrote Kevin Powell in *Horizon* magazine. "Beautiful, multitalented, whipsmart," wrote *Harper's Bazaar*. "Catalyst...shining star...a divine singing voice and an up-front rhyme flow that ranks her among hip hop's dopest MCs," assessed *Vibe*. Public Enemy's Chuck D compared her to reggae legend Bob Marley. After creating, as *Essence* declared, "a new image of womanhood in the world of hip-hop" with her group the Fugees in the mid-1990s, Hill went on to score with her own phenomenally successful solo debut, 1998's *The Miseducation of Lauryn Hill*. Just when Hill's stardom seemed to reach its zenith, she stepped out of the limelight, taking a several-year hiatus from the public eye. When she resurfaced in the early 2000s, Hill revealed new depths of her musical talents.

Explored Music from an Early Age

Hill was born on May 22, 1975, and grew up in South Orange, New Jersey, not far from its public-housing projects. Her father Mal, who once sang professionally, was a computer analyst, while mother Valerie taught school in nearby Newark. Hill recalled many hours as an adolescent spent listening to her parents' old R&B records, which gave her an appreciation for the likes of Gladys Knight, Curtis Mayfield, and others. The Hills, however, stressed academic achievement for their children—she has an older brother, Malaney— and she won entry to Columbia High School, an academically challenging school, where she became acquainted with a friend of her brother's named Prakazrel "Pras" Michel. A Haitian immigrant, Michel formed a rap group and asked Hill to join.

Hill, who also ran track, was a popular and magnetic personality even in high school. She once asked her father if she could have a birthday party in their backyard, and he agreed as long as it was kept small. "By the end of the night, 250 people must have showed up," Mal Hill told *Rolling Stone* reporter Alec Foege. By this time, she had ventured out on a few auditions, and won a recurring role on the CBS soap opera As the *World Turns*. "You'll see that my house is right on the borderline of the suburbs and the ghetto," Hill pointed out to Foege, who was visiting Hill at her family's home in South Orange. "I always had this duality. I went to school with a lot of white kids—it was really like a suburban environment—but I lived with black kids."

Formulated New Sound with the Fugees

Hill, Michel, and another girl had formed a group called the Fugees-Tranzlator Crew. The "fugee" part was taken from the word "refugee," based on their conviction that all blacks outside of Africa are, in a sense, refugees. They cut demos in which they rapped in other languages. One day Michel's cousin, Wyclef Jean, came by the studio to hear them. Jean was also from Haiti, but grew up in a rough section of Brooklyn in a strict household headed by his minister father.

At a Glance . . .

Born on May 25, 1975, in South Orange, New Jersey; daughter of Mal (a computer analyst) and Valerie (a teacher) Hill; married Rohan Marley, date unknown; children: Zion David, Selah Louise, Joshua, John. *Education*: Attended Columbia University.

Career: Actress, singer, songwriter, and producer. The Fugees, member, 1988-1997; solo artist, 1997–; The Fugees, brief reunion performances, 2004, 2005; The Refugee Project, youth outreach program, founder, 1996-2000.

Awards: Two Grammy Awards for Best R&B song by a duo or group, for "Killing Me Softly with His Song," and for best rap album, *The Score*; 1997; triple platinum certification, November 1998, for *The Miseducation of Lauryn Hill*, Recording Industry Association of America; five Grammy Awards, including two for *The Miseducation of Lauryn Hill*, best R&B song for "Doo Wop (That Thing)," best new artist, and best female R&B vocalist; *Essence* Award, for humanitarian work, 1998; three NAACP Image Awards, 1999; two American Music Awards, for *The Miseducation of Lauryn Hill*, 2000.

Addresses: *Web*—www.laurynhill.com.

"When I heard Lauryn sing, I was like 'Wow!'" Jean told Edwige Danticat in *Essence*. "It clicked. I knew it was meant to be."

By this time, Hill had already won a billed film role opposite Whoopi Goldberg in the 1993 film *Sister Act II: Back in the Habit,* as insubordinate student Rita Watson. Accepted to several colleges, including Yale and Spelman, Hill chose to stick close to home and concentrate on her recording career by enrolling at Columbia University. After the other member departed for college, the three of them—Hill, Jean, and Michel—began performing in local talent shows and in New Jersey clubs; they also dropped the "Tranzlator" part of their name. "We sang, we rapped, we danced," Hill recalled for Foege in the *Rolling Stone* interview. "As a matter of fact, we were a circus troupe," she added. They won a recording contract with the Philadelphia rap label Ruffhouse, who released *Blunted on Reality* in 1993.

Hill and the others were unhappy with the finished product, however. Like many other young, inexperienced artists, they were shut out of the production and creative process, and the album was an edgy, quick-paced work of rap. "Hailed in Europe as a glimpse of the future, *Blunted* was summarily trashed in the American hip-hop press for missing the mark altogether," noted *Rolling Stone*'s Foege. It languished on the charts, but when a producer remixed two of the tracks, the songs became underground club favorites. Then word of mouth began spreading about the female rapper who could also sing, and Hill soon became the focus of attention for the group. She, Michel and Jean fought for and won producer rights for their next effort, *The Score*, and their perseverance paid off. Bolstered by singles that showcased Hill's talents, such as a cover of the 1973 Roberta Flack hit "Killing Me Softy with His Song," and "Ready or Not," and the 1996 release sold millions and was the number-three pop album in the country at one point while in first place on the Billboard R&B charts. With sales of 17 million, the Fugees became the biggest selling rap act in history.

Solo Star Rose

Hill's appearance on magazine covers without her bandmates may have fueled speculation early on that she would ditch them for a solo career. The issue became one of the most overreported non-events during the peak of Fugee success. She emphatically dismissed such talk—"It's not a compliment when people tell me to break off from them," Hill told *Vibe* magazine in early 1996. "That's like telling me to drop my brothers," she continued. The group toured heavily in 1996, but by the time they performed at the Grammy Awards ceremony in early 1997, Hill was three months pregnant. She had met Rohan Marley, son of the late reggae giant Bob Marley, when he showed up for a Fugee show and tried to talk to her. At first, she was uninterested in the beginning because of a past relationship that soured. "But back then I wasn't really checking for anybody," Hill told *Essence* writer Monifa Young. "I was very much into my music. You know, I'd spent so many years working at a relationship that didn't work that I was just like, 'I'm going to write these songs and pour my heart into them.'"

Yet Marley persisted, a romance developed, and soon the fact that Hill was carrying the grandchild of late Bob Marley only added to the aura of divinity that seemed to surround her. She had initially refused to disclose who the father was, and took heat for taking the "single mother" route at such a young age. "A lot of people told me, 'Don't do it. It's not the right time, you're a superstar,'" Hill recalled in an interview with Daisann McLane in *Harper's Bazaar*. "But I looked at my life, and I said, 'Well, God has blessed me with a whole lot in a little bit of time.' At the end of the day, the only reason for me not to have a child would have been that it was an inconvenience to my career, and that wasn't a good enough excuse for me not to have my son."

Carrying a child, Hill has said, gave her even more energy—she recorded a track with gospel star CeCe

Winans the day before she gave birth—and she wrote over two dozen songs for her own project. Hill's solo debut, *The Miseducation of Lauryn Hill*, was released in August of 1998. Writing in *Essence*, Young called it "one of the most anticipated albums of the year by fans and industry insiders." It debuted to platinum sales. On it was a tribute to her son, named Zion David, titled "Joy of my World Is in Zion." *Time* magazine put Hill on the cover, and inside wrote about her and other African American artists such as Maxwell and Erykah Badu who were producing a fresh wave of "emotionally relevant" music that seemed to embody what writer Christopher John Farley called the "neo-soul" movement. Farley termed Hill's solo debut "the kind of galvanizing work neo-soul needs: unabashedly personal, unrelentingly confrontational, uncommonly inventive."

Hill has also become one of the most lauded of behind-the-scenes talents as well. She executive-produced *Miseducation*, and went to Detroit to work with Aretha Franklin and wrote the song "A Rose Is Still a Rose" for the Queen of Soul, which became the title track for Franklin's album. Hill also directed its video. "She's positive, detailed, conscientious," Franklin said of Hill to McLane in *Harper's Bazaar*. "Frankly, I was surprised to see that in such a young woman," she continued. Still, Hill found that fighting for control over her talents was not easy in the music industry, and she ultimately realized that success of her vision brought with it its own demons. "This is a very sexist industry," Hill told Young in the *Essence* interview. "They'll never throw the 'genius' title to a sister. They'll just call her diva and think it's a compliment."

In addition to her musical career, Hill sought opportunities to give back to her community. In 1996 she founded the Refugee Camp Youth Project, an outreach organization aimed at improving the lives of children in places like Haiti, Zaire, Kenya, Uganda, and New Jersey. The organization's projects included a day camp for inner-city kids in New Jersey and well-building projects in Africa. Hill's charity put on the first ever concert by an American act in Haiti. Over 75,000 showed up, including the country's president, for the benefit concert for the country's orphanages and rehabilitation camps. The money was mismanaged, some say by the Haitian government, but a second concert in Miami also garnered money for the foundation. Hill also organized "Hoodshock" in Harlem, which featured the late Notorious B.I.G. and the Fugees among others. In July of 2001, she teamed with Marc Anthony and Luther Vandross in a benefit concert, called "Aftershock," to provide relief to earthquake victims in India and El Salvador. The Refugee Camp Youth Project closed its doors in late 2000.

Turned from the Limelight

At the height of her popularity, Hill did something unusual: she retreated from the public eye. Hill bought her parents' house in South Orange, New Jersey, and eventually had three more children with Marley, whom she eventually married. And though she did not grant interviews and limited her appearances, Hill continued to compose her music. Her 2002 release of a performance on *MTV Unplugged* highlighted a new side of Hill, a side full of pain and emotion. Her emotional acoustic performance shocked fans who had pigeonholed her music talents into the hip-hop renditions of her earlier work, but her commanding lyrics and vocal performance marked a new high in her artistic career.

Slowly, Hill sought out performance opportunities, appearing with the Fugees for the first time since the late 1990s at various concerts in 2004 and 2005. Hill reemerged with a keen focus on her artistic vision, not a desire to please critics. In *Trace* magazine, her first interview in five years, Hill declared that the music she creates from now on "will only be to provide information to my own children," adding "If other people benefit from it, then so be it." She spoke of work on a new solo album and the possibility of a new album with the Fugees.

Selected works

Albums

(With the Fugees) *Blunted on Reality*, Ruffhouse/Columbia, 1993.
(With the Fugees) *The Score*, Ruffhouse/Columbia, 1996.
The Miseducation of Lauryn Hill, Ruffhouse/Columbia, 1998.
The Lauryn Hill Story, Chrome Dreams, 2000.
MTV Unplugged No. 2.0, Columbia, 2002.
Greatest Hits, 2003.

Films

Sister Act II: Back in the Habit, 1993.
Restaurant, 2000.

Sources

Periodicals

Essence, August 1996, p. 85; June 1998, p. 74.
Harper's Bazaar, April 1998, pp. 204-208.
Rolling Stone, September 5, 1996.
Time, July 6, 1998, pp. 85-86.
Trace, July 14, 2005.
Vibe, March 1996; June/July 1996; August 1998.

On-line

Lauryn Hill, www.laurynhill.com (August 4, 2005).
"Lauryn Hill Returns to the Limelight," CNN, www.cnn.com/2005/SHOWBIZ/Music/07/13/people.laurynhill.ap/?section=cnn_showbiz (August 4, 2005).

"Lauryn Hill: She Knows Why the Caged Bird Sings," *Horizon Magazine,* http://horizonmag.com/1/hill.htm (August 4, 2005).

—Carol Brennan and Sara Pendergast

Wendy Hilliard

196?—

Gymnast and founder, Wendy Hilliard Foundation

The first African-American rhythmic gymnast to represent the sport on a U.S. national team, Wendy Hilliard has won several medals in international competition. She has also gone on to promote the sport among inner-city children. The Wendy Hilliard Foundation, which she formed in 1995, provides funding and support for aspiring gymnasts in New York City, and to date has served more than 4,500 local children.

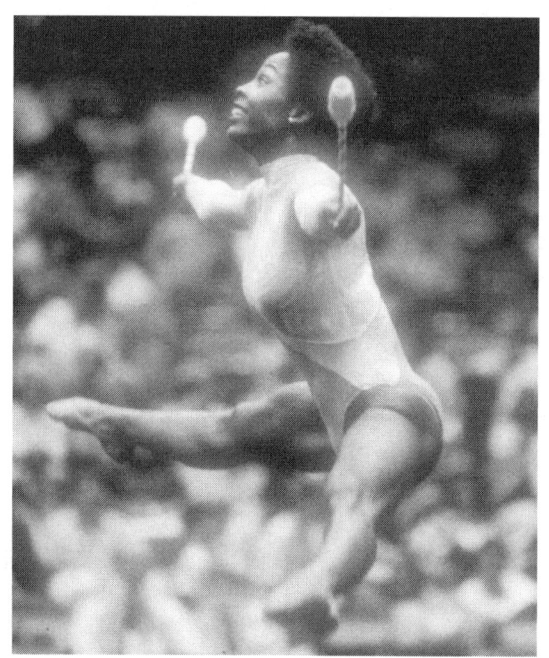

Hilliard, Wendy, photograph. Tony Duffy/Getty Images.

Was Drawn to Artistry of Rhythmic Gymnastics

Hilliard was born and raised in Detroit, Michigan, where there were few sports programs available in her neighborhood. She began training as a traditional gymnast after discovering the sport at a local gym. At a practice session one day, however, she noticed the ribbon used by a rhythmic team using the same gym. Inspired by the artistry of that sport, she decided to switch to rhythmic gymnastics.

Rhythmic gymnastics combines traditional gymnastic moves with elements of performance. Athletes perform jumps, splits, tumbles, or other moves while using props such as hoops, ribbons, or balls. The sport traces its roots to the early 1800s, when Swedish educator Per Henrik Ling developed a system of free exercise in which students would express their emotions through bodily movement. Over the years, trainers began incorporating apparatuses such as balls, ropes, and clubs into the sport. The first rhythmic gymnastics national championship was held in 1949 in the Soviet Union, and the first international competition took place in 1961. Rhythmic gymnastics became an Olympic sport in 1984.

Hilliard quickly excelled as a rhythmic gymnast, and in 1978 earned a spot on the U.S. national team, making her the first African American to represent a U.S. team. Her nine-year tenure on the team set a record, and she served two years as national team captain. As a member of the team, she competed in more than 15 foreign countries and in three World Championships, earning both national and international gold medals. After retiring from competition in 1998, Hilliard was named U.S. national team coach—a position she held

At a Glance . . .

Born in Detroit, Michigan; married to Robert Mensah ; children: one son. *Education:* Attended Wayne State University; graduated (with honors) from New York University.

Career: Rhythmic gymnast. Competed internationally, 1978-1988; U.S. National Rhythmic Gymnastics Team, coach, 1988-97; television broadcaster and sports analyst, 1989–; ANTIGRAVITY dance/gymnastics company, founding member, associate director, choreographer, and featured performer, 1990–; Wendy Hilliard Foundation, founder and president, 1995–; NYC2012, director of sports, 1999–.

Memberships: USA Gymnastics; Women's Sports Foundation.

Addresses: *Office*—c/o The Wendy Hilliard Foundation, 1 Liberty Plaza, 33rd floor, New York, NY 10006.

for four years. One of her athletes, Aliane Baquerot, went to the Olympic Games in 1996.

A tireless advocate for her sport, Hilliard served for ten years as National Spokesperson for Rhythmic Gymnastics, and chaired the Athletes' council of USA Gymnastics. She also served as athlete representative for Men's, Women's and Rhythmic Gymnastics to the U.S. Olympic Committee. In 1998, the Board of Directors of USA Gymnastics elected her Vice President for Rhythmic Gymnastics. Hilliard has also worked to promote athletic opportunities for girls, serving as president of the Women's Sports Foundation from 1995 to 1997. She was the first African American and the first gymnast to hold this position.

Started Program in Harlem

Growing weary of the high-pressure world of international athletics, Hilliard decided to realize her dream of inspiring children. In particular, she wished to make sports programs available to kids who had few resources to seek out elite athletic training. In 1994 she opened a free neighborhood program in rhythmic gymnastics to serve children in Harlem, where she was then living. Within the first year, more than 200 girls were enrolled in classes held at the Central Baptist Church in Manhattan's Upper West Side. The following year, Hilliard opened Rhythmic Gymnastics NY in the same location. Also that year, she formed the Wendy Hilliard Foundation to help provide funding for rhythmic gymnastics programs; at the competitive level, the cost of training per athlete can exceed $5,000 per year. Sponsors of the foundation include the U.S. Olympic Committee, the New York City Department of Youth and Community Services, the Hospital for Special Surgery, the Aetna Foundation, and the YWCA of the USA.

"There is just something about the discipline you learn doing this sport," she told *New York Times* writer Lynn Zinser. "These kids learn about nutrition, how to take care of themselves. You have to show up. You have to be on time. We watch their report cards. We want to keep kids in sports at this age."

Gymnastics has proved quite popular among Hilliard's young clients, who look up to her as a role model. "It's awesome to be coached by Wendy," said one Harlem 15-year-old to Zinser in the *New York Times*. "She's the person I want to be like." Hilliard's programs, which include a six-week free summer gymnastics camp for 350 students each year, have introduced competitive gymnastics to more than 4,500 New York City children—including more than 150 each year who live in homeless shelters.

Continues to Promote Excellence in Sports

In addition to her work with children, Hilliard has worked as a television analyst and interviewer, including coverage of the 1992 summer Olympic Games for NBC. She also conducts gymnastic clinics worldwide and appears as a guest performer in gymnastic tours and TV specials. Among the gymnastic superstars with whom she has performed are Nadia Comaneci, Shannon Miller, and Kurt Thomas. Hilliard also choreographs routines for top gymnasts, including Olympic gold medalist Dominique Dawes.

Hilliard is associate director, choreographer, and featured performer in the dance/gymnastics company AntiGravity, based in New York City. A founding member of the company, which was formed in 1990, she made her AntiGravity performance debut in 1997 in the Broadway musical, *Candide*. The company's performances, described by the *Village Voice* as "innovative, swanky, and mind-boggling," focus on movements in the air, and incorporate elements from classical dance, athletics, and theater. According to AntiGravity's Web site, the company's "unique movement vocabulary seamlessly incorporates acrobatic skills from many unrelated physical disciplines merging athletics and aesthetics into its own art form." The company has received commissions from leaders in several fields, including Bill Gates, Steve Forbes, Diddy, Giorgio Armani, Paul Newman, and Franco Zeffirelli.

Also keeping Hilliard busy is her work as director of sports for NYC2012, an organization promoting New York City's bid to host the 2012 summer Olympic Games. In this position, she serves as liaison between

NYC2012 and national governing bodies, the city's amateur sports community, and the region's Olympic athletes on all sports issues. Recognizing the importance of youth sports programs such as Hilliard's, NYC2012 noted on its Web site that "Sports make a difference in the lives of New York kids. Through hundreds of youth sport development programs...kids involved in sport develop healthier lifestyles, self-confidence, discipline, and a sense of teamwork and fair play."

Sources

Periodicals

Village Voice, October 2002.

On-line

"AntiGravity Bio," *AntiGravity,* www.anti-gravity.com (June 16. 2005).
"New York City's 2012 Olympic Bid," NCY2012, www.nyc2012 (June 16, 2005).
"Wendy Hilliard Biography," *Wendy Hilliard Foundation,* www.wendyontheweb.org (May 18, 2005).

—E. M. Shostak

Michael Jackson

1958—

Singer, songwriter, dancer

A powerfully creative and disciplined artist, Michael Jackson is a distinctive vocalist, an imaginative and original songwriter with a gift for turning his own experiences into powerful lyrics, and a dancer almost without peer. Keeping control over his own career, he ruled pop and rhythm-and-blues music charts throughout the 1980s. Jackson's private life has proven just as fascinating as his music and dance moves.

The lead singer of the beloved family group the Jackson 5, Michael Jackson was in his early twenties when *Thriller* catapulted him into the ranks of the rich and famous. He has never matched the success of *Thriller*, and in the 1990s his career suffered serious reversals, the most damaging of which may have been the accusations of child abuse leveled against the singer in 1993. By the late 1990s, the star of the self-proclaimed "King of Pop" seemed to have dimmed, especially after 2003, when he was arrested on a number of charges including ten counts of child molestation. But no one who remembered the explosion of his talent during the previous decade could doubt either his overall impact as a performer or his ability to once again seize the limelight.

Singing with the Jackson 5

Jackson was born on August 29, 1958, in the steel-manufacturing center of Gary, Indiana, outside of Chicago. His father Joseph had played guitar in a local group called the Falcons; his mother Katherine was a country music enthusiast who instilled in her eight children a love of singing. Joseph, very demanding and rumored by his children to be an abusive man, aimed to turn his five male children—Jackie, Tito, Jermaine, Marlon, and Michael—into musical stars. By 1964, before Michael's sixth birthday, he had formed them into the Jackson 5. The group played in local arenas and traveled throughout the Midwest performing before they were noticed. Attracting the attention of hit singer Gladys Knight and pianist Bobby Taylor—not Diana Ross as some have claimed—the Jackson 5 were signed in 1968 to the Motown label, whose roster of youthful black acts had reliably been generating hits for several years.

Michael's exuberant vocals defined such catchy Jackson 5 hits as "I Want You Back," "The Love You Save," "ABC," and "I'll Be There," all of which hit Number One in 1970. He released three albums for Motown as a solo artist, with singles such as "Ben," "Rockin' Robin," and "Got to Be There" reaching top chart levels. With Michael as lead vocalist and choreographer, the group toured extensively, giving audiences electrified shows that made the Jackson 5 more popular with each new show. Joseph Jackson and label founder, Berry Gordy, Jr., never saw eye to eye. Joseph always believed his sons could produce and write, but were limited by Motown's management. The Jacksons, minus Jermaine, left Motown after a dispute over artistic control and signed with CBS's Epic label in 1976.

Motown sued and the Jackson 5 lost its name. The brothers now known as The Jacksons—added to the

At a Glance . . .

Born Michael Joseph Jackson on August 19, 1958, in Gary, Indiana; son of Joseph (a heavy equipment operator and part-time musician) and Katherine (a sales clerk, maiden name Scruse) Jackson. Married Lisa Marie Presley, 1994 (divorced 1996); married Debbie Rowe, 1996 (divorced 1999); children: (with Rowe), Prince Michael Jackson Jr. and Paris Michael Katherine; (with unknown mother), Prince Michael Jackson II.

Career: Performing and recording artist, 1963–. Vocalist with the Jackson 5, 1963-76; group signed with Motown Records, 1969; signed as solo artist with Motown, 1972–.

Awards: Numerous Grammy awards for *Thriller*, including album of the year, record of the year, best male rock vocal performance for "Beat It", and best new R&B song for "Billie Jean"; Song of the Year for "We Are the World," 1986; special humanitarian award from President Ronald Reagan, 1984; American Music Awards, Special Award of Achievement, 1989; World Music Awards for Best-Selling American Artist, World's Best-Selling Pop Artist, and World's best-Selling Artist of the Era, 1993; Grammy Award, Living Legend Award, 1993; Best R & B Single for "Remember The Time," 1993; Bambi Award, for Pop Artist of the Millennium, 2002.

Addresses: *Web*—http://mjjsource.com.

group was youngest brother, Randy—went on to be successful on the Epic label with such hits as "Blame It On The Boogie," "Shake Your Body," and "Heartbreak Hotel," all of which were written by various Jackson brothers.

As the Jackson 5, the brothers appeared in their first TV special, *Goin' Back to Indiana*, an ABC network presentation that also starred comedians Bill Cosby and Tom Smothers. ABC also aired a Saturday morning animated series *The Jackson Five* which featured the Jacksons' singing voices. As The Jacksons, they performed in Las Vegas with their sisters Rebbie, La Toya, and Janet. (Incidentally, Janet in the 1990s would eclipse Michael in popularity.)

Striking Out as a Solo Artist

Michael sought to carve out a career independent of his siblings'. Though he made solo albums as a child on the Motown label, it was on Epic that Michael became a superstar in his own right. He played the Scarecrow in the 1978 film *The Wiz* (opposite longtime friend Diana Ross in the role of Dorothy), and during the making of the film met music executive and producer Quincy Jones.

Jones would become one of the architects of Jackson's grand successes, creating a light, sophisticated production style that effectively showcased Jackson's quiet yet intensely dramatic vocals. A musical eclectic since his jazz days in the early 1960s, Jones also encouraged Jackson to experiment with novel stylistic fusions. The first fruit of their efforts was Jackson's 1979 release *Off the Wall*, which mixed disco and ballad elements and spawned four Top Ten singles.

Jones also produced *Thriller*, the long-awaited follow-up to *Off the Wall*. After the release of the mild novelty song "The Girl Is Mine" (a duet with ex-Beatle Paul McCartney) as the first single, the album's sales built slowly. But with subsequent single releases Jackson emerged spectacularly as a personality who could appeal to diverse audiences like no one else in American music had been able to for years. "Beat It," featuring rock guitarist Eddie Van Halen, crossed over to attain popularity even among fans of heavy metal music; "Billie Jean" drew on Jackson's own experience of unjust paternity accusations. Both songs reached number one, and "Billie Jean" made him the first artist to be number one on the pop single, pop album, R & B single, and R & B album charts simultaneously. *Thriller* went on to generate an unprecedented total of seven Top Ten singles. The album roosted atop *Billboard* magazine's sales charts for thirty-seven weeks, and at its peak was reported to be selling more than 500,000 copies every week.

Inspired Dance Moves

In 1985 Jackson co-wrote the international famine-relief single "We Are the World," one of the biggest-selling singles of all time. It seemed that everything Jackson touched turned to gold or platinum. His videos for the *Thriller* album helped to put the Music Television Channel, or MTV for short, on the map. His videos also showcased his dance moves that were still being imitated well into the 1990s. His most famous move, the Moonwalk, became a dance craze. Jackson first displayed the Moonwalk in his video for his song, "Billie Jean." He also began wearing one glove that was covered with rhinestones. He was asked by Barbara Walters on the television show *20/20* why he wore one glove, Jackson replied, "Cooler than two." Glove aside, many were impressed with Jackson's style and moves. Jane Fonda in *Time* magazine, described his music as "A fresh, original sound. The music is energetic, and it's sensual. You can dance to it, work out to it, make love to it, sing to it. It's hard to sit still to."

Jackson could also count as fans of his dancing, such pros as Bob Fosse, Gene Kelly, and Fred Astaire, who was quoted in *Time* as saying, "My Lord, he is a wonderful mover. He makes these moves up himself and it is just great to watch.... I don't know much more dancing he will take up, because singing and dancing at the same time is very difficult. But Michael is a dedicated artist."

Jackson reunited with his brothers, including Jermaine, for a *Motown 25* television special in 1983. Afterward, the Jacksons released another album, titled *Victory*, and then went on tour. Pepsi, who had signed Michael to a lucrative contract, decided to make a commercial with all the brothers performing. During production, an accident occurred and Michael's hair and scalp was badly burned, but he fully recovered. The tour was his swan song exit. After the end of the tour, Michael left the group and soon afterward, they disbanded.

Growing Popularity

His next album release, 1987's *Bad*, sold 22 million copies internationally, a disappointment only by the lofty standard *Thriller* had established. Bad included five number one singles: "I Just Can't Stop Loving You," "Bad," "The Way You Make Me Feel," "Man in the Mirror," and "Dirty Diana." *Dangerous*, released in 1991 with new producer Teddy Riley at the helm, likewise topped 20 million in total sales. *Dangerous* produced "Remember The Time," that won R & B's best single at the Grammys. The album also featured kid rap duo Kriss Kross, rapper Heavy D, and Princess Stephanie of Monaco.

Jackson continued to produce videos. As his popularity grew, he was able to premiere each video during primetime television and MTV. Most videos were short form, that is, lasting the length of the songs, but some were long form, which included dialogue, and some were mini-movies.

His song "Thriller" began the tradition, and the video *The Making of Michael Jackson's 'Thriller'* garnered sales in the millions. Most notable among the long form videos were "Bad"—which also starred an unknown actor by the name of Wesley Snipes—"Black or White," which featured Macauley Culkin of *Home Alone* fame, and the infamous crotch-grabbing dance routine, and also "Remember The Time," with comedian Eddie Murphy, basketball great Magic Johnson, and supermodel Iman. "Remember The Time" also featured Jackson's first on-screen romantic kiss and one of the best choreographed dance routines of the 1990s.

Jackson's songs "Smooth Criminal" and "Leave Me Alone" were featured in his film, *Moonwalker*. His other film, *Captain Eo*, was shown at Disneyworld and Disneyland theme parks. Although he was not given credit, Michael Jackson's voice appeared on the animated television series *The Simpsons*.

Personal Life Scrutinized

In the years following the release of *Thriller*, Jackson found himself subject to the isolation that artists in the top echelon of fame inevitably experience. A devout Jehovah's Witness, he adopted a disguise and went door to door to promote the religion shortly after the album was released. But the pressures of stardom eventually made it impractical for him to continue his religious activities, and he renounced his membership in the sect in 1987 after his video "Thriller" was condemned by the group. A public perception of Jackson as a curious recluse began to take shape about this time. He was a constant subject of stories in the nation's tabloid press. Some—such as the story that he slept in a levitating "hyperbaric chamber" for the purpose of extending his life span—were planted by Jackson's own operatives as a way of garnering publicity. Jackson's skin seemed to become progressively lighter, leading to rumors that he was bleaching his skin in order to appear white.

Jackson countered this rumor in a February 1993 interview with television talk show host Oprah Winfrey, claiming that he suffered from vitiligo, a skin disease. But public unease with the star increased markedly as a result of much more serious allegations that surfaced in August of that year. Jackson was accused of sexually molesting a thirteen-year-old boy at his Encino, California, compound, called Neverland. The singer had long enjoyed surrounding himself with children; in September, his sister La Toya claimed that he had sometimes spent nights together with them in his bedroom. Jackson strongly denied any wrongdoing, maintaining that he was the victim of an extortion plot on the part of the father of the thirteen-year-old. The case was settled privately for an undisclosed sum in January of 1994, and charges were dropped, but it cost Jackson a lucrative endorsement contract with Pepsi-Cola. He has continued to deny the charges.

Jackson's musical successes since the time of these allegations have been sporadic, but his personal life continued to provide surprises. In August of 1994 it was revealed that Jackson had married Lisa Marie Presley, daughter of legendary rock and roll innovator and pop megastar Elvis Presley, ten weeks earlier in a ceremony in the Dominican Republic. The couple was amicably divorced in January of 1996; in November of that year, Jackson married Debbie Rowe, a nurse who had reportedly been artificially inseminated and was pregnant with the singer's child. A son, Prince Michael Jackson Jr., was born in early 1997, and the couple was graced with the birth of a daughter, Paris Michael Katherine, in April of 1998. The couple divorced in

1999, with Jackson receiving full custody of the children in the settlement. Jackson soon added another son, Prince Michael II, with an unknown woman.

Jackson's public outings with his children were eagerly followed by the press. Jackson covered his children's heads with cloth in public as a precaution against kidnapping, according to *Jet*. In 2002 Jackson brought on public scorn for holding his infant son over the edge of a fourth-floor balcony to show fans. Soon after, Jackson released a statement saying "I made a terrible mistake. I got caught up in the excitement of the moment. I would never intentionally endanger the lives of my children," as quoted in *Jet*.

Struggled to Stay on Top

Despite a $30 million marketing campaign, Jackson's 1995 release *HIStory: Past, Present, and Future Book I* fell short of expectations with its sales of two million units domestically, twelve million internationally; controversies over the songs "Scream" and "They Don't Care About Us" (the latter contained an allegedly anti-Semitic lyric reference for which Jackson later apologized) and an award for song "You Are Not Alone," did not keep the album from dropping out of the U.S. Top Ten within weeks of its release. A 1997 album, *Blood on the Dance Floor: HIStory in the Mix*, fared even worse, with little marketing and domestic sales in the hundreds of thousands; it consisted largely of remixes by various hit producers of songs from the 1995 HIStory release. Jackson seemed to be attempting to update his style to fit with the technology-driven musical trends of the 1990s.

During the late 1990s the singer was occupied with grandiose schemes to build entertainment complexes in such diverse locales as Poland, South Korea, Paris, and Detroit, where he joined with gambling magnate Don Barden to push for a proposed casino and amusement park. This effort fell through in Detroit, when the people voted no on their proposal to allow the two to bid for a casino license in August of 1998. His charitable foundation Heal the World was reported by *People* magazine to be cutting back on donations as Jackson's total income dropped from an estimated $65 million in 1989 to $20 million in 1997.

Jackson continued to release records on Epic in the early 2000s, including *Invincible* in 2001 and *Michael Jackson: The Ultimate Collection* in 2003. While *Invincible* cost $30 million to make, it only sold six million copies worldwide by mid-2002. Though the record label spent $25 million to promote the record, Jackson believed they did not provide support in promoting the record and were trying to sabotage his career. As Jackson's musical career continued to become more irrelevant, his income also fell further. In the early 2000s, it was reported that he heavily borrowed against his assets to maintain his lifestyle.

Alleged Molestation Goes to Trial

In February of 2003, an unflattering television documentary by British journalist Martin Bashir called *Living with Michael Jackson* was broadcast. In the program, Jackson defended as "loving" his practice of letting young boys sleep in his bed. In November of 2003, California authorities searched Jackson's Neverland Ranch, following allegations that he molested a young boy who had visited the Neverland Ranch and spent the night there several times. Jackson was booked on child-molestation charges that month and released on $3 million bail. Formal charges against Jackson were filed in December 2003. A grand jury indicted the 46-year-old pop star in April 2004 on charges of molesting the boy at the center of the trial, giving him alcohol and conspiring to hold him and his family captive in 2003. The case remained in the public eye through 2004, with both sides allegedly leaking information. Because of the leaks and related issues, the judge issued a gag order for both sides. This order did not prevent some of the grand jury testimony of the young victim from being released shortly before the trial was to begin.

Jury selection began on January 31, 2005, and Jackson's trial started at the end of February. According to CNN.com, testimony and closing arguments lasted nearly 14 weeks before the jury got the case. "Prosecutors alleged that, following the broadcast of the Bashir documentary in 2003, Jackson and five associates plotted to control and intimidate the accuser's family to get them to go along with damage-control efforts, including holding them against their will at Neverland. The molestation charges relate to alleged incidents between Jackson and the accuser after the Bashir documentary aired. Jackson's lawyers, however, consistently portrayed the singer as a naive victim of the accuser's family, who, they claimed, were grifters—schemers—with a habit of wheedling money out of the rich and famous," CNN.com summed up. On June 13, 2005, the jury exonerated Jackson of all ten charges against him. If he had been convicted, he could have been sent to prison for nearly 20 years. As Jackson recuperated at his Neverland home, his fans wondered what the future would hold for him.

Michael Jackson described the importance of his music career to his personal life in his 1993 Grammy Living Legend Award acceptance speech: "My childhood was completely taken away from me. There was no Christmas, there was no birthdays, it was not a normal childhood, nor the normal pleasures of childhood.... But as an awful price, I can not re-create that part of my life. However, today, when I create my music, I feel like an instrument of nature. I wonder what delight nature must feel when we open our hearts and express our God-given talents." Millions of fans, young and old, black or white, are happy Michael Jackson chose to share those talents with the world. And after Jackson's trial, Michael Sands, a Hollywood media publicist related to *People* that Jackson's future still held promise. "He's still an icon, and his fans worldwide love him." Jackson seemed to agree, as he still referred to himself as the King of Pop.

Selected works

Albums, solo

Got to Be There, Motown, 1972.
Ben, Motown, 1972.
Music and Me, Motown, 1973.
Forever, Michael, Motown, 1975.
The Best of Michael Jackson, Motown, 1975.
Off the Wall, Epic, 1979.
Thriller, Epic, 1982.
Bad, Epic, 1987.
Dangerous, Epic, 1991.
HIStory: Past, Present, and Future Book I, Epic, 1995.
Blood on the Dance Floor: HIStory in the Mix, Epic, 1997.
Invincible, Epic, 2001.
Michael Jackson: The Complete Collection, Epic, 2004.

Albums, with the Jackson 5

Diana Ross Presents the Jackson 5, Motown, 1969.
ABC, Motown, 1970.
Third Album, Motown, 1970.
The Jackson 5 Christmas Album, Motown, 1970.
Maybe Tomorrow, Motown, 1971.
Goin' Back to Indiana, Motown, 1971.
The Jackson 5's Greatest Hits, Motown, 1971.
Looking Through the Windows, Motown, 1972.
Skywriter, Motown, 1973.
Get It Together, Motown, 1973.
Dancing Machine, Motown, 1974.
Moving Violation, Motown, 1975.
Joyful Jukebox Music, Motown, 1976.
The Jackson 5 Anthology, Motown, 1976.
The Jacksons, Epic, 1976.
Goin' Places, Epic, 1977.
Destiny, Epic, 1978.
Off the Wall, Epic, 1979.
Boogie, Motown, 1980.
Triumph, Epic, 1980.
The Jacksons Live, Epic, 1981.
Farewell My Summer Love, Motown, 1984 (recorded 1973, previously unreleased).
Victory, Epic, 1984.

Books

Moonwalk, Doubleday, 1988.

Films

The Wiz, 1978.

Sources

Books

Chandler, Raymond, *All that Glitters: The Crime and the Cover-Up*, Windsong Press, 2004.
Jackson, Michael, *Moonwalk*, Doubleday, 1988.
Jones, Bob, as told to Stacy Brown, *Michael Jackson, The Man behind the Mask: An Insider's Story of the King of Pop*, SelectBooks, 2005.
Lewis, Jel D., and Michael Jackson, comp., *The King of Pop: The Big Picture: The Music! The Man! The Legend! The Interviews: An Anthology*, Amber Books 2, 2005.
Perel, David, *Freak!: Inside the Twisted World of Michael Jackson: New Information of Jackson's Indictment and Trial*, HarperEntertainment, 2005.
Romanowski, Patricia, and Holly George-Warren, eds., *The New Rolling Stone Encyclopedia of Rock and Roll*, Fireside, 1995.
Taraborrelli, J. Randy, *Michael Jackson: The Magic and the Madness*, Birch Lane Press, 1991.

Periodicals

Associated Press, January 13, 2005.
Atlanta Journal, November 26, 1996, p. A14.
Billboard, March 30, 1991, p. 5.
Detroit Free Press, August 3, 1998, p. B2.
Jet, December 9, 2002, p. 16; January 19, 2004, p. 55.
Los Angeles Times, February 28, 1998, p. D1.
MacLean's, April 20, 1998, p. 11.
Newsweek, December 1, 2003, p. 38.
New York Sun, November 16, 2004, p. 19.
New York Times, March 20, 1996, p. D4; June 23, 1997, p. D6.
People, March 1, 1993, p. 46; September 6, 1993, p. 40; May 4, 1998, p. 6; July 22, 2002, p. 15; December 8, 2003, p. 84; January 12, 2004, p. 64; June 27, 2005, p. 57.
Time, March 19, 1984, p. 54; September 14, 1987, p. 85; December 1, 2003, p. 48.
Washington Post, August 2, 1994, p. F1; January 19, 1996, p. D1.

On-line

Michael Jackson, http://mjjsource.com/ (August 15, 2005).
"The Michael Jackson Trial," *CNN*, http://www.cnn.com/SPECIALS/2005/jackson.trial (August 15, 2005).

Other

Barbara Walters' interview with Michael Jackson on 20/20 and Jackson's 1993 Grammy Award acceptance speech was found at the Michael Jackson Internet Fan Club at www.fred.net/mjj/.

—James M. Manheim, Ashyia N. Henderson, and Sara Pendergast

Wayne Jones

1952—

Engineer

Jones, Wayne, photograph. Courtesy of Wayne Jones.

National Society of Black Engineers (NSBE) 2004 Golden Torch for Lifetime Achievement in Government recipient Wayne Jones attended college during a period of enormous growth and development in the computer sciences. Deeply interested and excited by the possibilities of this new technology, he specialized in computer systems engineering and worked for several major corporations in the field. However, it was not only his expertise as a systems engineer that would influence his career choices, but also his affection for his home and family. He eventually applied for an engineering job at Oklahoma's Tinker Air Force Base to please his father, and took the job because it would allow him to live closer to his parents. His own skill, combined with the determination and confidence he had first learned from his mother and father, helped him to rise to increasingly responsible positions on the job and to achieve his personal goal of earning his doctoral degree in industrial engineering.

Taught to Reach for His Goals

Jones was born in Oklahoma City on July 29, 1952. His father, Booker T. Jones worked for many years as a civilian machinist for the United States Air Force at Tinker Air Force Base on the outskirts of Oklahoma City. His mother, Louise Jones worked in the home caring for her husband and their eleven children. The Joneses were a close family, and young Wayne grew to admire both of his parents for their hard work and devotion to their children. From his father, who worked long hours without complaint, Jones learned persistence. His mother's unfailing optimism encouraged him to reach for his goals. "It doesn't hurt to ask," she often told her children. "All they can do is say no."

Young Wayne was unhappy at first about leaving home to go to school, but by junior high school he began to enjoy his classes, especially math and science. He played basketball, ran track, and played tenor saxophone in the band. Weekends and summers were spent working with his father, who ran a side business taking care of lawns in addition to his full time machinist job. Booker T. Jones maintained this second business largely to teach his sons about the value of work. Working alongside their father, the Jones boys stayed out of trouble and earned their own spending money.

At a Glance . . .

Born Wayne Jones on July 29, 1952, in Oklahoma City, Oklahoma; married Brenda Harbin, 1973 (divorced); children: Lashawn, Julian; married Amber Booth, 1997; children: Amy, John. *Education:* Langston University, BS, mathematics, 1973; Arizona State University, MS, systems engineering, 1977; University of Oklahoma, PhD, industrial engineering, 2001.

Career: Boeing Computer Services, systems engineer, 1974; Honeywell Inc., systems engineer, 1974-79; Codex Corporation, systems engineer, 1979-80; Oklahoma City Air Logistics Center, project engineer, 1980-85; engineering management, 1985-91; chief engineer for the B-1B weapon system, 1991-92; chief systems engineer and chief of the science and engineering division, 1991–.

Memberships: University of Oklahoma, Industrial Engineering Advisory Board; Oklahoma Christian University, Engineering Executive Council; Oklahoma Engineering Foundation, Board of Trustees; Center for Aircraft Systems/Subsystems and Infrastructure (CASD); Oklahoma City National Society of Black Engineers, Alumni Extension Chapter.

Awards: National Society of Black Engineers, Golden Torch Award, Lifetime Achievement in Government, 2004.

Addresses: *Office*—3821 Randie St., Oklahoma City, OK 73150.

The Joneses assumed their children would attend college. Wayne Jones' uncle had been one of the first blacks to receive a Ph.D. in biological sciences from the University of Oklahoma, and his success inspired young Wayne to work toward a higher education. In 1969, he entered Oklahoma's Langston University, an historically black college that had been established as the Colored Agricultural and Normal University in 1897, when Oklahoma was still a territory.

It was in college that Jones first became interested in computers. An older student who had gone to high school with Jones had specialized in computer science and encouraged Jones to enter the field. Jones immediately became fascinated with the new machines. In 1973, he received his bachelor's degree in mathematics, with a minor in computer science.

Began Career at Boeing

The friend who had sparked Jones' interest in computers had gone to work for Boeing, a manufacturer of aircraft and related products. He recommended Jones for a job, and by January 1974, Jones had moved to Wichita, Kansas, to work as a systems analyst for Boeing.

Working for Boeing in Wichita was not a good experience for Jones. Though he had grown up during the segregation of the 1950s and the civil rights activism of the 1960s, Jones had remained fairly sheltered, living in a large, secure family in a black neighborhood. His parents had been protective, keeping their children close to home. He had attended a black high school and a black college. Jones and his friends were aware of injustice around them. They noticed, for example, that black schools often received inferior books and equipment. However, Jones was an adult before he lived in an integrated environment, and Boeing's Wichita plant was a culture shock.

For the first time in his life, he worked with people who disliked him simply because he was black. Unused to rude and unfair treatment, Jones reacted angrily. He was determined to get the recognition and opportunity that he felt his hard work deserved. When one of his supervisors asked him, "Why can't you be more like JJ?" Jones was deeply offended. JJ was the name of a character on the 1974-79 CBS comedy *Good Times.* He was a clownish black teenager with many stereotypical characteristics, and many black viewers of the program found his portrayal to be insulting. As a serious computer engineer, Jones did not want to be expected to behave like a comedian. He began to look for a new job.

Advanced Through Education and Experience

When he heard of a job available with a Phoenix aerospace company called Honeywell, Jones wrote them a letter, outlining his qualifications for the job and adding that he would not change jobs if he could expect the same racist experience that he had had at Boeing. His honesty and directness appealed to the Honeywell management, and they invited Jones for an interview. Jones was pleased to be treated respectfully and agreed to take the job. His work at Honeywell involved developing computer operating systems and designing tests for the company's giant supercomputers.

Jones found his work at Honeywell interesting and challenging. The company encouraged him to continue his education, so he returned to school and earned a masters degree in systems engineering at Arizona State University. His new degree made him even more valuable to employers, and in 1979 a small subsidiary of Motorola called Codex offered Jones a higher-paying job.

Though he only worked at Codex for a year, Jones learned a lot about the way a business operates. Because Codex was a smaller company than either Boeing or Honeywell, employing only about seventy people, Jones had more direct experience with more aspects of the business. However, the small size of the company also meant it was less stable and Jones did not feel secure about his job.

On one of Jones' visits to his parents' home in Oklahoma City, his father suggested he apply for an engineering job at Tinker Air Force Base. Though he had not intended to look for a job, he took his father's suggestion. To his surprise, the Oklahoma City Air Logistics Center at Tinker Air Force Base offered him a job. The chance to move closer to his parents appealed to him and he took a job as project engineer for cruise missile software.

Jones' first work at Tinker AFB involved designing embedded flight computer systems, that is, built-in systems with specific functions, such as guidance systems. In 1985, Jones was promoted to a management position, and he rose quickly to become a senior manager by 1991. That year, he became the chief engineer for the B1 bomber aircraft. Also in 1991, he became the Center Chief Systems Engineer. In this position, he supervised twelve hundred engineers and scientists, as well as helping to set policy and coordinate support for engineers working in all areas of the base. Jones became the representative for these engineers on Tinker's corporate board.

Earned His Doctorate

In 1995 Jones began the venture that he would consider the biggest accomplishment of his career. He decided to return to school at the University of Oklahoma. Though he had only intended to take a few refresher courses, he quickly became immersed in the subjects he studied. What had started as a brief project quickly became a long-term goal: Jones decided to pursue a Ph.D. in industrial engineering. Engineers apply the principles of science for practical purposes, and industrial engineers learn about all aspects of industry in order to make the manufacturing process work better. As usual, Jones was especially interested in the ways that innovative computer systems, such as artificial intelligence and computer simulation, could be used in industry.

Nothing in Jones' work required him to obtain his doctorate; he did not expect to earn a higher salary as a result. He was motivated by his interest in the field and by the challenge of achieving his goal and becoming the second member of his family to earn his doctorate at the University of Oklahoma. Though it required years of hard work, attending classes while working full time, Jones felt supported by his religious faith and the values of persistence and optimism he had learned from his parents. In 2001 he proudly received his doctorate.

As often happens, accomplishing one goal created other goals. For Wayne Jones, this new goal became giving something back to the black community and the historically black colleges that nurtured and helped him during his youth. He actively encourages African-American students to pursue careers in technological fields, and would like to return to the academic world as a teacher and researcher in order to give direct support to the new generation of black engineers.

Sources

On-line

National Society of Black Engineers Website. "Lifetime Achievement In Government: Wayne Jones, Ph.D." www.nsbe.org/publicrelations/winner_bios.php (May 12, 2005).

University of Oklahoma College of Engineering Website. "Board of Advisors: Wayne Jones, PhD." www.coe.ou.edu/ie/alumni/advisory/jones.htm (May 12, 2005).

Other

Information for this profile was obtained through an interview with Dr. Wayne Jones on June 3, 2005.

—Tina Gianoulis

Al Loving

1935-2005

Artist

The 20th-century artistic style known as abstract expressionism, with its emphasis on patterns, geometrical shapes, and works that focus on the process of making art, has grown into a generally accepted part of the American cultural vocabulary. But when Alvin Loving began his career, abstract art was not practiced by many black artists. At the time Loving began working in the 1960s and 1970s, most black artists were exploring ways of depicting the black experience or black culture. Loving, however, heeded a different call. Loving became recognized as the foremost African-American exponent of abstract expressionism. His works always bore a distinct personal stamp, especially in the way he extended abstract expressionist ideas in highly original ways.

Loved Painting from Early Age

Alvin Loving Jr., often known as Al, was born in Detroit on September 19, 1935. His father, the first black teacher in Detroit's public high schools, had worked as a sign painter and taken some art classes. The elder Alvin Loving would later become a pioneering educator, ascending to a university professorship and then a deanship in the University of Michigan system and serving in teaching and administrative posts in India and Nigeria on special leaves. When his son was twelve, Alvin Loving Sr. had him copy landscapes and watercolors he had done himself. Soon Loving was painting sets for plays presented at Detroit's Northern High School.

Loving moved to Cass Tech High School after exhausting Northern's art offerings, and graduated in 1954. He took classes at Wayne State University and a local art school the following year, but then moved with his family to India for a year instead of continuing school. The distance from his home gave Loving perspective on his ambitions, and he decided to pursue a career in the fine arts—at a time when the number of working African-Americans fine artists was minuscule—rather than as a commercial artist.

At this crucial formative stage, Loving came under the influence of artist Al Mullen, who himself had been a student of the German abstract expressionist Hans Hoffmann. Hoffmann's paintings featured large, intensely colored rectangles with indistinct edges that seem to float in backgrounds of a related color; he is regarded as one of abstract expressionism's pioneers, and his style influenced Loving directly. Having settled on his choice of career, Loving proceeded methodically to acquire his education as an artist; he was interrupted only by two years during which he worked as a propaganda illustrator at Fort Bragg in North Carolina. Loving received an associate's degree from Flint Junior College (now Mott Community College) in 1958, a Bachelor of Fine Arts degree from the University of Illinois in 1963, and a Master of Fine Arts from the University of Michigan in 1965.

Driven to Realize His Own Artistic Vision

Loving taught briefly at Eastern Michigan University in

At a Glance . . .

Born on September 19, 1935, in Detroit, MI; died on June 21, 2005, in New York, NY; son of Alvin Loving, an educator and Mary Helen (Green) Loving; married Eleanor Jean Randles (divorced); married Wyn Cortes Reiser, 1969 (died 1990); married Mara Kearney; children: (first marriage) Alvin III, Lauri (died, 2001), (second marriage) Alicia, Ann. *Education*: Flint Junior College, associate's degree, 1958; University of Illinois, BFA, 1963; University of Michigan, MFA, 1965.

Career: Artist, 1960s-2005; guest lecturer and artist-in-residence posts at University of California at San Diego, Ohio University, Skowhegan School of Painting and Sculpture, Maryland Institute, University of Kansas, Virginia Commonwealth University, Notre Dame University, University of Vermont at Johnsonville, Cornell University; City College of New York, instructor, 1988, associate professor, 1992-?.

Selected awards: National Endowment for the Arts fellowships, 1970, 1971, 1975, 1976, 1985; Guggenheim fellowship, 1986.

the late 1960s, but he felt the need to make an impact with his own art and headed for New York, the art world's mecca. Later, ironically, he would find a strong market for his work in Detroit and would come to be impressed by the sophistication of that city's art buyers. A Detroit gallery owner smoothed the way by introducing Loving to her counterparts in New York, and his career took off with surprising speed. Producing new works inspired by Hoffmann and by another arch-abstractionist, Josef Albers, Loving hit on what would for a time become a trademark style: representations of open-insides cubes whose edges interlock.

In 1969 Loving snared the Holy Grail of many a young artist: a one-person show at New York's Whitney Museum of American Art. The show was part of a series intended to explore the world of African-American art, and Loving's work stood out for its seeming disengagement from the turbulent racial issues of the late 1960s. But it likewise was distinctive on its own terms, brilliantly fusing pure abstraction with the feel of the optical-illusion paintings of the popular Hungarian artist Viktor Vasarely. The result was that in the 1970s, Loving found his work in demand for gallery and museum shows all over the country—and himself in demand as a university teacher and artist-in-residence.

University residencies at the University of California at San Diego, Ohio University, the University of Kansas, Notre Dame University, and other institutions helped to pay the bills, but Loving began to feel trapped by his trademark style. "Basically, I was trying to liberate myself from those cubes, that box," he told the *Detroit Free Press*. "I couldn't find a way out." But the series of experiments Loving undertook continued to raise his standing in the art world. By the late 1990s, Loving's major works would sell for over $70,000 apiece.

Thrived on Experimentation

In the mid-1970s Loving began to create works that used the gallery space itself as his "canvas," tacking strips of actual painted canvas to the walls and ceilings and draping them across the room—an idea counted as quite radical at the time, although it later became fairly common. Once again, Loving fused two trends in contemporary art, for his work retained an element of geometric abstraction—the hung pieces of canvas would be sewn into various geometrical shapes. In the next stage of Loving's career he collapsed this style based on sewn cloth back into the space of the traditional picture frame, creating woven-fabric surfaces that critic John Canaday (later quoted in the *Boston Globe*) dubbed "soft sculpture." The tactile nature of Loving's works during this period suited them for public spaces such as a station of the Detroit People Mover downtown parking shuttle.

In the 1980s and 1990s, Loving continued to make new stylistic turns, building at each point on his own previous work. He turned to the collage medium, working at first with paint and corrugated cardboard that, sculpture-like, jutted out from the surface plane of the work. Loving also became known for a signature use of color; he tended toward "hot" colors, such as red, accented with cool touches. Collage, Loving told the *Detroit Free Press* (in an interview quoted by Michigan State University's Shannon Bonner) "has a wonderful ability to make a string of extreme things go together." In the 1980s Loving learned the craft of papermaking and incorporated his own handmade paper into his collage works.

It is tempting to liken Loving's abstract creations with the vivid abstract patterns that appear in certain traditions of African art. Nevertheless, asked by Bonner whether he consciously tried to incorporate African elements into his work, Loving replied, "I absolutely never think about it." Loving has argued that African Americans will produce works that differ stylistically from those of their white counterparts, but he is skeptical about the existence of a specifically African-American aesthetic or artistic outlook.

Loving, who joined the faculty of the City University of New York in 1988, soon began to work in a style he calls material abstraction. His work in this style was marked by the use of paper spattered or sprayed with paint, cut into shaped pieces, and then arranged on a surface. In the 1990s and early 2000s the prices his works commanded were helped by the emergence of a strong market for art among African Americans. His works were often shown at the G. R. N'Namdi galleries in Detroit and Chicago, and he found that Detroit, from which he had fled as a young man in the late 1960s, actually provided him with his strongest sales.

In 2001 Loving completed what would be his last commission: a mosaic wall of colorful glass windows for the Metropolitan Transportation Authority on display at the Broadway-East New York subway station. Loving died in New York, on June 21, 2005, from complications of lung cancer. Erik Chan wrote in his *Detroit Free Press* obituary for Loving: "Like one of the spirals he was so known for painting, Al Loving's life spread continuously outward in concentric rings, touching and teaching and awing and astonishing more people than an art museum could contain." Loving's work remains on permanent display in several art museums.

Selected works

Permanent collections

Detroit Institute of Arts, MI.
Metropolitan Museum of Art, New York, NY.
Philadelphia Museum of Art, PA.
Studio Museum, Harlem, NY.
Whitney Museum of American Art, New York, NY.

Sources

Books

St. James Guide to Black Artists, St. James Press, 1997.

Periodicals

Boston Globe, September 29, 1988, p. 79.
Christian Science Monitor, June 22, 2001.
International Herald Tribune, July 1, 2005, p. 8.
Jet, June 1, 1992, p. 18.
New York Times, June 30, 2005, p. B9.

On-line

"Al Loving: Maker of Art." www.msu.edu/~bonnersh/alov.htm (July 31, 2005).

—Ashyia Henderson, James M. Manheim, and Sara Pendergast

Marilyn McCoo

1943—

Singer, actress

In a career spanning forty years, Marilyn McCoo has become one of the most successful female recording artists in American music. With super group The 5th Dimension, her husband Billy Davis Jr., and as a soloist, McCoo has earned seven gold albums, five gold singles, six Grammy awards, and a star on the Hollywood Walk of Fame. Her own fame was cemented as a singer when she helped the hippie generation "Let the Sunshine In" and showed the world that "You Don't Have to Be a Star" to find lasting love.

Began Singing as a Child

Marilyn McCoo was born on September 30, 1943, in Jersey City, New Jersey. At the age of seven she moved with her family to Los Angeles. Her parents, Mary and Waymon McCoo, were both doctors who provided McCoo, her two sisters, and one brother with a solid middle-class upbringing. McCoo sang before she took her first step. Dance, piano, and voice classes followed and by the time she was a teenager McCoo was set on a career in entertainment. At 15 she entered Art Linkletter's *Talent Scouts*, a local Los Angeles talent show. Tall, with striking good looks, McCoo soon began modeling. Meanwhile, she graduated high school and enrolled in UCLA, where she earned a degree in business administration.

In 1962, McCoo entered the Miss Bronze California contest. After sweeping the talent competition she went on to earn the crown. At the event she met Lamonte McLemore, a photographer for *Jet* and a part-time vocalist. McLemore's photos of McCoo were featured in the magazine's column "Beauty of the Week." He also invited her to join his singing group, The Hi-Fi's. She accepted and began performing with them in Los Angeles clubs. Soul legend Ray Charles caught one of their gigs and invited The Hi-Fi's to join him on tour. Charles also produced the group's single "Lonesome Mood."

The Hi-Fi's disbanded in 1965 and that same year McCoo, McLemore, Florence LaRue, Ron Townson, and Billy Davis Jr. joined forces as The Versatiles. At first the group sang for fun. "We started out as friends, singing as a hobby," McCoo told the *St. Louis Post-Dispatch*. In between gigs, McCoo worked for a department store and later as a job developer in Watts for a group called Economic Youth Opportunities. Davis, however, had brought to the group a connection with the recording industry, and a record deal was soon in the works.

Found Fame with The 5th Dimension

The Versatiles briefly signed with Bronco Records where future R&B icon Barry White was working as a music director. When that deal collapsed, they joined the Soul City label and changed their name to The 5th Dimension. With a crew of veteran session musicians, the five singers recorded their first hit in 1966, "Go Where You Wanna Go." They followed that release with the full-length album *Up, Up, and Away*. Catchy pop with an R&B attitude, the title track highlighted the group's vocal acrobatics and lodged itself at number seven on the charts. Another standout track was

At a Glance . . .

Born on September 30, 1943, in Jersey City, NJ; married Billy Davis Jr. (1969). *Education:* University of California-Los Angeles, BS, business administration.

Career: The Fifth Dimension, singer, 1965-75; solo, and with Billy Davis Jr., singer, 1975–; actress, 1977–.

Memberships: Children's Miracle Network, board member; Los Angeles Mission, board member; Cancer Research Foundation, board member; Soldiers for the Second Coming, founder.

Awards: Miss Bronze California, 1962; Grammy Award, Record of the Year (with Billy Davis Jr.), "You Don't Have to Be a Star," 1977; earned a star on the Hollywood Walk of Fame (with The Fifth Dimension), 1991; Children's Miracle Network, Achievement Award, 2002; Grammy Hall of Fame, inductee (with The Fifth Dimension), "Aquarius/Let the Sunshine In," 2004.

Addresses: *Management*—The Sterling/Winters Company, 10900 Wilshire Blvd., Suite 1550, Los Angeles, CA 90024. *Web*—www.mccoodavis.com.

"Learn How to Fly," driven by McCoo's clear vocals.

Up, Up, and Away snagged The 5th Dimension four Grammy awards in 1967, including Best Pop Performance by a Group and Record of the Year. McCoo and company became stars. A follow-up album, *The Magic Garden,* also released in 1967, was tepidly received, but did nothing to hurt the band's popularity. 1968's *Stoned Soul Garden,* widely considered the group's best work, featured two chart-topping singles—the title track and "Sweet Blindness."

In 1969 The 5th Dimension hit the upper stratosphere of stardom with *The Age of Aquarius*. The album's first single, "Aquarius/Let the Sunshine In," became a mega-hit, occupying the number one spot on the charts for six weeks and becoming the un-official anthem of the 1960s. It earned the group two more Grammy Awards, including Record of the Year. A second song, "Wedding Bell Blues," also went to number one. In this gospel-tinged ballad, McCoo took center stage, infusing the lyrics with tender yearning when she crooned, "C'mon and marry me, Bi-ill." Fittingly, 5th Dimension co-singer Billy Davis Jr. did just that.

Partnered with Davis in Marriage and Music

McCoo and Davis had developed a strong friendship from the moment The 5th Dimension formed. "When we met, there was no immediate physical attraction because we weren't each other's physical type," McCoo told *Jet*. "So, Billy and I became friends." After four years of constant togetherness—performing, touring, rehearsing—the duo realized they were in love. "Our relationship was built on being around each other all the time," McCoo told *Jet*. They were married on July 26, 1969, setting off a 30-plus year partnership.

In 1970 The 5th Dimension released yet another chart-topping album, *Portrait*. It is home to one of McCoo's strongest performances, "One Less Bell to Answer," a steamy, torch song dripping in soul. The group released nearly a dozen more albums over the next five years, though they never again reached the success they had in 1969. McCoo recorded several powerful solos including "Loves Lines, Angles, and Rhymes" from the album of the same name, "(Last Night) I Didn't Get To Sleep at All" from *Greatest Hits on Earth,* and "If I Could Reach You" from *Individually and Collectively*. All three songs made it to the Billboard Top Ten.

By 1975 McCoo and Davis had decided to leave the group. "In the back of our minds, we still had that desire to see where our careers could go as individuals," McCoo told NPR radio host Tavis Smiley. "The 5th Dimension had a wonderful sound...and every sound has its run. And we had had our run. Well, Billy and I weren't ready to accept that, so we were saying, 'Let's do something different. Let's do something new." Recording as a duo, they released 1976's *I Hope We Get To Love In Time* featuring the single, "You Don't Have to Be a Star (To Be in My Show)." The song went straight to number one and earned the duo a Grammy for Best R&B Performance by a Group.

Broke into Broadway and Books

McCoo moved into television in 1977, co-hosting *The Marilyn McCoo and Billy Davis, Jr. Show* on CBS. The prime-time variety show featured comedy sketches by Jay Leno and Tim Reid and, of course, lots of singing. In the 1980s McCoo hosted *Solid Gold*, a music show that featured a count down of that week's top ten songs interpreted by the famous, spandex-clad *Solid Gold* dancers. McCoo also made guest appearances on *The Love Boat* and *Night Court*, and had a recurring spot on the soap opera *Days of Our Lives*. Onstage, McCoo began appearing in musicals—*The Man of La Mancha*, *Anything Goes,* and *A... My Name is Alice*—with the dream of appearing on Broadway. "I had hoped those shows would lead to a Broadway opportunity; but in any case, I felt that if I was serious about my dream, I needed experience," she told *The Philadelphia Tribune*. Her dream came true in 1996 when she landed the role of Julie in a Broadway production of *Showboat*.

As her acting career unfolded, her singing career steadily rolled along. She and Davis released *The Two of Us* and *Marilyn and Billy*. On her own, McCoo released *Solid Gold* in 1983 and *The Me Nobody Knows* in 1991. The latter was a contemporary gospel album that reflected McCoo's spiritual beliefs. Incorporating jazz, soul, and Caribbean beats, the album made the Christian music charts and was nominated for a Grammy for Best Gospel recording. She and Davis also maintained a busy schedule of touring and performing, particularly on the Gospel circuit. In 1990 they joined the original members of The 5th Dimension for a national reunion tour.

In 1999 McCoo and Davis took two musical productions on the road: *The Duke Ellington Songbook Tour* and *It Takes Two*. Of the latter, Davis told the *St. Louis Post-Dispatch*, "It's a love, unity, and togetherness kind of show. Songs were picked for two people, and it just kind of fell into place for us because of who we are and what we represent." McCoo and Davis further shared what they represented with the 2004 publication of *Up, Up and Away: How We Found Love, Faith and Lasting Marriage in the Entertainment World*. The book came with a CD of love songs including "I Believe in You and Me" and "Because You Love Me." Not only a testament to lasting marriage, the book was a testament to a lasting career. It came out as McCoo was entering her fourth decade as an entertainer. Like her marriage, her career showed no signs of stopping.

Selected works

Albums

(With the 5th Dimension) *Up, Up, and Away,* Soul City, 1967.
(With the 5th Dimension) *Stoned Soul Picnic,* Soul City, 1967.
(With the 5th Dimension) *The Age of Aquarius,* Soul City, 1969.
(With the 5th Dimension) *Portrait,* Bell, 1970.
(With the 5th Dimension) *Love's Lines, Angles, and Rhymes,* Bell, 1971.
(With the 5th Dimension) *Individually and Collectively,* Bell, 1972.
(With the 5th Dimension) *Greatest Hits on Earth,* Arista, 1972.
(With Billy Davis Jr.), *I Hope We Get to Love in Time,* ABC Records, 1976.
(With Billy Davis Jr.), *The Two of Us,* ABC Records, 1977.
(With Billy Davis Jr.), *Marilyn and Billy,* Columbia, 1978.
Solid Gold, RCA, 1984.
The Me Nobody Knows, Warner Brothers, 1991.
(With Billy Davis Jr.), *Spirituals: Songs of the Soul,* Discovery House Music, 2004.

Books

With Billy Davis Jr. and Mike Yorkey, *Up, Up and Away: How We Found Love, Faith and Lasting Marriage in the Entertainment World*, Northfield Press, 2004.

Plays

Showboat, Broadway, 1996.

Television

The Marilyn McCoo and Billy Davis Jr. Show, CBS, 1977.
Solid Gold, 1980s.

Sources

Periodicals

Jet, August 15, 1994; October 16, 1995; August 9, 1999; October 18, 2004.
St Louis Post-Dispatch, August 14, 1996; November 11, 1999.

On-line

Marilyn McCoo and Billy Davis, Jr., www.mccoo-davis.com/marilyn.htm (June 10, 2005).
The Original 5th Dimension, http://members.aol.com/laruemccoo/ (August 16, 2005).

Other

"Marilyn McCoo and Billy Davis Jr. Discuss the Music Business and Their Book," interview on *The Tavis Smiley Show*, National Public Radio, March 1, 2004.

—Candace LaBalle

Terry McMillan

1951—

Novelist, educator

"Terry McMillan has the power to be an important contemporary novelist," stated Valerie Sayers reviewing *Disappearing Acts* in the *New York Times Book Review* in 1989. "Watch Terry McMillan. She's going to be a major writer," predicted a short but positive review of the same novel in *Cosmopolitan*. McMillan had already garnered attention and critical praise for her first novel, *Mama*, which was published in 1987, but it wasn't until 1992 that these predictions came true with the publication of *Waiting to Exhale*, McMillan's third novel. The book became a runaway hit with an appeal that crossed racial lines, and the movie that followed, starring Whitney Houston and Angela Bassett, was just as much of a blockbuster.

"Seriously, I just don't get it; I really don't," the unpretentious author mused during an interview with Audrey Edwards for *Essence*. But McMillan's honest, unaffected writings have clearly struck a chord with the book-buying public, particularly with her enthusiastic African American audience. Paperback rights for *Waiting to Exhale* fetched a hefty $2.64 million, making the deal with Pocket Books the second largest of its kind in publishing history, and future McMillan titles could earn the author as much as six million dollars. With her fourth novel, *How Stella Got Her Groove Back*, described as a "chatty, dishy, you-go!-girl tale" by an *Entertainment Weekly* reviewer and the movie rights already sold, McMillan has found success at the top of the *New York Times* bestseller list.

Enjoyed Reading from an Early Age

McMillan was born on October 18, 1951, and grew up in Port Huron, Michigan, a city approximately 60 miles northeast of Detroit. Her working-class parents did not make a point of reading to their five children, but McMillan discovered the pleasure of reading as a teenager, shelving books in a local library. Prior to working in the library, she had no exposure to books by black writers. McMillan recalled feeling embarrassed when she saw a book by James Baldwin with his picture on the cover. In a *Washington Post* article, she was quoted as saying, "I...did not read his book because I was too afraid. I couldn't imagine that he'd have anything better or different to say than [German essayist and novelist] Thomas Mann, [American nature writer] Henry Thoreau, [American essayist and poet] Ralph Waldo Emerson.... Needless to say, I was not just naive, but had not yet acquired an ounce of black pride."

Later, as a student at Los Angeles City College, McMillan immersed herself in the classics of African American literature. After reading Alex Haley's *Autobiography of Malcom X*, McMillan realized that she had no reason to be ashamed of a people who had such a proud history. At age 25, she published her first short story. Eleven years after that, her first novel, *Mama*, was released by Houghton Mifflin.

Knew the Power of Publicity

McMillan was determined not to let her debut novel go unnoticed. Typically, first novels receive little publicity other than the press releases and galleys sent out by the publisher. When McMillan's publisher told her that they

At a Glance . . .

Born on October 18, 1951; raised in Port Huron, MI; married Jonathan Plummer, 1998 (divorced 2005); children: Solomon (with Leonard Welch). *Education*: University of California, Berkeley, BA, journalism, 1979; Columbia University, MFA, 1979.

Career: Writer. Worked as a word processor; participated in Harlem Writers Guild literary workshop; attended MacDowell and Yaddo artists colonies, 1983; University of Wyoming, Laramie, instructor, 1987-90; University of Arizona, Tucson, professor, 1990-92.

Memberships: Artists for a Free South Africa.

Awards: American Book Award; *Essence* Award for Excellence in Literature.

Addresses: *Publisher*—c/o Viking Publicity, 375 Hudson Street, New York, NY 10014.

could not do more for her, McMillan decided to promote the book on her own. She wrote over 3,000 letters to chain bookstores, independent booksellers, universities, and colleges. Although what she was doing seemed logical in her own mind, the recipients of her letters were not used to such efforts by an author. They found her approach hard to resist, so by the end of the summer of 1987 she had several offers for readings. McMillan then scheduled her own book publicity tour and let her publicist know where she was going instead of it being the other way around.

By the time *Waiting to Exhale* was published, it was the other way around. The scene at a reading from the novel was described in the *Los Angeles Times* this way: "Several hundred fans, mostly black and female, are shoehorned into Marcus Bookstore on a recent Saturday night. Several hundred more form a line down the block and around the corner. The reading...hasn't begun because McMillan is greeting those who couldn't squeeze inside.... Finally, the writer...steps through the throng."

Started with a Short Story

McMillan had come a long way since the publication of her first novel, which started out as a short story. "I really love the short story as a form," stated McMillan in an interview with *Writer's Digest*. "Mama" was just one of several short stories that McMillan had tried with limited success to get into print. Then the Harlem Writer's Guild accepted her into their group and told her that "Mama" really should be a novel and not a short story. After four weeks at the MacDowell artists colony and two weeks at the Yaddo colony, McMillan had expanded her short story into over 400 pages.

McMillan sent her collection of short stories to Houghton Mifflin, hoping that she would at least get some free editorial advice. McMillan was surprised, however, when the publisher contacted her about the novel she had mentioned briefly in her letter to them. She sent them pages from *Mama* and approximately four days later got word from Houghton Mifflin that they loved it.

Mama tells the story of the struggle Mildred Peacock has raising her five children after she throws her drunkard husband out of the house. The novel begins: "Mildred hid the ax beneath the mattress of the cot in the dining room." With those words, McMillan's novel becomes "a runaway narrative pulling a crowded cast of funny, earthy characters," stated Sayers in the *New York Times Book Review*. Because of McMillan's promotional efforts, the novel received numerous reviews–the overwhelming majority of which were positive–and McMillan gave 39 readings. Six weeks after *Mama* was published, it went into its third printing.

Exposed the Difficulties of Romance for Professional Women

Disappearing Acts, her second novel, proved to be quite different than *Mama*. For *Disappearing Acts*, McMillan chose to tell the story of star-crossed lovers by alternating the narrative voice between the main characters. Zora Banks and Franklin Swift fall in love "at first sight" when they meet at Zora's new apartment, where Franklin works as part of the renovating crew. Zora is an educated black woman working as a junior high school music teacher; Franklin is a high-school dropout working in construction. In spite of the differences in their backgrounds, the two become involved, move in together, and try to overcome the fear they both feel because of past failures in love.

Writing in the *Washington Post Book World*, David Nicholson pointed out that although this difference in backgrounds is an old literary device, it is one that is particularly relevant to African Americans: "Professional black women complain of an ever-shrinking pool of eligible men, citing statistics that show the number of black men in prison is increasing, while the number of black men in college is decreasing. Articles on alternatives for women, from celibacy to 'man-sharing' to relationships with blue-collar workers like Franklin have long been a staple of black general interest and women's magazines."

McMillan expressed her thoughts on this issue in an article she wrote entitled "Looking for Mr. Right" for the February 1990 issue of *Essence*. "Maybe it's just me, but I'm finding it harder and harder to meet men....

I grew up and became what my mama prayed out loud I'd become: educated, strong, smart, independent and reliable.... Now it seems as if carving a place for myself in the world is backfiring. Never in a million years would I have dreamed that I'd be 38-years-old and still single."

Throughout the rest of the article, McMillan discusses how she had planned to be married by age 24 but found herself attending graduate school instead. She ended up loving and living with men who did not, as she puts it, "take life as seriously as I did." When she was 32- years-old, she gave birth to her son, Solomon. Shortly after that she ended a three-year relationship with her son's father. Since then McMillan had been involved in what she called "two powerful but short-lived relationships," both of which ended when, without any explanation, the man stopped calling.

McMillan believes that "even though a lot of 'professional' men claim to want a smart, independent woman, they're kidding themselves." She thinks that these men do not feel secure unless they are with passive women or with women who will "back down, back off or just acquiesce" until they appear to be tamed. "I'm not tamable," declared McMillan in *Essence*. In response to a former boyfriend who told her that it is lonely at the top, McMillan replied, "It is lonely 'out here.' But I wouldn't for a minute give up all that I've earned just to have a man. I just wish it were easier to meet men and get to know them."

Reviewers commended McMillan on her ability to give such a true voice to the character of Franklin in *Disappearing Acts*. One reviewer for the *Washington Post Book World* called the novel "one of the few...to contain rounded, sympathetic portraits of black men and to depict relationships between black men and black women as something more than the relationship between victimizer and victim, oppressor and oppressed." In the *New York Times Book Review*, another reviewer stated: "The miracle is that Ms. McMillan takes the reader so deep into this man's head–and makes what goes on there so complicated–that [the] story becomes not only comprehensible but affecting." Not only did McMillan's second novel win critical acclaim, it also was optioned for a film; McMillan eventually wrote the screenplay for Metro-Goldwyn-Mayer.

Book Brought McMillan's Life into Limelight

Leonard Welch, McMillan's former lover and the father of their son, also found that portions of *Disappearing Acts* rung true–so true, in fact, that in August of 1990 he filed a $4.75 million defamation suit against McMillan. Welch claimed that McMillan used him as the model for the novel's main male character, and therefore the book defamed him. The suit also named Penguin USA (parent company of Viking, the publisher of the book) and Simon & Schuster (publisher of the book in paperback) as defendants.

The suit alleged that McMillan had acted maliciously in writing the novel and that she had written it mainly out of vindictiveness and a desire for revenge. In addition to believing that the novel realistically portrayed his three-year relationship with McMillan, Welch claimed that he suffered emotional stress. McMillan had dedicated the book to their son, and Welch feared that Solomon would believe the defamatory parts of the novel represented reality when he was old enough to read it.

Martin Garbus, the lawyer for Penguin USA, maintained that if McMillan had been an obscure writer who wrote an obscure book, there would not have been a lawsuit at all. One of McMillan's writing peers was quoted in the *Los Angeles Times* as saying, "I think it's just part of the general nastiness of the time, that people see someone doing well and they want part of it." The suit raised the issue of the delicate balance fiction writers must maintain. Many novelists draw on their experiences when writing, and most feel that they have an obligation to protect the privacy of an individual. In the *Los Angeles Times*, Garbus explained: "What Terry McMillan has done is no different than what other writers have done. It has to be permissible to draw on your real-life experiences. Otherwise, you can't write fiction." Most people involved in the suit, including Welch's lawyer, agreed that a victory for Welch could set an unfortunate precedent that would inhibit the creativity of fiction writers.

In April of 1991, the New York Supreme Court ruled in McMillan's favor. As reported in the *Wall Street Journal*, the judge in the case wrote that although "the fictional character and the real man share the same occupation and educational background and even like the same breakfast cereal...the man in the novel is a lazy, emotionally disturbed alcoholic who uses drugs and sometimes beats his girlfriend." The judge declared that "Leonard Welch is none of these things."

Edited an Anthology

In 1990 Viking published *Breaking Ice: An Anthology of Contemporary African- American Fiction*. Edited by McMillan, the anthology came into being as a result of the anger she experienced after reading a collection of short stories that did not include any black or Third World writers. Her research and book proposal were the first steps in correcting what McMillan felt was the publishing industry's neglect of black writers. She received almost 300 submissions for the anthology and chose 57 seasoned, emerging, and unpublished writers.

In reviewing *Breaking Ice* for the *Washington Post Book World*, author Joyce Carol Oates characterized the book as "a wonderfully generous and diverse collection of prose fiction by our most gifted African-

American writers." Oates credited McMillan's judgment for selecting such "high quality of writing...that one could hardly distinguish between the categories [of writers] in terms of originality, depth of vision and command of the language."

Found Great Success with Waiting to Exhale

McMillan's third novel, *Waiting to Exhale*, tells the stories of four professional black women who have everything except for the love of a good man. The overall theme of the book is men's fear of commitment; a sub-theme is the fear of growing old alone. The novel hit a nerve with its readers–both male and female. According to the *Los Angeles Times*, one black male from an audience of over 2,000 proclaimed: "I think I speak for a lot of brothers. I know I'm all over the book.... All I can say is, I'm willing to learn. Being defensive is not the answer." Women responded just as enthusiastically; one fan spoke for many in a *Newsweek* article when she said, "Terry talks about problems, but with humor and fun. I laugh through the tears. That's what I need." McMillan affirmed her own desire to portray the struggles of women in a positive, yet realistic, light, saying in the same article: "I don't write about victims. They just bore me to death. I prefer to write about somebody who can pick themselves back up and get on with their lives. Because all of us are victims to some extent." The movie that followed the success of the novel brought McMillan's voice to an ever-widening audience, grossing $66 million.

One issue that emerged from many reviews of McMillan's earlier books is the amount of profanity she uses. *Waiting to Exhale* met with the same criticism. One critic characterized her characters as male-bashing stand-up comedians who use foul language. For McMillan, reproducing her characters' profane language is her way of staying close to them. She believes that the language she uses is accurate. She told *Publishers Weekly*: "That's the way we talk. And I want to know why I've never read a review where they complain about the language that male writers use!"

Fourth Novel Returns McMillan's Personal Life to the Headlines

McMillan continued to employ the narrative style that made her such a popular author, to great success, in her fourth novel, *How Stella Got Her Groove Back*. The sensual, heavily autobiographical story chronicles a love affair between a successful African American woman and a Jamaican cook 20 years her junior. Needing to take some time off, McMillan stopped work on her novel *A Day Late and a Dollar Short,* which she had started in 1993, and traveled to Jamaica. There she grieved for the recent deaths of loved ones and unexpectedly found love. Her romance with and eventual marriage to Jonathan Plummer was widely publicized. "Stella is as close to autobiography as I've written in a long time," McMillan conceded to *Ebony*. "When she realizes that she is a breath away from the 21st century, alone, and unhappy, her heart skips a beat. She recovers. Acts. Adjusts. I felt my mom on that beach in Negril, Jamaica. She was telling me, 'I know you miss me, but you've got a life to live.'" Published in 1995, the novel had a first printing of 800,000 copies in hardcover—an unheard of number for an African American novelist—and the movie rights were quickly sold. While some reviewers have complained about McMillan's dependence on a stream-of-consciousness narrative technique, her use of language continues to appeal to her audience who find their voices in her own.

For her portrayal of feisty, tough, black heroines, McMillan has been compared to acclaimed black women writers Alice Walker, Gloria Naylor, and Zora Neale Hurston. McMillan acknowledges the compliment but asserts in the introduction to *Breaking Ice* that her generation of black writers is "a new breed, free to write as we please...because of the way life has changed." Life has changed for her generation but it has also stayed the same for many women in one fundamental way: the search for happiness and fulfillment continues. In an article in the *Los Angeles Times*, McMillan maintained: "A house and a car and all the money in the bank won't make you happy. People need people. People crave intimacy."

McMillan resumed work on *A Day Late and a Dollar Short* and published it in 2001. In the book, McMillan explored new issues. As she told *Essence*: "First, I wanted to write about a woman whose whole life revolved around her children. But I wanted her to have her own issues, though to some extent she was avoiding them. Viola [the protagonist] has very high expectations of her children; she only wants the best for them. Then I wanted to write about a husband [Cecil] who is estranged from the family, but who is basically a decent guy. And I also wanted to write about a family where everybody keeps secrets." McMillan's story hit home with readers who kept it on the *New York Times* best-seller list for 12 weeks.

McMillan released *The Interruption of Everything* in 2005. The novel delves into the issues of mid-life for women who have spent much of their lives focused on their children and their husband. McMillan tried to highlight the differences between female and male perspectives on family and marriage. Calling the book "fresh" and "funny," *People* reviewer Natalie Danford said, "Breathe easy, fans: It's been four years since her last book, but McMillan's still got her groove."

The publication of this novel coincided with the much publicized break up of McMillan's marriage. Unlike her protagonist, McMillan fully understood her own power over her life. She told *People:* "I never thought my happiness was contingent on having a man. A man should enrich it. But when that ceases to be the case, he's gotta go." She remained committed to living her life happily, and continuing to write. Her work remained at the forefront of the publishing craze for stories about middle-class black women that she "discovered" in the 1980s.

Selected writings

Books

Mama, Houghton Mifflin, 1987.
Disappearing Acts, Viking, 1989.
(Editor) *Breaking Ice: An Anthology of Contemporary African-American Fiction*, Viking, 1990.
Waiting to Exhale, Viking, 1992.
How Stella Got Her Groove Back, Viking, 1995.
A Day Late and a Dollar Short, Viking, 2001.
The Interruption of Everything, Viking, 2005.

Sources

Books

McMillan, Terry, *Mama*, Houghton Mifflin, 1987.
McMillan, Terry, *Disappearing Acts*, Viking, 1989.
McMillan Terry, editor, *Breaking Ice: An Anthology of Contemporary African-American Fiction*, Viking, 1990.
McMillan, Terry, *Waiting to Exhale*, Viking, 1992.

Periodicals

Black Issues Book Review, January-February 2002.
Cosmopolitan, August 1989.
Detroit News, September 7, 1992.
Ebony, May 1993, p. 23; December 1996, p. 116; July 2005, p. 32.
Emerge, September 1992.
Essence, February 1990; October 1992; January 2001; July 2005.
Los Angeles Times, October 29, 1990; June 19, 1992.
Newsweek, April 29, 1996, pp. 76-79.
New York Times Book Review, August 6, 1989; May 31, 1992.
New York Times Magazine, August 9, 1992.
People, July 20, 1992; July 11, 2005; July 25, 2005.
Publishers Weekly, May 11, 1992; July 13, 1992; September 21, 1992.
Wall Street Journal, April 11, 1991.
Washington Post, November 17, 1990.
Washington Post Book World, August 27, 1989; September 16, 1990.
Writer's Digest, October 1987.

—Debra G. Darnell and Sara Pendergast

Warren F. Miller, Jr.

1943—

Nuclear engineer, educator, and consultant

Growing up when the United States was still a racially segregated society, Warren F. Miller, Jr., learned a lot about the difficulties encountered when a member of a minority breaks barriers by entering a field traditionally dominated by whites. He broke many of those barriers himself, first by becoming one of a very small number of African Americans to graduate from the U.S. Military Academy at West Point during the early 1960s, then by going on to become one of the nation's most respected engineers in the complex field of nuclear engineering. However, Miller was concerned with more than the personal success and public recognition that he received for his accomplishments. Throughout his career he has promoted workplace diversity and encouraged young African Americans and women to seek careers in engineering, science and technology.

Grew Up in Chicago

Warren Fletcher Miller, Jr., was born in Chicago, Illinois, on March 17, 1943, one of five children of Warren F. Miller, Sr., and Helen Robinson Miller. His father worked as a milkman, delivering dairy products to homes in the Chicago area, and his mother worked as a secretary at the University of Chicago. His parents did not want to call their son "Junior," so, in order to distinguish him from his father, they gave him the nickname of a family friend, Peto. Warren Jr. would remain "Pete" to those who knew him for the rest of his life.

Growing up during the 1940s and 1950s, Miller attended an all black inner city school. He enjoyed his classes, especially science and math, and was such a good student that he was promoted directly from third to fifth grade, skipping fourth grade. In 1955, during the summer after fifth grade, Miller got a shocking and painful lesson in racism when one of his classmates, a 14-year-old boy named Emmett Till, was murdered by racist whites while visiting his mother's relatives in Mississippi. Till's murder—and the fact that the white men who killed him were never punished—energized the civil rights movement.

Miller excelled throughout his school years, inspired by the many excellent black teachers who taught at his segregated school. He especially valued his high school physics teacher in whose class he began to develop his love of advanced science. Along with his studies, he worked summers and every Saturday during the school year, helping his father deliver milk. He also enjoyed baseball and played on his high school baseball team.

Motivated by Military Opportunities

Boys entering Miller's Chicago high school were given the choice of physical education classes or participating in the Reserve Officers Training Corps (ROTC). ROTC is a military training program sponsored by many colleges and high schools. Because Miller had skipped a grade, he was younger and smaller than many of his classmates, and did not enjoy physical education classes. Choosing ROTC altered the course of his life.

He excelled in his ROTC training, becoming commander of his unit. The army sergeants who staffed the

At a Glance . . .

Born Warren Fletcher Miller, Jr., on March 17, 1943 in Chicago, Illinois; married Judith Hunter, February 21, 1969; children: David, Jonathan. *Education:* United States Military Academy at West Point, BS, engineering, 1964; Northwestern University, MS, engineering, 1970, PhD, engineering, 1972. *Military Service:* US Army, Captain, 1964-69.

Career: Northwestern University, Nuclear Engineering, assistant professor, 1972-74; Los Alamos National Laboratory, staff member, 1974-76, group leader, 1976-79, associate director, 1979-86, deputy director, 1986-90; University of California-Berkeley, Berkeley, CA, Pardee professor, 1990-92; Los Alamos National Laboratory, Research and Education, associate director, 1992-93, Science & Technology Base Programs, director, 1992-2001; private consultant, 2001–.

Memberships: National Academy of Engineering; National Research Council; American Nuclear Society Fellow.

Awards: US Army, Bronze Star, 1968; US Army, Commendation Medal, 1969; New Mexico Eminent Scholar, 1988; Northwestern University, Merit Award, 1993; National Society of Black Engineers, Golden Torch Award for Distinguished Engineer, 2004.

program began to advise Miller that he should attend college at the United States Military Academy in the New York town of West Point. Admission is free for those who are accepted at West Point, and students receive a percentage of an officer's pay while they study there. In return, graduates are required to serve in the U.S. Army for five years.

Miller earned admission to West Point, but his years there were difficult. During the early 1960s, as civil rights workers fought against discrimination, overt racism was still present in many institutions. There was only one other black cadet in Miller's class of 800, and the entire college of 2,500 students included only eleven African Americans. Racial prejudice was widespread and blatant, creating a hostile atmosphere for the small number of black students.

During the 1960s, all West Point cadets received bachelor's degrees in engineering upon graduation. Though they could not choose any other major, they could choose between civil engineering and nuclear engineering. Miller quickly scanned the texts for each, decided that nuclear engineering seemed the more interesting, and chose that as his field of study.

After his graduation from West Point in 1964, Miller underwent further army training at Airborne school and Army Ranger school. He then went to California to start his first assignment at an air defense artillery unit. Still interested in math and science, Miller sought the opportunity to work with computers, still a fairly new technology during the mid-1960s. One way the army used computers was to keep track of the vast amounts of supplies sent to troops all over the world, so Miller went to supply school to learn about computers.

It was as the commander of a supply unit that Captain Warren Miller saw combat. He served for 13 months in Southeast Asia during the U.S. conflict in Vietnam. By the late 1960s, the civil rights movement had effected some changes in attitudes and policies, and Miller's army career was not marked by the prejudice and racism of his college years. However, he was not really happy in the army. The large, complex organizational structure of the military often frustrated him, seeming too bogged down in forms and procedures to accomplish tasks efficiently. After his tour of duty in Vietnam was over, he gave the U.S. Army a year's notice and resigned his commission.

Deepened His Interest in Computers

In September 1969, three months after leaving the army, Miller entered Northwestern University, near his hometown of Chicago, to continue his education. In three years he earned both his master's and doctoral degrees in nuclear engineering. He took a job at Northwestern and enjoyed both teaching and academic research. However, his intellectual curiosity and fascination with evolving computer technology would continue to impel him toward another career change.

Miller's work in nuclear engineering had involved using computer models to develop and test theories of nuclear technology. When Los Alamos National Laboratory offered him a job that included a chance to work with a new supercomputer, he left Northwestern and moved to New Mexico.

Established in 1943, Los Alamos National Laboratory (LANL) is a United States Department of Energy research facility which is managed by the University of California. LANL was established during World War II to research and develop an atomic weapon for the war. The laboratory employs physicists, engineers, chemists, and other scientists and mathematicians to participate in a variety of scientific research projects, along with its continued work on nuclear weaponry.

Miller remained at LANL for 27 years. During his career he held many different positions, rising from his entry-level job to associate lab director for math and physics, associate lab director for energy research, and senior research advisor. In these management positions, he learned many organizational skills in addition to his expertise as an engineer and research scientist. As associate lab director he was responsible for overseeing the work over 2000 scientists. As senior research advisor, his job included deciding which research projects the lab should undertake, recruiting the best scientists to work on those projects, and finding the best laboratory facilities for them to use. Another part of his job was speaking with Congress to gain government funding for research projects.

Several times during his career at LANL, Miller took time off from his work to return to teaching. He is also the author of many research papers and journal articles about his work, including, with a colleague, the book *Computational Methods of Neutron Transport,* published in 1984, which became a standard textbook for engineering students around the world.

Activism Brought Rewards

One of the most personally satisfying moments in Miller's career came during the 1990s when he became one of the scientists honored by President Bill Clinton for his efforts to establish a program to research the human genome. "Human genome" is the term used to describe all of the genetic material required to produce a human being. Though as a nuclear engineer he had not actually worked in the field of genetic biology, Miller had long been interested in promoting the study of the genome and in 1990 had helped initiate a workshop in Santa Fe, New Mexico, to consider the use of laser, robotic, and computer technologies to determine the correct order, or sequence, of the approximately 30,000 human genes in the genome. He then testified before Congress to persuade them to grant the funds needed for the work on the genome.

Another important part of Miller's career has been his work on increasing workplace diversity. Having been one of very few blacks both during his college years and on the job, he has devoted much time and energy increasing the number of African Americans and other minorities in science and engineering. At Los Alamos, he worked for a time as diversity director, encouraging the laboratory to recruit more minority scientists, and acting as mentor to other employees of color and women, who are also often a minority in scientific fields. He has also frequently spoken out publicly about the need for more racial equality in the workplace, such as his keynote speech at the 2000 annual meeting of the American Chemical Society, titled, "Affirmative Action, Mend It, End It, Or What?" During Miller's tenure at LANL, the number of African American employees there almost tripled.

Miller retired from his job at LANL in 2001. He has continued to work as a private consultant, both for the laboratory at Los Alamos and for other national laboratories, helping them plan their research programs. He has also continued to encourage young people to study science and engineering. Though he remains an honored and respected member of the scientific community, Miller considers his greatest achievement to be the successful lives of his two sons, David and Jonathan.

Selected writings

(With E.E. Lewis) *Computational Methods of Neutron Transport*, 1984.

Sources

Periodicals

LANL Newsletter, March 1, 2004, p. 6.
Profiles in Diversity Journal, January/February 2003, p. 67.

On-line

"Browne Selects Deputy for Science, Technology And Programs," *Los Alamos National Laboratory*, www anl.gov/news/index.php?fuseaction=home.story&story_id=1800 (April 22, 2005).
"Distinguished Engineer of the Year: Warren F. "Pete" Miller, Jr." *National Society of Black Engineers*, www.nsbe.org/publicrelations/winner_bios.php (April 22, 2005).
"Warren F. Miller, Jr." *Biography Resource Center*. http://galenet.galegroup.com/servlet/BioRC (April 22, 2005).

Other

Information for this profile was obtained through an interview with Warren F. Miller, Jr., on April 30, 2005.

—Tina Gianoulis

Youssou N'Dour

1959—

Singer, composer, drummer

Youssou N'Dour is an international star in the field of popular music that has come to be known as "Afro-pop" or "world beat." He is a singer, composer, and drummer whose style has been given the name "mbalax." N'Dour's own particular brand of mbalax has become so popular and widespread that he is often credited with inventing the genre, although Ronnie Graham stated in his authoritative book on contemporary African music that mbalax is a generic Senegalese music characterized by a percussion base and featuring an improvised solo on the sabar drum. Mbalax has also been described as modern Senegalese rock.

Graham described Senegalese pop music of the late 1980s as "a sophisticated blend of the old and the new," with the old being primarily Cuban-influenced melodies and rhythms that dominated Senegalese music prior to the 1970s. The development of local styles was seriously hindered by the French philosophy of exporting their own culture; and local idioms, instruments, and traditions did not begin to appear in urban contemporary music until the 1970s, after Senegal had achieved independence. The tama, a small talking drum, was introduced in the 1970s and became a popular lead instrument.

N'Dour calls his music "African storytelling on the wings of 21st-century instrumentation," according to *Vanity Fair.* N'Dour's own mbalax features a rhythmic dance band consisting of as many as 14 members, including multiple percussionists, guitarists, saxophonists, and backing vocalists. As N'Dour achieved greater recognition and acceptance among Western audiences in Europe and the United States during the late 1980s, he began to use more traditional African and Arabic sounds in his music. Although he is fluent in French, Arabic, and his native Wolof, his English is not very good. Thus, he is at his best when able to present an appealing and authentic brand of African pop, with its own unique rhythms and vocalizations sung in Wolof, one of Senegal's major native languages.

Inspired by His Roots

N'Dour was born on October 1, 1959, in Dakar, the capital of Senegal, on the west coast of Africa. Historically, Senegal is a part of French or francophone Africa. Musically, external influences within Senegal and other parts of francophone Africa were more restricted than in anglophone or British Africa. N'Dour grew up in a traditional African community within the Medina section of the city, a place has continued to offer great inspiration for his music. He related to *Interview* that Dakar was to him "a living poem, a place of unbridled energy, remarkable ambition and legendary artistic flair. I know of no other city on earth where people do so much with so little."

The story of N'Dour's upbringing is that his father was a mechanic who discouraged him from a musical career. His mother, however, was a griot in the community. A griot is a historian and storyteller within the community. N'Dour's mother was a respected elder who kept the oral tradition of the community's history alive through traditional songs and moral teachings.

With his mother's encouragement, N'Dour would sing at kassak, a party to celebrate circumcision. As N'Dour

At a Glance . . .

Born on October 1, 1959, in Dakar, Senegal; father was a mechanic; mother was a griot (a community historian and storyteller).

Career: Singer at ceremonial parties throughout childhood; Star Band, recording/performing group, member, 1970s-?; Etoile de Dakar (Star of Dakar), member, c. 1979-84(?); Super Etoile de Dakar (Superstar of Dakar), member, c. 1984; Joko, Senegalese internet training company, founder, 2001.

Memberships: Ambassador to the United Nations, Ambassador to UNICEF, Ambassador to the International Bureau of Work.

Awards: Best African Artist, 1996; *fRoots,* Best African Artist of the Century, 2000; Critics Award, BBC Radio 3, 2005; Grammy Award, for Best Contemporary World Music Album, 2005, for *Egypt.*

Addresses: *Office*—Youssou N'Dour Head Office, Route des Almadies Parcelle, No. 8 BP 1310, Dakar, Senegal; *Web*—www.youssou.com.

described his work then, "Sometimes on one street there would be four or five kassaks going on at the same time. They would start in the evening and I would go to one and sing two numbers, then on to the next.... Sometimes I used to sing at 10 kassaks a night. Gradually, my friends and others encouraged me and gave me confidence, because they liked my singing."

Made It Big with the Super Etoile

By the age of 14, N'Dour was performing in front of large audiences and had earned the nickname, "Le Petit Prince de Dakar," or "The Little Prince of Dakar." As a teenager he joined the Star Band, the best known Senegalese pop band of the time, recording with them and performing in clubs in Dakar. By the time he was 20, he had left the Star Band to form his own group, Etoile de Dakar (Star of Dakar). They recorded three albums in Dakar and had a hit with their first single, "Xalis (Money)." Then they relocated to Paris and reformed as the Super Etoile de Dakar (Superstar of Dakar).

Living in Paris and the European milieu provided N'Dour with a range of new musical influences to contend with. He says, "When I started to play music, I was playing traditional music. But when I came to Europe to listen to the sounds around me, by 1984 I had a new attitude. I'm a new person now [1990], opening fast. I like to change. I'm African, yes, but I like to play music for everybody. But my identity is African. That will never change."

From his base in Paris, N'Dour and the Super Etoile began to win over Western audiences to the sound of mbalax. The Super Etoile consisted of 14 members, probably the largest aggregation N'Dour would ever perform with. The group used traditional Wolof and African rhythms behind N'Dour's unique tenor. N'Dour sang and continues to sing in Wolof, his vocal style often compared to Islamic chanting reminiscent of mosques and temples.

Gained International Attention

By the mid-1980s, the group was ready for a major international breakthrough. They had toured the United States, Great Britain, and Holland, in addition to playing at N'Dour's nightclub in Dakar, the Thiosanne. Remembering his audiences in Dakar and his friends from the Medina, N'Dour made it a point to return there. A song he wrote, "Medina," celebrates his old neighborhood and his old friends, who "are still my friends today and are the people I have around me." As his career progressed, N'Dour remained in touch with his roots and made his home base in Dakar. He told *Time* in 2001 that living in Dakar "gives me a certain inspiration; it allows me to keep my passion for music alive."

N'Dour and Super Etoile released an album in 1985 that became a classic in the Afro-pop field, *Immigres*. It was released in the United States three years later. N'Dour increased his exposure to Western audiences in 1986 by appearing as a drummer on Paul Simon's *Graceland* album. He recorded the *Nelson Mandela* album in Paris that year and toured the United States twice with Super Etoile, once on their own and once opening for Peter Gabriel. N'Dour sang backing vocals on Gabriel's *So* album, and it is Gabriel who is the Western musician most responsible for bringing Youssou N'Dour to America and other Western nations.

N'Dour continued to tour with Peter Gabriel in 1988, reducing the size of his band to six pieces and a dancer. In the summer of that year, N'Dour played New York's first International Festival of the Arts at the Beacon Theatre. The influence of American pop on N'Dour was revealed in his playing half a set's worth of American pop and soul, with Nona Hendryx joining him for a song in English and Wolof. *New York Times* writer, Jon Parelis, wrote of N'Dour, "What makes Mr. N'Dour an international sensation, along with the dance rhythms of mbalax, is his unforgettable voice, a pure, pealing tenor that melds pop sincerity with the nuances of Islamic singing." Noting that mbalax has always combined international influences with Senegalese traditions, Parelis expressed his concern that

American pop was diluting the effect of N'Dour's singing and the band's rhythms. N'Dour would later echo this concern in *Rolling Stone*, when he said, "It's a very difficult balance to keep the roots and bring in a bit of the Western world."

Leveraged His Fame for the Needy

In the Fall of 1988, N'Dour gained even greater international exposure as part of Amnesty International's "Human Rights Now!" world tour. At London's Wembley Stadium, N'Dour joined Bruce Springsteen, Sting, Peter Gabriel, and Tracy Chapman to sing Bob Marley's classic reggae song, "Get Up, Stand Up." It was the start of a 44-day tour of five continents, including such Third World and Eastern bloc nations as Hungary, India, Zimbabwe, Argentina, and Brazil. Only two U.S. dates were included, Los Angeles and Philadelphia.

Over the years, N'Dour has tried to leverage his celebrity to benefit others. To help his country, he bought a newspaper, a nightclub, a radio station, and a recording studio in order to offer employment to his people. He has participated in several charity album recordings. He has campaigned for the debt relief of developing nations. He has served as Ambassador to the United Nations, Ambassador to UNICEF, and Ambassador to the International Bureau of Work. In 2001 he also started an internet training company called Joko in order to introduce a greater number of Senegalese to the World Wide Web. N'Dour's original songs also include political and social commentary.

Personal Messages Woven into His Music

N'Dour is also capable of writing and performing songs with a personal lyric content, songs about his old neighborhood and childhood pals, about the youth of his country, and about roaming the countryside with a friend. In 1989, Virgin Records released a new N'Dour album, *The Lion (Gaiende)*. It was recorded in Paris, England, and Dakar and was produced by George Acogny and David Sancious, who have combined backgrounds in jazz, pop, and rock. The Super Etoile, by now reduced to an eight-piece band, was joined by some Western musicians, including pop-jazz saxophonist David Sanborn. Peter Gabriel and N'Dour sing a duet on one of the album's tracks, "Shaking The Tree." N'Dour sings in Wolof on the album, but English translations of the lyrics are provided. In a review of the album, *New York Times* reviewer Jon Parelis again expressed his concern that too much Western influence was creeping into N'Dour's music, and he wrote, "Despite an undercurrent of Senegalese drums, the rippling vocal lines and dizzying polyrhythms that made Western listeners notice him are usually truncated."

By the Fall of 1989, Super Etoile was back to full strength with 12 pieces for N'Dour's club dates in the United States. The extra percussion and instrumentation helped restore the driving rhythm of N'Dour's music. Reviewing a performance at New York's the Ritz, Jon Parelis described the "two percussionists whose doubletime and tripletime rhythms restored mbalax's sense of swift, sprinting momentum." He noted that the intricate cross-rhythms combined well with a firm downbeat to provide a mix of Western and Senegalese styles. The show ended with a song about toxic wastes that would be released in 1990 as a single from N'Dour's Virgin album, *Set*.

N'Dour's songs on *Set* deal with personal emotions, social problems, and political issues. He says, "Most of the songs I heard in my youth were either love songs or traditional songs recounting the history of the people that I come from—praise songs, historical songs. The lyrics of my own works today I consider to be about the society in which I live, the world in which I live. I want my words to have an educational function."

Dubbed King of West African Music

The international success of *Set* set the stage for N'Dour to broaden his international fame. It inspired *Rolling Stone* contributor Brian Cullman to comment that "If any third-world performer has a real shot at the sort of universal popularity last enjoyed by Bob Marley, it's Youssou, a singer with a voice so extraordinary that the history of Africa seems locked inside it." Indeed, his star continued to rise. His 1994 album *The Guide* garnered two Grammy nominations. He wrote and performed, with Axelle Red, the anthem for the 1998 World Cup in France. By 2000, N'Dour was recognized as the "king of West African music," according to *Billboard*.

His greatest success came in 2004 when he released the album, *Egypt*. N'Dour deftly combined Senegalese percussion traditions with Arabic instrumental arrangements. The songs explore his Islamic faith. N'Dour has said that the songs were so personal that he did not intend to release the album, which he recorded with both Egyptian and Senegalese musicians in 1999. But world events soon changed his mind. "My religion needs to be better known for its positive side," he told *Billboard*. "Maybe this music can move us toward a greater understanding of the peaceful message of Islam." Reviewer Chris Nickson wrote in *Sing Out!* that *Egypt* is "one of those rare records that truly deserves to be called stunning, quite possibly the best thing N'Dour has ever achieved which is saying something indeed." His effort was honored with his first Grammy award in 2005.

Selected works

Albums

Nelson Mandela, Polydor, 1986.
Immigres, Virgin, 1988.

The Lion (Gaiende), Virgin, 1989.
Set, Virgin, 1990.
Eyes Open, Columbia, 1992.
The Guide (Wommat), Chaos/Columbia, 1994.
Lii, Jololi, 1996.
St. Louis, Jololi, 1997.
Rewmi, 1999.
Joko, Wea/Atlantic/Nonesuch, 2000.
Batay, Jololi, 2001.
Le Grand Bal, 1 and 2, Jololi, 2001.
Et Ses Amis, Universal International, 2002.
Nothing's in Vain, Warner/Nonesuch, 2002.
Egypt, Nonesuch, 2004.

Sources

Books

Graham, Ronnie, *The Da Capo Guide to Contemporary African Music*, Da Capo Press, 1988.

Periodicals

Billboard, June 10, 2000; April 17, 2004.
Detroit Free Press, October 5, 1990.
Detroit Metro Times, October 3-9, 1990.
Detroit News, October 5, 1990.
Down Beat, May 1987.
Interview, May 2001, p. 76.
New York Times, July 2, 1988; July 2, 1989; November 8, 1989.
Newsweek, September 12, 1988.
People, October 10, 1988.
Rolling Stone, July 13-27, 1989; November 15, 199D.
Sing Out!, Fall 2004, p. 110.
Time, September 15, 2001, p. 66.
Vainty Fair, November 2004.

On-line

"Youssou N'Dour," *Nonesuch,* www.nonesuch.com/Hi_Band/index_frameset2.cfm?pointer=ndour.gif (August 12, 2005).
Youssou N'Dour, www.youssou.com (August 12, 2005).

—David Bianco and Sara Pendergast

Arthel Neville

1962—

Television broadcaster

Though her last name is revered in musical circles, Arthel Neville was on her own when she decided to pursue a career in television. "Believe me, the name Neville didn't do anything for me in the field of journalism," she told *New Orleans Magazine*. Nonetheless, Neville has gone from a station intern for a local Texas channel to a nationally famous broadcaster with a proven track record in both hard news and celebrity reporting. She is now not only a reporter, but a celebrity in her own right.

Juggled TV Career with College

Arthel Neville was born on October 20, 1962, into a home thumping with New Orleans funk. Daughter of keyboardist Art Neville, one of the founding members of the Grammy Award-winning Neville Brothers, young Neville grew up surrounded by music. Uncle Aaron, internationally famous for his warbling falsetto, performed at Neville's high school. Local and world-famous musicians paid regular visits to the Neville home. In an *Essence* interview Neville recalled "a rainbow of races" at her childhood birthday parties. Unfortunately, the multiculturalism in her living room did not protect her from the harsh realities of race lingering just outside the front door. "I was maybe the fourth Black student to attend my private Catholic school, so I'm not naive about racial differences," she told *Essence*.

Neville did not veer towards her family's musical legacy, however. "I'm not without musical talent, it's just I was always into writing," she told *New Orleans Magazine*. Her mother Doris wholly supported that choice. "[She] was the only role model I needed. She taught me that I can do anything I put my mind to," Neville told the Web site *Divabetic*. After graduating from St. Mary's Dominican High School in 1980, Neville traveled to New York to pursue acting and modeling. She landed a few commercials and even a recurring role on the soap opera *Days of Our Lives* before returning to New Orleans. She enrolled in a pre-pharmacy program at Xavier University before switching to journalism at Southern Methodist University. She finally landed at the University of Texas in Austin, where she earned a bachelor's in journalism in 1986.

Even before graduating, Neville began blazing her broadcasting career. As a junior she landed a job as a general assignment reporter for Austin's KVUE-TV, becoming the station's first African-American on-air reporter. After a morning full of classes, Neville spent her afternoons rushing all over Austin to cover everything from breaking news to human interest stories for the evening news broadcast. "It was extremely tough. I was very overwhelmed and considered quitting college several times," she told the *Los Angeles Sentinel*.

Became Celebrity by Interviewing Celebrities

Neville's first job after graduation was in New Orleans as a reporter/anchor for WWL-TV. In 1988 she moved back to Texas for a one-year stint on the anchor team of Houston's KHOU. Neville next went to Chicago

At a Glance . . .

Born on October 20, 1962, in New Orleans, LA; married Derrick Lassic, 1995 (divorced 1998); married Taku Hirano, 2001. *Education:* Attended Xavier University and Southern Methodist University; University of Texas, BA, journalism, 1986.

Career: WWL-TV, New Orleans, LA, reporter/anchor, 1986-88; KHOU-TV, Houston, TX, anchor/reporter, 1988-89; *Travel & Adventure,* Chicago, IL, host, 1989-90; WVUE-TV, New Orleans, LA, 1990; *Extreme Close-Up,* E! Entertainment TV, anchor, 1991-94; *Extra,* Warner Brothers TV, co-anchor, 1994-96; *Arthel & Fred,* NBC, co-host, 1997; *Fox Files,* Fox TV, senior correspondent, 1998-2001; *The O'Reilly Factor,* Fox TV, contributor, 2001; *TalkBack Live with Arthel Neville,* CNN, host, 2002-03; CNN, on-air personality, 2002-04; *Good Day Live,* Fox TV, co-host, 2004-05; *A Current Affair,* Fox TV, West Coast correspondent, 2005–; *Celebrity Hobbies,* DIY Network, host, 2005–.

Awards: University of Texas, Outstanding Young Texas Ex Award, 2003.

Addresses: *Home*—Atlanta, GA.

where she worked as a host and correspondent for *Travel & Adventure*, a nationally-syndicated travel television show. The following year it was back to New Orleans and an anchor spot for WVUE-TV. This early criss-crossing of the country was just the beginning for Neville. "Change is the name of the game in my career," she told *Divabetic*. "Fortunately, all of the many changes have meant progress."

Neville's next change not only propelled her into the inner circle of the nation's brightest stars, but made Neville a star in her own right. In 1991 she landed the host spot on *Extreme Close-Up,* a one-on-one celebrity interview show for E! Entertainment TV. During three years with the program she logged over 200 interviews with stars from Will Smith to Tom Cruise to Sharon Stone. "Mr. [Bill] Cosby was definitely one of the highlights," Neville told the *Los Angeles Sentinel*. Cosby had initiated the interview and specifically requested Neville. It was an indication of how far she had come—Neville had become the nation's first high-profile black female entertainment reporter.

In 1994, at the special request of Dick Clark, Neville traveled to San Padre Island, Texas, to co-host the Miss USA pageant. There she met Derrick Lassic, NFL free agent and former Dallas Cowboy. The two wed the following year in New Orleans. Her uncle Aaron performed during the ceremony and the Neville Brothers performed at the reception. The couple settled into a bi-coastal lifestyle with Neville living near Los Angeles and Lassic in North Carolina. Unfortunately things did not work out and the couple split in 1998.

Forged Path for Black TV Personalities

Meanwhile, Neville's fame was growing. In 1994 she beat out over 1,000 hopefuls to earn the anchor spot for the Warner Brothers network's new show, *Extra*. Landing the job was the result of not only her experience, but also careful planning. "You definitely have to have foresight when you're making career decisions," she told the *Los Angeles Sentinel*. "Therefore over my 11 years officially in the business, I have made calculated moves, knowing that if I do this, if I work in this market, then I can make it to this market, and if I work here, then I can make it here." Neville's role on *Extra* was also notable because it made her the first African-American female to host a prime-time network show. As a result Neville was able to open the door for African-American reporters following in her footsteps.

Neville remained with *Extra* until 1996 when the program was revamped. In 1997 she teamed up with famed sportscaster Fred Roggin to host *Arthel & Fred*, a daytime entertainment news program on NBC. A year later, Neville left Los Angeles for New York and joined Fox Broadcasting as a senior correspondent for the newsmagazine show *Fox Files*. She also became the Fox News Channel's entertainment anchor. During this time Neville made cameo appearances on television sitcoms such as *Moesha*, *Fresh Prince of Bel Air* and *Cybill*.

Found New Love and Open Doors

In 1999 Neville was backstage at a concert in New Orleans when she met Taku Hirano, a drummer from Japan. After a two-year, long-distance relationship, Hirano asked Neville's parents for permission to marry her. It was granted. "Of course," she told *Essence*, "the initial hope in any Black family is that you will marry someone Black. But ultimately they want you to have someone who loves you and is good to you." Hirano proposed on a gondola in Venice, Italy, the couple married on a beach in Hawaii, and they honeymooned in Japan, where Neville met Hirano's family.

As her personal life was blossoming, Neville's professional life was hardening. On *The O'Reilly Factor*, Neville flexed her journalistic muscles, serving as the liberal challenger to O'Reilly's contentious conservatism. The two debated everything from race relations to labor unions, and the audience loved it. Neville did also.

"Taking on Bill O'Reilly was the highlight of my week," she told *New Orleans Magazine*. "We had a really great chemistry on the air; we were an unlikely couple together."

In 2002 Neville joined CNN to become host of *Talk-Back Live with Arthel Neville*. The show presented news of the day and featured live interaction with audience members and guests via phone and internet. "It's a juggling act, a challenge to make the show appear seamless," she told *New Orleans Magazine*. Neville also worked for CNN as a fill-in anchor and covered high profile celebrity events such as the Oscars and the Grammys before jumping back to Fox in 2004 to co-host the daily morning show *Good Day Live*. Though the show was cancelled in 2005, Neville quickly landed not one, but two, on-air positions: West Coast correspondent for the newsmagazine *A Current Affair* and host of the DIY Network's *Celebrity Hobbies*. The new opportunities illustrated a philosophy she expressed in an interview with the *Los Angeles Sentinel*. "Know that no one's going to give you anything. You work hard for it, and don't give up when doors close, because other doors will open."

Sources

Periodicals

Essence, July, 2003.
Los Angeles Sentinel, August 2, 1995.
New Orleans Magazine, September 2002.
Times Picayune, (New Orleans, LA), November 01, 2004.

On-line

"Arthel Neville, Co-host of *Good Day Live*," *Divabetic,* www.divabetic.com/pals.php (May 28, 2005).

—Candace LaBalle

Terrell Owens

1973—

Professional football player

Owens, Terrell, photograph. Frederick M. Brown/Getty Images.

Known as one of the National Football League's top wide receivers, Terrell Owens has made his mark in football history, not just for his talent as an athlete, but for his controversial behavior both on and off the field that gained him the label of football's most misunderstood star.

Born to a 17-year-old girl who eventually abandoned him to an abusive grandmother, Owens turned to sports in part to help him escape a tortured home life. He played basketball, baseball, and football, and also loved to swim. In high school, Owens' athletic talent blossomed and he was eventually recruited by the University of Tennessee at Chattanooga (UTC). He soon distinguished himself as an explosive receiver for the UTC Moccasins, and he gave the same high energy as a starting forward on the basketball team that qualified for the NCAA tournament in 1995. He also ran track for the school, anchoring the 4x100 relay team. The San Francisco 49ers drafted Owens in 1996, and he played there until 2003 amid increasing conflicts with teammates and media. After the 2003 season, Owens was traded to the Philadelphia Eagles where he quickly established himself as one of the most prolific receivers in Eagles history in just one season. Known as an inspirational leader who gives everything to his team, Owens is as divisive as he is talented. As a dominant figure in the football arena, he is considered by some the ultimate NFL athlete.

Played Multiple Sports in High School and College

Terrell Eldorado Owens was born December 7, 1973, in Alexander City, Alabama, to Marilyn Heard. Just 17 years old at the birth of her son, Marilyn continued living with her mother, Alice, after Terrell was born, and eventually had three more children. Bouncing from job to job, Marilyn eventually found a house of her own, taking her three younger children with her. Because there wasn't enough room for him in his mother's small house, young Terrell stayed with his grandmother, and when her failed marriage turned her to alcohol, Terrell often cared for her until she sobered up.

At Benjamin Russell High School in Alexander City, Alabama, Owens was a star football, basketball, baseball, and track athlete. He wore the number 80 on his football jersey to honor his idol, San Francisco 49er

At a Glance . . .

Born December 7, 1973, in Alexander City, Alabama; children: Terique. *Education:* Attended University of Tennessee at Chattanooga, 1993–96.

Career: San Francisco 49ers, professional football player, 1996-2003; Philadelphia Eagles, professional football player, 2004–.

Selected Awards: First team, All-Southern Conference, 1995; first team All-Pro, Associated Press, 1998, 2000, 2001, 2002; Pro Bowl selection, National Football League, 2000-2004; Athletics Hall of Fame, University of Tennessee at Chattanooga, 2003.

Addresses: *Office*—c/o Philadelphia Eagles, One NovaCare Way, Philadelphia, PA 19145. *Web*—www.terrellowens.com.

Jerry Rice. Terrell's athletic career blossomed when he entered high school, and he lettered four times in football and track, three times in basketball, and once in baseball. He was recruited by the UTC Moccasins out of high school, and for three years went on to prove his amazing athleticism and talent on the football field.

As a sophomore at UTC, he played all 11 games of the season and set a new Moccasin record with four touchdowns in a game against Marshall. During his junior year at UTC, Owens became the team's most powerful offensive weapon, earning him the honor of second-team All-Southern Conference. The following season, however, Owens' game statistics declined as a result of double coverage by the opposition. Although his statistics were not overly impressive, he was drafted by the San Francisco 49ers to start the 1996 season. Owens was thrilled to be working alongside his idol, Jerry Rice. By the end of the preseason, Owens was second to Rice in catches and receiving yards; by the season's end his 35 receptions for 520 yards made him the likely successor to Jerry Rice as the 49ers number one receiver.

In the years that followed, Owens racked up increasingly impressive numbers and fulfilled that early promise. He caught 60 passes for 936 yards in 1997; 67 passes for 1097 yards in 1998; and 60 passes for 754 yards in 1999. Then, Owens' productivity exploded: he made 97 catches for 1451 yards in 2000, 93 catches for 1412 yards in 2001, and 100 catches for 1300 yards in 2002. With these stats, Owens was widely considered one of the great receivers in the league.

Courted Controversy

In his most productive season, however, Owens also displayed a real talent for generating controversy. Early in the 2000 season, after catching a touchdown pass against the Dallas Cowboys, Owens ran to the center of the field to celebrate. The 49ers had come off a disappointing 1999 season and Owens' could not contain his excitement over the 49ers lead. A second score by Owens brought on another celebration, much to the offense of both the Cowboys and the 49ers. He was suspended for a week and fined $24,000, leaving him feeling angry and abandoned by his teammates.

Owens' best season as a professional football player with the 49ers merged with Rice's final campaign with the 49ers, in which Rice was shown one loud ovation after another. But Owens did not let the tumult of Rice's departure distract him. In a December game against Chicago, Owens set a new NFL record of 20 receptions for 283 yards. By year-end, he was on his way to his first Pro Bowl in Hawaii.

During the off-season, however, Owens was hounded by the press. Criticisms of his attitude, his locker room explosions, and his touchdown celebrations came to define his reputation. Spending time alone, he isolated himself from reporters, fans, and teammates. His isolation was noted as discontent, and predictions for the 49ers 2001 season was grim. Owens made no excuses for his behavior. He just went out and played. By the season's end, Owens had another stellar season and was selected for the Pro Bowl a second time, earning him first team All-Pro honors.

In the coming seasons, Owens continued to court controversy. The first game of the 2002 campaign against the Seattle Seahawks ended with a game-winning touchdown by Owens. After the score, Owens pulled a Sharpie pen from his sock and signed the football, then handed it to his financial advisor who sat in the stands. Seahawks' coach Mike Holmgren claimed that Owens had dishonored the game. After ESPN analysts ripped Owens for his on-field behavior, he invited a camera into his home in order to defend himself on live television. He argued that the league targeted black players with its strict rules against touchdown celebrations. "You'd have thought I committed a crime, like some other players we could talk about in pro sports today," Owens later wrote in his autobiography *Catch This! Going Deep with the NFL's Sharpest Weapon*. Not only that, Owens claimed that his mother, whom he is now very close to, is the reason for his touchdown tactics. "I wanted her to see me on television," he said in his autobiography. "Before each game I tell my mom to stay tuned for something new." But in spite of his motivations, the 2002 season ended with a mutual agreement that Owens and the 49ers would part ways after the next season.

Although the Sharpie incident spawned immense criticism by the media and fans, Owens found a way to turn it into good will, testifying to his claim that the most important things in his life are his faith and his family. The Sharpie Company agreed to pledge money to the Alzheimer's Association for every touchdown that Owens makes. Owens' grandmother, Alice, suffers from the disease, and he has testified to the U.S. Senate committee about its effects.

Set New Records

Over the eight years that Owens played for the San Francisco 49ers, he caught 592 passes, 100 of those in 2002. He ranks second among the 49ers for lifetime touchdown receptions, behind his idol Jerry Rice. He broke a 50-year record in 2000 with 20 receptions in a game against the Chicago Bears, and established himself as one of the best blocking receivers ever.

In 2003 Owens was traded to the Philadelphia Eagles, where his impact on its offense was immediately obvious. During a seven-game Eagles winning streak, Owens topped 100 yards receiving per game—but he also increased his touchdown celebrations. The winning streak ended with a defeat against the Steelers, but a controversial television promotion that had appeared before the Monday Night football game overshadowed Owens' six receptions for 134 yards and three scores during the game. The sensual television promotion featured Owens in the locker room with barely clad actress Nicollette Sheridan from the television show *Desperate Housewives.* Ultimately Owens apologized for the promo, but not before a barrage of media criticism.

Although Owens may have made mistakes in the eyes of some fans and the media, his passionate personality and performance captured the hearts of many. In a 2004 game against the Lions he responded to e-mails from Navy and Air Force members stationed in the Middle East who had asked him to salute if he scored a touchdown. He gave the salute after scoring a 29-yard touchdown early in the game.

Played in the Super Bowl

Later in the 2004 season in a game against the Cowboys, Owens fractured his leg, causing concerns that the Eagles would be ineffective without their star receiver. But receiver Freddie Mitchell took up the slack for Owens, and after 20 years Eagles fans were celebrating a return to the Super Bowl. Owens was ready to play again by the Super Bowl XXXIX kickoff in Jacksonville, Florida, only 46 days after surgery on his leg. Although the team lost to the Patriots, Owens finished the game with a heroic effort of nine catches for 122 yards.

The second season of Owens' seven-year contract began badly. Owens wanted the Eagles to renegotiate his $48.97 million contract. When the Eagles refused, he threatened to skip training camp completely. Roundly criticized by players and the media, Owens reported to camp, but was distant and aloof. Soon, he was ejected for a week after arguing with head coach Andy Reid. As always, Owens refused to apologize for his behavior. "They don't pay me to go in there and talk to everybody and be friendly to everybody," he told reporters. "They paid me to play and they paid me to perform. That's what I've been going in there and doing."

Among his many accomplishments as a football player, Owens was the second NFL player to record five seasons with 13 or more touchdowns, and the first to score a touchdown in seven straight Monday Night Football games. He is known as an inspirational player and leader of his team—an athlete who gives the ultimate effort in each practice and each game. His intense drive to succeed has earned him the respect and admiration of his fellow football players, though many fans criticize him for his arrogant and antagonistic attitude. Terrell Owens seems likely to continue to grab attention, both on the field and off.

Sources

Books

Owens, Terrell, and Stephen Singular, *Catch This! Going Deep with the NFL's Sharpest Weapon,* Simon and Schuster, 2004.

Periodicals

Lindy's Pro Football, August 2005, pp. 96-97.
Philadelphia Magazine, February 2005.
Pro Football Weekly, August 15, 2005, p. 119.
Sporting News, December 1, 1997; August 27, 2001; October 28, 2002; September 29, 2003; October 13, 2003; March 1, 2004; June 14, 2004; November 15, 2004.
Sports Illustrated, December 14, 1998; October 16, 2000; November 26, 2001; August 1, 2005.
Time, October 28, 2002.

On-line

"Eagles' Owens Returns to Training Camp," *Fox Sports,* http://msn.foxsports.com/nfl/story/389 502 (August 17, 2005).
"Terrell Owens," *Philadelphia Eagles,* www.philadel hiaeagles.com (August 17, 2005).
"Terrell Owens," *Biography Resource Center,* www. galenet.galegroup.com/servlet/BioRC (April 5, 2005).
Terrell Owens, www.terrellowens.com (August 29, 2005).

—Cheryl A. Dudley

Fritz Pollard

1894-1986

Professional football player, coach, businessman

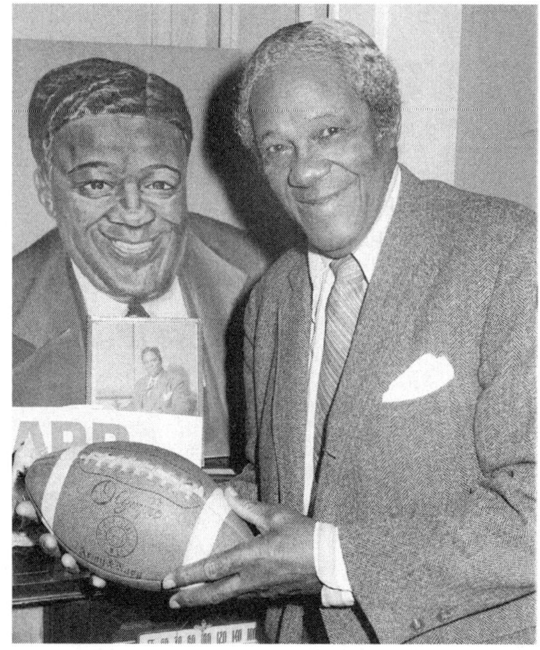
Pollard, Fritz, photograph. AP/Wide World Photos. Reproduced by permission.

A highly successful football and track athlete, Fritz Pollard became the first African American to play in the Rose Bowl when he played for Brown University in 1916 and the first African American to coach in the National Football League (NFL) in 1922. During the early days of professional football, Pollard was an energetic promoter of integrated rosters, recruiting prominent black players to the NFL and organizing exhibition games to showcase their talents. He assembled and coached the all-black Chicago Black Hawks football team, which became one of the most popular teams from 1929 to 1932. After retiring from his successful coaching career, Pollard founded a number of businesses and established a weekly black tabloid. He then became a successful casting agent, producing videos and a film that featured African-American entertainers. Among his many honors, he was the first African American to be elected into the National College Football Hall of Fame as well as the recipient of an honorary doctorate from Brown University. Along with his own amazing athletic ability and accomplishments, Pollard was a courageous advocate for confronting racial barriers and creating opportunities for African Americans, both in the athletic and business world.

Frederick Douglass Pollard was born in an affluent neighborhood in Chicago on January 27, 1894, to John William, a barber, and Catherine Amanda Hughs Pollard, a seamstress. The seventh of eight children, he was affectionately called Fred, but later nicknamed "Fritz" by neighborhood residents, a name that stuck with him throughout life. He was, however, named after civil rights leader Frederick Douglass, a famous abolitionist whom his parents had heard speak the preceding year. Pollard attributed much of his success in life to his ancestors, who—through tremendous hard work, courage, and a pioneering spirit—thrived and prospered during the era of slavery. Even though his grandparents and great grandparents had been Virginia slaves, the family became free yeomen farmers after the Revolutionary War and through hard work overcame tremendous odds. The John William Pollard family was well-educated and had moved from Missouri to Chicago in order to give their eight children a better life and more opportunity. Fritz

At a Glance . . .

Born January 27, 1894, in Rogers Park, Illinois; married Ada Laing, 1914 (divorced, 1940); married Mary Ella Austin (1947); children: three daughters, one son. *Education:* Attended Brown University, 1915-18.

Career: Professional football player and coach; business entrepreneur; theater agent; tax consultant.

Selected Awards: Named to National College Football Hall of Fame, 1954; named to R.I. Heritage Hall of Fame, 1967; named to Brown Athletic Hall of Fame, 1971; named to National Black Hall of Fame, 1973; Brown University, honorary doctorate, 1981; named to Pro Football Hall of Fame, 2005.

Pollard embraced these opportunities and proved that through hard work and the spirit of his ancestors, he could accomplish great things.

By the time Fritz graduated from Lane Technical High School in 1912, he had become a talented running back, baseball player, and a three-time county track champion. In June 1914 he married Ada Laing. The couple, who had three daughters and one son, separated in the early 1920s and was later divorced. Their son, Fritz Pollard Jr., was also an athlete, won a bronze medal in the 1936 Olympic Games and was named an All-American football player at the University of North Dakota in 1938.

Prior to receiving a Rockefeller scholarship to attend Brown University in 1915, Pollard played football briefly for Northwestern, Harvard, and Dartmouth. As a freshman at Brown University, the 5' 9", 165-pound halfback led his team to the Rose Bowl in 1915 against Washington State, gaining notoriety as the first African American to ever play in the Rose Bowl. During the 1916 football season, Pollard scored 12 touchdowns and led Brown to an 8-1 record. Not only that, in the spring of 1916 he set a world record for Brown University's track team in low hurdles and qualified for the Olympic Team. Additionally, Pollard played his best games against the two premier college football teams, Yale and Harvard, leading Brown to unprecedented victories in both games. He was selected by famed coach Walter Camp for a halfback position on the All-America team in 1916, becoming the first African American to play a backfield position on an All-America team, and only the second to be selected by Camp for the team.

A 1916 *New York Times* report posted on the Brown University Web site said of Pollard's performance in a game between Brown University and Yale, "At every stage of this dazzling performance sturdy arms clad in blue yawned for him, but Pollard trickily shot out of their reach. Tacklers charged him fiercely enough to knock the wind out of any ordinary individual, but Pollard had the asset which is the greatest to a football player—he refused to be hurt. It required a terrific shock to upset him. An ordinary tackle did nothing more than make him swerve slightly out of his course."

In 1918 Pollard dropped out of school after becoming ineligible to play for Brown's team because of academic neglect. He then became head coach of Lincoln University in Pennsylvania until 1920. In 1919 Pollard also joined the Akron Pros, which in 1920 joined the American Professional Football Association (APFA), later known as the National Football League (NFL). The Akron Pros went undefeated during Pollard's first season, winning the league's first crown. As one of just two African Americans in the new league, Pollard earned a place in football history. Accounts of Pollard's football talent on the Pro Football Hall of Fame Web site claim that he was "an exciting elusive runner" and "the most feared running back in the fledgling league."

In 1921 the Pros named Pollard co-coach of the team, earning him the distinction of the first African American to coach in NFL history. After becoming a coach for the NFL, Pollard was known to coach up to four different teams in a single season. He also continued playing in the 1923 and 1924 season for an independent pro team in Pennsylvania called the Coal League. Then in 1928 he organized a professional all-African American team in Chicago known as the Chicago Black Hawks. Playing against white teams around Chicago, the Black Hawks enjoyed great success and became a highly popular team until the Depression caused the team to fold in 1932.

In addition to his athletic endeavors, Pollard was involved in several business enterprises. He began an investment firm that served the African-American community in 1922, and after its bankruptcy in 1931 he ran a coal company in New York and also served as a casting agent during the production of the1933 film *The Emperor Jones*. From 1935 to 1942 Pollard founded and operated the *New York Independent News*, the first African-American tabloid newspaper, then in 1943 he managed Suntan Studios in Harlem, auditioning African-American entertainers for scripts and modeling. He also began producing short music videos featuring black entertainers—called Soundies—for the Soundies Distribution Corporation of America. The company was sold after World War II. In 1947 Pollard married Mary Ella Austin.

Following the sale of the Soundies Distribution Corporation of America, Pollard became a booking agent for nightclubs, radio, and television, and eventually produced his own movie in 1956 entitled *Rockin' the Blues*. The film, similar to his music videos, featured new African American artists. During the 1950s-1975, when he retired, Pollard dedicated his time to being a successful tax consultant. He died of pneumonia on May 11, 1986, in Maryland at the age of 92. In 2005, he was finally inducted into the Pro Football Hall of Fame.

Sources

Books

Carroll, John M., *Fritz Pollard: Pioneer in Racial Advancement,* University of Illinois Press, 1999.

Periodicals

Sports Illustrated, December 15, 2003.

On-line

"Frederick Douglass Pollard," *Biography Resource Center.* www.galenet.galegroup.com/servlet/BioRC (April 5, 2005).

Frederick Douglass Pollard, www.fritzpollard.com (July 6, 2005).

"Fritz Pollard," *Pro Football Hall of Fame*, www.profootballhof.com/hof/member.jsp?player_id=242 (April 16, 2005).

"Fritz Pollard and Early African American Professional Football Players," *Brown University*, www.brown.edu/Administration/News_Bureau/2003-04/03-078f.html. (April 16, 2005).

"Fritz Pollard Was a Football Architect," *The African American Registry*, http://www.aaregistry.com/african_american_history/39/Fritz_Pollard_was_a_football_architect (April 5, 2005).

—Cheryl Dudley

Omara Portuondo

1930—

Cuban vocalist

The elegant vocalist Omara Portuondo, nearly 70 years old at the time, was the only female artist showcased in the successful *Buena Vista Social Club* album and film that reintroduced classic Cuban music to American audiences in the late 1990s. It wasn't only because she was a woman that Portuondo stood out, however. In contrast to the Afro-Cuban roots music made by the other *Buena Vista Social Club* stars, Portuondo brought to life a different kind of Cuban song, one with a thoroughly romantic spirit and with a strong influence from American jazz and pop. "In Cuba we have always had the opportunity to get to know many parts of the world, the music of South America, North America, Latin America. I take the best from everywhere," Portuondo told *San Diego Union-Tribune* writer Andrew Gilbert through an interpreter (she speaks Spanish in interviews).

Portuondo, Omara, photograph. Staton R. Winter/Getty Images.

Portuondo was born in 1930 in the modest but musically rich Cayo Hueso neighborhood of Havana, Cuba. Her parents were an odd and fairly controversial couple for the time: her mother was a high-born woman of Spanish descent who was expected to marry a man of similar background but instead chose an Afro-Cuban baseball star. Neither was particularly musical, but sometimes they sang romantic duets around the house. Portuondo's father had been a schoolmate of Cuban song composer Ernesto Grenet, and musicians and artists were always welcome in the household.

Started Out in Chorus Line

A silent type, Portuondo was a reluctant performer at first. Her sister Haydee became a member of the chorus line at Havana's Tropicana Club, and when Omara was 15 she was asked to join as well after another dancer fell ill. "I was very shy and ashamed to show my legs," Portuondo recalled to Rob Adams of Scotland's *Glasgow Herald*. "Then my mother said, 'Do it for me. You'll see, one day you'll represent your country all over the world with your art.'" Portuondo, despite her shyness, had closely studied the dancers' routines in rehearsal and had no trouble picking up their steps.

She and Haydee soon began doing a vocal-harmony act in Havana's nightclubs as well, performing American songs for the throngs of tourists who came to the city for a taste of the tropical life. Portuondo began to

At a Glance . . .

Born in 1930 in Havana, Cuba; married (divorced); children: Ariel (son).

Career: Began performing at age 15 in chorus line at Tropicana Club, Havana; Loquibambla Swing, lead vocalist; Cuarteto las d'Aida, member, 1952-1967; toured United States and Europe, 1957-62; solo artist, 1959–; toured U.S. and Europe, 2000-04.

Addresses: Agent—International Music Network, 278 Main St., Gloucester, MA 01930.

perform as lead vocalist with a group called Loquibambla Swing, fronted by a blind pianist named Frank Emilio Flynn. That group, appearing daily on Cuban radio, pioneered a new style called *filín* that merged Cuban sounds with jazz and Brazilian bossa nova music. Portuondo began to find favor among Cuban audiences, who dubbed her "La novia del filín"—the fiancee of feeling.

In 1952, Portuondo formed the group Cuarteto las d'Aida with her sister Haydee, Elena Bourke, and Moraima Secada. The group took its name from pianist and director Aida Diestro, but another key creative contributor was Cuban jazzman Chico O'Farrill, who wrote many of their vocal arrangements. Cuarteto las d'Aida toured the United States and Europe beginning in 1957, and Portuondo released a solo album, *Magía Negra,* in 1959. Two years later, the rising career of Cuarteto las d'Aida was blocked by the unsuccessful Bay of Pigs invasion of Cuba assisted by the United States Central Intelligence Agency and the subsequent Cuban missile crisis showdown between the United States and the Soviet Union. Relations between the United States and Cuba deteriorated, and Portuondo, a supporter of Cuban leader Fidel Castro, returned to her homeland. Her sister remained in the United States.

Toured World, Except for United States

Unlike the other musicians featured in the *Buena Vista Social Club* album and film, Portuondo was a longtime star. "Omara is a legend in Cuba, and it's safe to say there's no one of my age who didn't grow up under her influence," 31-year-old Cuban-born ballet dancer Carlos Acosta told Jenny Gilbert of the London (England) *Independent.* Portuondo headlined shows at the Tropicana. She worked with some of Cuba's top musicians, including future Gloria Estefan arranger Juanito Marquez. America was off limits to Portuondo, but she toured both Western and Eastern Europe with the Orquesta Aragón, a legendary Cuban dance band.

The music Portuondo made as a solo artist showed the cultural influences with which she had grown up; her shows often included a Spanish translation of George and Ira Gershwin's "The Man I Love." Her specialties were the Latin song genres known as son and bolero—romantic ballads centered on the themes of love, memory, and loneliness. Not an explosive salsa singer like her contemporary Celia Cruz, Portuondo was a classic vocal stylist sometimes compared to the melancholy American jazz diva Billie Holiday or the French chanteuse Edith Piaf. Portuondo married and divorced; her son, Ariel, became her manager.

Omara, a documentary film about her career, won a prize at the Cannes Film Festival in France in 1986. By the early 1990s, Portuondo's schedule had slowed down a bit, but the *Buena Vista Social Club* projects brought her a whole new generation of admirers. Her involvement with the group came about after its organizer and producer, slide guitarist and world music enthusiast Ry Cooder, heard her on a visit to Havana in the mid-1990s. As Cooder brought together his group of aging Cuban musicians at Cuba's state-owned Egrem studios in 1996, Portuondo happened to be recording a new album of her own in the same building. Bandleader Juan de Marcos Gonzalez, Portuondo recalled to Adams, "looked in on me and said: 'We need a female voice for a duet with Compay Segundo, why don't you do it?'" The 66-year-old Portuondo thought, "'What, a love duet with that old guy?' I hadn't seen him for years."

Featured in Duet in Film

For her duet with Segundo, which appeared on the *Buena Vista Social Club* album, Portuondo chose a song called "Veinte Años" that she had originally learned from her parents years before. On the soundtrack of the *Buena Vista Social Club* film (1998) directed by German filmmaker Wim Wenders, however, she was featured in a different duet: in "Silencio," her duet partner Ibrahim Ferrer was seen using a handkerchief to wipe away a tear that fell from her face. After the film won an Academy Award nomination for best documentary feature, Portuondo became better known among U.S. audiences.

The *Buena Vista Social Club* projects proved to be much more than a last hurrah for Portuondo as well as for many of the other performers involved. In 2000 she launched her first U.S. tour since the Cuban missile crisis, and she performed frequently in the United States, Mexico, and Europe over the next five years. Her 2004 album *Flor de Amor* saw her undertaking new experiments with Brazilian sounds, and she showed no signs of being ready to retire. "What we are doing is so much full of love ...," Portuondo told *Washington Post* writer Richard Harrington as she reflected on her new popularity and that of her compatriots. "Love moves the world, and in our case we love so much what we are doing, that's probably the main secret of our success."

Selected works

Albums

Magía Negra, 1959 (reissued Vedisco, 1997).
Soy cubana, Artex, 1993.
Palabras, Intuition, 1996.
(with other artists) *Buena Vista Social Club,* World Circuit, 1996.
(with Chucho Valdes) *Desafinos,* Intuition, 1999.
Buena Vista Social Club Presents: Omara Portuondo, Elektra/Asylum, 2000.
Omara Portuondo: Roots of Buena Vista, Egrem, 2000.
Dos Gardenias, Tumi, 2001.
La gran Omara Portuondo, Egrem, 2002.
Flor de Amor, World Circuit, 2004.

Films

Omara (documentary), 1983.
Buena Vista Social Club (documentary), 1999.

Sources

Periodicals

Boston Globe, July 30, 2004, p. C13.
Daily Telegraph (London, England), April 29, 2004, p. 23.
Herald (Glasgow, Scotland, U.K.), May 1, 2004, p. 3.
Independent (London, England), April 16, 2004, p. 18; June 6, 2004, Features section, p. 5.
Plain Dealer (Cleveland, OH), April 17, 2002, p. E1.
San Diego Union-Tribune, March 28, 2002, Night & Day section, p. 9; October 30, 2003, Night & Day section, p. 19.
Washington Post, October 20,. 2000, p. N15.

On-line

"Omara Portuondo," *AfroCubaWeb,* http://www.afrocubaweb/portuondo.htm (April 22, 2005).
"Omara Portuondo," *All Music Guide,* http://www.allmusic.com (April 22, 2005).

—James M. Manheim

Willie Randolph

1954—

Major league baseball manager, player

Randolph, Willie, photograph. Peter Kramer/Getty Images.

A star second baseman with the powerhouse New York Yankees baseball teams of the 1970s and 1980s, Willie Randolph became New York's first African-American pro baseball manager when he was named to that post by the New York Mets in 2004. Randolph rose to prominence as a player and manager the hard way: he earned it. As a player he was a quiet, determined presence who clawed his way up to the major leagues from street baseball games in Brooklyn. His hiring by the Mets marked the end of a long, patient effort to ascend to a managerial position from among the ranks of coaches.

William Larry Randolph Jr. was born in Holly Hill, South Carolina, on July 6, 1954, but grew up in the rough-and-tumble Brownsville area in the New York borough of Brooklyn—also home to future boxing champion Mike Tyson. "Any kid coming out of that neighborhood has a toughness most kids don't, brings an energy most kids don't, and has a drive most people don't," Randolph's friend Mel Vitter told Lee Jenkins of the *New York Times*. "Willie was never blessed with huge physical ability. He was never the strongest or the fastest. He made himself with his attitude." From the time he first put on a Jackie Robinson model baseball glove, Randolph showed a drive to excel at sports.

Went to Mets Game on Date

At Samuel J. Tilden High School, baseball coach Herb Abramowitz recalled to T.J. Quinn of the New York *Daily News,* Randolph volunteered for extra work after regular practice was over. "I'd lay a mat on the floor of the gym and he practiced how to dive for a ball," Abramowitz said. "Did you ever hear of a player practicing diving for a ball? We practiced that for hours." An important milestone in the teenaged Randolph's personal life also had to do with baseball: he saved up his entire allowance to take his future wife, Gretchen, on a date to see the New York Mets play the Chicago Cubs at Shea Stadium.

Some baseball scouts avoided traveling to Brownsville to see Randolph play. Nevertheless, just before he turned 18 in 1972, Randolph was drafted by the Pittsburgh Pirates. He played for four minor-league teams over the next four years before ascending to the

At a Glance . . .

Born on July 6, 1954 in Holly Hill, SC; married Gretchen; children: Taniesha, Chantre, Andre, and Ciara. *Education:* Attended Samuel J. Tilden High School, Brooklyn, NY.

Career: Major league baseball player, coach, and manager. Pittsburgh Pirates farm system, professional baseball player, 1972-74; Pittsburgh Pirates, professional baseball player, 1975; New York Yankees, professional baseball player, 1976-88; Los Angeles Dodgers, professional baseball player, 1989-90; Oakland Athletics, professional baseball player, 1990; Milwaukee Brewers, professional baseball player, 1991; New York Mets, professional baseball player, 1992; New York Yankees, assistant general manager and coach, 1993-2004; New York Mets, manager, 2005.

Selected awards: James P. Dawson Award, 1976; Topps All-Rookie team, 1976; American League All-Star Team, 1976, 1977, 1980, 1981, and 1987; National League All-Star Team, 1989.

Address: *Office*—New York Mets, Shea Stadium, 123-01 Roosevelt Ave., Flushing, NY 11368.

Pirates squad and playing 30 games at the end of the 1975 season. He got into two playoff games with the Pirates that year, but after the end of the season he was traded to the Yankees. He began to flourish almost immediately, batting .267 and drawing 58 walks for an on-base percentage of .355 in his first season with the team. Randolph appeared in the 1976 All-Star Game, an honor he received again in 1977, 1980, 1981, 1987, and 1989.

Randolph's fortunes paralleled those of the Yankees in the late 1970s; as he hit his stride as a player, he became a key member of the World Series-winning Yankees teams in 1977 and 1978. Randolph played at a consistently high level over 13 seasons with the Yankees, always pushing a .300 batting average (and exceeding it in 1987 with a .305 mark). He stole more than 30 bases four times, rarely struck out, and in 1980 drew a team-high 119 walks. By 1986 his salary topped $1,000,000.

Left Yankees for Dodgers

Never graced with an outgoing personality, Randolph nevertheless was a key motivator and linchpin of the Yankees squad. "He was quiet. Very quiet," former Yankee catcher Fran Healy told Quinn. "You could see there was more there, though. This was when all sorts of crazy stuff was going on there—with Reggie [Jackson], with Thurman Munson. But Willie, with all the turmoil in those years, he was the professional." Randolph became a free agent in 1986 and signed on for two more years with the Yankees before departing for the Los Angeles Dodgers in 1989.

The last several years of Randolph's career were unusually successful ones. He moved to the Oakland Athletics in 1990, making World Series appearances for the fourth time, and then had the best year of his career in 1991, batting .327 over 124 games for the Milwaukee Brewers at age 37. Randolph returned home to close out his career in 1992 with the Mets. His lifetime batting average over 18 years was .276.

With four children to raise, Randolph and his wife settled into life in New York as Randolph took a job as a third-base coach with the Yankees. As the Yankees recaptured their former glory, winning three championships in four years at one point, Randolph tutored Derek Jeter and other star players. As a player himself he had worked under the legendary scrapper Billy Martin and other top managers, and now he absorbed lessons in the managerial art from Yankees skipper Joe Torre. Back at Tilden High School, Randolph revived a moribund baseball program with a donation of uniforms and bats. In 1993, Randolph added the title of assistant general manager to his Yankees resume.

Persisted After Unsuccessful Interviews

Randolph had his eye on bigger things than coaching, however. "From Day One as a coach I've been saying I want to go to the next level," he told John Harper of the New York *Daily News*. He had numerous interviews over more than a decade as a Yankees coach—up to a dozen according to some counts. In 2000 there were reports that he had been offered the manager's job with the Cincinnati Reds but turned it down due to the low salary offer of $300,000 annually. Randolph later denied those reports, and he openly began to muse about leaving organized baseball to teach the game to children.

A lingering reluctance among baseball team owners likely played a role in Randolph's repeated rejections, but Randolph himself pointed out that he needed to learn a more aggressive style. "They [the network of baseball decision makers] know of me, they don't really know me," he told William C. Rhoden of the *New York Times*. "In this business you have to get into the mix. I needed to be exposed to people, to let them know me." Randolph began preparing more intensively for interviews, stressing the wisdom he had picked up from a series of baseball's greatest managers.

Finally Mets general manager Omar Minaya, himself a newcomer to the team, announced Randolph's hiring as manager on November 4, 2004. "I think my wife had to pull me off the ceiling, I was so excited,"

Randolph told *Jet*. "It's a lot of emotion running through your body, the fact that you finally get your opportunity, you're doing it in your hometown, for the team you rooted for as a kid."

Randolph laid down strict rules for his new team, governing everything from hair length to behavior in practice. The first games of the 2005 season were every new manager's nightmare: the Mets lost five in a row. But Randolph showed no nervousness, telling reporters that he had slept well throughout the ordeal. By May of 2005 the Mets had a winning record and were contending for first place in their division, before slumping to eight games back of division-leading Atlanta by August. The long-delayed managerial career of Willie Randolph was off to a good start.

Sources

Periodicals

Daily News (New York), February 26, 2002, November 4, 2004; November 5, 2004, p. 90.

Jet, November 22, 2004, p. 51.

New York Times, July 7, 2001, p. D1; November 3, 2004, p. D1; November 4, 2004, p. D1; April 2, 2005, p. D1.

Newsday (New York), April 21, 2005, p. A89.

Philadelphia Inquirer, October 25, 2000.

Sporting News, March 11, 2005, p. 10.

On-line

"Willie Randolph," *Baseball Library*, www.baseballlibrary.com/baseballlibrary/ballplayers/R/Randolph_Willie.stm (August 11, 2005).

"Willie Randolph," *Baseball Reference*, www.baseball-reference.com/r/randowi01.shtml (May 5, 2005).

"Willie Randolph," *New York Mets*, http://newyork.mets.mlb.com/NASApp/mlb/team/coach_staff_bio.jsp?c_id=nym&coachorstaffid=120927 (August 11, 2005).

—James M. Manheim

Reginald R. Robinson

1972—

Ragtime composer, pianist

Robinson, Reginald R., photograph. AP/Wide World Photos. Reproduced by permission.

Reginald Robinson makes new piano music in a genre that flourished a hundred years ago. Ragtime, the music that brought African-American syncopated rhythms to a broad American public in the early years of the twentieth century, marked an important stage of American musical history. Yet in recent years it has been mainly cultivated by predominantly white musical nostalgia buffs—until Robinson, a young African-American Chicagoan, came along and extended the ragtime tradition with exciting new compositions. After years of laboring in obscurity, Robinson found his efforts rewarded with a $500,000 MacArthur Foundation fellowship in 2004.

Although he looked backward into musical time, Robinson's story is a thoroughly contemporary one: part of the impetus for his creative activity came from the often violent streets of Chicago's West and South sides, where he grew up. Robinson was born in Chicago in 1972, the year before the film *The Sting* sparked a short-lived revival of ragtime's popularity. The teenaged Robinson would one day find a copy of that film on video and watch it repeatedly, but as a child he and his five siblings had more immediate problems on their minds. Gunfire in the streets was a common occurrence near their apartment in the notorious Henry Horner Homes project, and one time the family returned from a movie to find burglars in the process of ransacking their apartment. "The front door had melted," Robinson recalled to Howard Reich of the *Chicago Tribune.* "I guess they used some kind of heating apparatus or something to get in."

Introduced to Ragtime by Ice-Cream Truck

Music provided a respite from the chaos. Robinson immersed himself in his parents' record collection, which ranged from jazz to classical music. One day his attention was snared by an ice-cream truck whose speaker played a catchy, deceptively simple tune. The melody came from a piece called "The Entertainer," composed by Scott Joplin and featured in *The Sting*—neither one of which Robinson had heard of. A few years later, however, Robinson was attending seventh grade at the Robert Emmet school in Chicago's west-

At a Glance . . .

Born 1972 in Chicago, IL; one of six children. *Education:* Mostly self-taught; took classes at the American Conservatory of Music, Chicago, and at a music store on the South Side of Chicago.

Career: Musician. Performed at Green Mill Lounge, Chicago, early 1990s; signed to Delmark label, 1993; toured extensively, 1993-95.

Awards: MacArthur Foundation Fellowship winner, 2004.

Addresses: *Office*—Reginald R. Robinson Publishing, P.O. Box 2964, Chicago, IL 60690-2964.

side Austin neighborhood, and a jazz musician from a youth arts program called Urban Gateways happened to play "The Entertainer" on the piano.

"Something was really pulling me into that music," Robinson told Reich. "It's strange to me; I'm still trying to figure that out." Having learned that the music was called ragtime, he proceeded to learn everything he could about it. He collected records and watched silent film comedies that featured ragtime accompaniment. He started asking his parents for a piano and finally got a small electric keyboard and then a spinet model that a neighbor wanted to discard. Meanwhile, the net of urban violence drew closer as Robinson hit his teenage years. His classmates began carrying guns to school, and he saw several get shot. During his freshman year he dropped out and began to spend most of his time teaching himself to play ragtime on the piano. The *Tribune*'s Reich reported that he rarely left his bedroom for three years. He hung red curtains and arranged lamps so that the room resembled a century-old brothel where a ragtime pianist might have played. "I became ragtime," Robinson told Lloyd Sachs of the *Chicago Sun-Times.* The isolation helped him find a very distinctive musical voice; he later reflected that if he had known at the time about the festivals devoted to classic ragtime, he would have been too intimidated to try to write music of his own.

By the time he was 16, Robinson could amaze relatives with his piano skills and original compositions. He got a job at a T-shirt printing shop (the first of many day jobs whose proceeds would go to his music) and used his earnings to take a few music classes at the American Conservatory of Music in Chicago's central Loop. A professor, astonished by how much Robinson had learned without lessons, agreed to continue teaching him for a while, and he also took lessons at a South Side music store. Robinson learned to read music—ragtime, unlike jazz, was usually written down in musical notation—and gained a deeper understanding of the harmonies and forms that gave ragtime its classic sense of balance. On the side, he became an accomplished calligrapher.

Befriended by Chicago Pianist

Finally, local musicians began to get wind of Robinson's talent, and he began appearing on Sunday afternoons at the classic-jazz Green Mill club on Chicago's North Side. Stride-style pianist Jay Weber helped Robinson record a demo tape, consisting mostly of original ragtime pieces, like "The Strongman" and "Poker Face Blues," that he had written in his late teens. Robinson took the tape to Bob Koester, of Chicago's Delmark Records. "When he came in, I thought he was a rap artist, based on the way he looked and the photo of him on his tape," Koester told Sachs. "I started to get my rap ready on the kind of things we don't record. Then I saw the word 'rag' on the end of some of the titles and couldn't believe it." Robinson's debut album, *The Strongman,* came out on Delmark in 1993; it opened with Robinson's rendition of Scott Joplin's "Maple Leaf Rag" and followed with 17 Robinson originals.

By that time, the ragtime boom stimulated by *The Sting* had mostly subsided. Ragtime might be heard on a reconstructed riverboat, in the home of a serious music fan interested in early jazz and its ancestors, or at a festival devoted to the music. But few composers, and fewer still who were African American, were writing new piano rags. Robinson created a sensation with *The Strongman.* He appeared on National Public Radio's *Piano Jazz* and signed a management contract with the agent who handled the show's septuagenarian host, Marian McPartland. Soon Robinson was sharing a bill with ragtime veteran Dick Hyman and releasing a sophomore album, *Sounds in Silhouette* (1994). He delved more deeply into the history of ragtime, discovering a photograph of Joplin at Nashville's Fisk University that showed a snatch of sheet music containing a previously unknown Joplin composition propped on a piano. Robinson performed that Joplin fragment in 1998 on his third Delmark album, *Euphonic Sounds.*

The title track of that album was a piece Joplin had written near the end of his life, full of unexpected harmonic turns and a freeform approach to ragtime's usually strict sectional structure. Robinson's own music often followed similar lines. At times he seemed almost able to channel the spirit of Joplin, whose music he had learned by ear as a teenager from an album featuring Joplin's performances of his own works on piano rolls. His performances of Joplin's rags resembled Joplin's own, departing from the notated music in similar ways without reproducing them note for note. And Robinson's originals were complicated pieces that seemed to push, both structurally and technically, against the boundaries of the classic ragtime language. Robinson's rags were difficult for even experienced jazz pianists to play. "God, it would take me hours—years—to learn them," McPartland told Sachs. Occasionally Robinson ventured into vocal music or recorded other music of the ragtime era; *Euphonic Sounds* featured his rendition of the so-called "Negro National Anthem," James Weldon Johnson's "Lift Ev'ry Voice and Sing."

Faced Financial Problems

Despite praise from well-known figures like McPartland, Robinson fell on hard times after his first flash of celebrity faded. His albums on the small Delmark label brought him advances of between $1,000 and $3,000, plus royalties—not nearly enough to live on even though he moved in for a time with his mother, Janet. On the more lucrative ragtime festival circuit, Robinson was a fish out of water. "When you go to those ragtime festivals you see those little group of people with suspenders and ragtime buttons jumping around doing the cakewalk," Robinson explained to the Chicago *Reader.* "It's different for me. I live in Chicago and when I write a rag I can hear gunshots outside." He began taking odd jobs to make ends meet: at a packaging company in Chicago's suburbs, as a porter for a downtown car-rental agency.

Robinson assembled his fourth album; self-produced, it was entitled *Man Out of Time.* (One of his earlier pieces had been called "The Ragtime Pauper.") Those who heard the new album included Reich, who wrote that it "contains one intricate ragtime opus after another, each a world of pitch and rhythm unto itself." Robinson took the album to various labels, feeling that to agree to the $2,000 advance offered by tiny Delmark would be to sign his soul away, but he found no other takers. By 2002 Robinson had become discouraged about his musical prospects. He gradually stopped composing and even practicing. When the MacArthur Foundation called in the fall of 2004 to inform Robinson that he had received one of its $500,000 cash awards, he was lying in a West Side apartment in which the heat had been cut off.

Popularly termed "genius grants," the MacArthur Foundation fellowships are given to individuals not just in recognition of past accomplishments but to enable them to bring their new ideas to fruition. Things turned around in a hurry after Robinson received the award. "Engagements are here now that once seemed impossible to get," Robinson told the *Tribune.* "This has meant big respect." Looking to the future, Robinson hoped to educate younger audiences about the fascinating but often-forgotten music to which he had devoted his life. He enjoyed performing for young audiences. "Every school I play at, children are fascinated and affected by what I do," he told *Down Beat.* And he was an energetic advocate for ragtime's continuing relevance. "The syncopation that's in ragtime is in rap," he pointed out to the magazine. "Ragtime back then is like rap today. It wasn't considered music and it was pushed off, and now it's classic."

Selected discography

The Strongman, Delmark, 1993.
Sounds in Silhouette, Delmark, 1994.
Euphonic Sounds, Delmark, 1998.
Man Out of Time, self-issued, 2003.

Sources

Periodicals

Chicago Defender, March 30, 2004, p. 13.
Chicago Reader, June 19, 1998.
Chicago Sun-Times, January 30, 1994, p. 1; September 28, 2004, p. 4.
Chicago Tribune, November 21, 1993, p. 14; December 27, 2004, p. 1; May 1, 2005, p. 12.
Columbian (Vancouver, WA), February 12, 1995, p. 1.
Down Beat, December 2004, p. 24.
Milwaukee Journal-Sentinel, December 7, 1999, p. 6.
St. Louis Post-Dispatch, September 10, 2000, p. C4; September 28, 2004, p. A2.
Winston-Salem Journal, May 19, 2000, p. E5.

On-line

"Reginald R. Robinson," *MacArthur Fellows Program,* www.macfdn.org/programs/fel/fellows/robinson_reginald.htm (May 3, 2005).

—James M. Manheim

Marcus Samuelsson

1970—

Chef

Samuelsson, Marcus, photograph. Adam Rountree/Bloomberg News/Landov.

Celebrity chef Marcus Samuelsson and the New York City restaurant he co-owns, Aquavit, have each done their share to make Swedish cuisine one of the hot new culinary trends of the early twenty-first century. Born in Ethiopia but raised in Sweden, Samuelsson took over the executive chef's post at the Manhattan landmark eatery when he was just 24 years old, and "what then was a respectable Scandinavian restaurant best known among Swedish expatriates and comrades began to build a national reputation," noted Laura Yee in *Restaurants & Institutions.* In 2003 Samuelsson's first cookbook, *Aquavit and the New Scandinavian Cuisine,* was published to enthusiastic reviews that extolled his talents and the Aquavit dining experience.

Samuelsson was born in Ethiopia in 1970, but when he was three years old his parents died in a tuberculosis epidemic that swept the land. He and his sister were adopted by a Swedish couple, and grew up in Gothenburg, Sweden's second largest city and a major seaport on the North Sea. Though the country was a relatively homogenous place during Samuelsson's youth, with a scarce number of foreign-born residents, he said he never felt like an outsider. "Color was not an issue in Sweden," he told *Restaurant Business* writer Patricia Cobe. "My upbringing was very open-minded, and I never saw a hurdle I couldn't work through."

Samuelsson spent a great deal of time with his adoptive grandparents, and learned to cook at the side of his grandmother, who had once been the private chef for a well-to-do family. He learned the kitchen basics from her, but also a deeper appreciation for the art of sustenance. "We'd do things like go hunting for mushrooms, or go out fishing on our own when I was nine," he explained to Melissa Ewey Johnson in a *Black Issues Book Review* article. "By spending time with her and being raised around food and nature, I didn't just learn how to cook, I learned where food comes from, how to identify different things and combine ingredients to create unique flavors."

Samuelsson's first job was in a bakery, and he entered the Culinary Institute of Goteburg at the age of 16. Swedish cuisine was not considered at the same level as French or Italian, however, with Swedish meatballs perhaps the best-known dish outside of Scandinavia.

At a Glance . . .

Born in 1970 in Ethiopia; emigrated to Sweden, c. 1973, and to the United States, 1994. *Education:* Trained at the Culinary Institute of Goteborg, Sweden.

Career: Apprenticed at fine-dining establishments in Switzerland and Austria, late 1980s; Aquavit, New York City, chef's apprentice, 1991; Georges Blanc restaurant, Lyon, France, assistant chef, c. 1992-94; Aquavit, executive chef, 1994–, and partner, 1997–.

Awards: James Beard Foundation, rising-star chef award, 1999; James Beard Award for Best Chef, 2003.

Addresses: *Office*—Aquavit, 65 E. 55th St., New York NY 10022.

Sweden was for centuries an isolated northern land, and fish and other fruits of the sea were the mainstay of the national diet; the Swedes' devotion to herring, especially in pickled form, remained a solely national passion. The herring and other chilled fish delicacies were usually served with *akvavit,* a distilled alcoholic beverage similar to vodka but flavored with caraway or other spices, during an appetizer course.

While still in school, Samuelsson worked in a restaurant kitchen at night, and then completed apprenticeships at fine-dining establishments in Switzerland and Austria. He even worked on a cruise ship for a time. In 1991 he traveled to New York City and began an eight-month apprenticeship at Aquavit, the well-known New York City eatery. In business since 1987, the Upper East Side restaurant was considered the top Swedish-cuisine restaurant in North America.

After that, Samuelsson returned to Europe and worked at the legendary restaurant Georges Blanc, near the French city of Lyon. In 1994 Aquavit owner Hakan Swahn invited him back to New York. Swahn had recently hired a new executive chef and offered Samuelsson the second-in-command job. Two months later the executive chef died unexpectedly, and Samuelsson took over the job. He was just 24 years old at the time. Aquavit's daring new menu soon earned it three stars from the influential *New York Times* restaurant reviewer, making Samuelsson the youngest chef ever to win such an honor. In 1997 Swahn made him a partner in the restaurant, and two years later they opened a second Aquavit, this one in Minneapolis, Minnesota, a state that is home to a large number of Americans of Scandinavian heritage.

New York Times food critic William Grimes returned to the Manhattan Aquavit in 2001 and found its chef still "restlessly inventive" and "a fully mature artist with a distinctive style, the culinary version of counterpoint, in which precisely defined flavors talk back and forth to each other rather than blending into a single smooth harmonic effect. He keeps your palate on edge." Grimes wrote approvingly of several innovative dishes that came out of Samuelsson's kitchen, among them the Swedes' beloved dish. "Aquavit's herring plate, served with an icy shot of aquavit and a Carlsberg beer, amounts to a dazzling showcase for the national fish," Grimes wrote. "It's an infectious, show-off medley of marinades and herbal accents that makes the humble herring seem, for once, like a star."

Critics generally marvel, often in superlative terms, over the amalgam of flavors and textures that Samuelsson seems to invent out of thin air; at Aquavit, careful attention is also paid to what is sometimes a stunning moment of arrival. "A dish such as house-smoked salmon with poached quail egg, goat cheese parfait and osetra caviar is a testament to Aquavit's out-of-the-ordinary presentations—it arrives on an ice block—and attention to texture and temperature," wrote Yee in *Restaurants & Institutions*. "The parfait is frozen, while the quail egg contributes to the richness."

Samuelsson worked for years on his first book, *Aquavit and the New Scandinavian Cuisine,* which was published by Houghton Mifflin in 2003. Translating his elaborate Aquavit dishes into ones that were attainable in the kitchen of the average reader and cook was a particular challenge, he noted, but he was enthusiastic about broadening culinary horizons with his mix of old and new. The recipes in the book included some traditional items, such as gravlax—thinly sliced, cured salmon—and Swedish meatballs, but also some new items, such as Pickled Herring Sushi Style. He even found inspiration in his Ethiopian heritage with entrees like coffee-roasted duck breasts.

A *Publishers Weekly* review gave *Aquavit and the New Scandinavian Cuisine* high marks. "Samuelsson is one of our great chefs, and a warm-hearted and generous writer to boot," its reviewer noted. The publication of his first cookbook was just one of many notable achievements for Samuelsson in 2003: he won the James Beard Award for Best Chef and also opened Riingo, a new fusion restaurant with a heavily Japanese influence, in New York City. Aquavit moved to stunning new quarters in early 2005 on 65 E. 55th St., and it continued to win high marks from patrons and hard-to-please critics alike. Still, Samuelsson was pragmatic about the challenges of his profession. "You make more bad food than good," he said in a *Restaurant Hospitality* interview with Pat Fernberg. "When you cook, your goals are always changing, and you need to find a medium in which you can be happy—but not satisfied. It's bad for an artistic person to he satisfied, I think."

Selected writings

Aquavit and the New Scandinavian Cuisine, Houghton Mifflin, 2003

Sources

Periodicals

Black Issues Book Review, May-June 2004, p. 38.
Crain's New York Business, January 31, 2000, p. 27; February 14, 2005, p. 22.
Interview, September 2000, p. 148.
New York Post, March 16, 2005, p. 44.
New York Times, May 23, 2001, p. F9; October 26, 2003, p. 25.
Publishers Weekly, July 7, 2003, p. 67, p. 68.
Restaurant Business, August 15, 2003, p. 20.
Restaurant Hospitality, November 2003, p. 34; July 2004, p. 120.
Restaurants & Institutions, May 15, 2001, p. 63.
Star Tribune (Minneapolis, MN), October 23, 2003, p. 1T.
Time, October 20, 2003, p. 84.

—Carol Brennan

Barry Sanders

1968—

Professional football player

Barry Sanders was one of the greatest football players of the 1990s and perhaps of all time. Although he always described himself as an "average person," Barry Sanders' accomplishments playing football are truly extraordinary. In his three years at Oklahoma State University, Sanders broke or tied 24 NCAA records on his way to winning college football's top honor, the Heisman Trophy. He followed by signing a $6.1 million pro football contract with the Detroit Lions, one of the largest ever offered to a first-year player. His rookie year in the National Football League was also impressive: he fell ten yards shy of the season individual rushing title, was selected as a starter for the Pro Bowl, and was named the league's Rookie of the Year. Over the course of ten seasons, Sanders was consistently one of the top performers in the league, and by averaging over 1,500 yards rushing per season he was on pace to shatter the all-time NFL rushing record. Sanders took football fans by surprise, however, when he announced in 1999 that he had lost the desire to compete and retired from the NFL.

Slow Starter

Barry James Sanders was born on July 16, 1968, in Wichita, Kansas. He was one of 11 children born to William (a roofer) and Shirley (a registered nurse) Sanders. From early on, the Sanders siblings learned the value of hard work and dedication. As soon as they could handle the tools of the trade, he and his two brothers were pressed into service as roofer's assistants by their father. Of Sanders' boyhood apprenticeship, Mitch Albom of the *Detroit Free Press* wrote: "All day they would labor, with the hammers, with the tar, sweating in the hot summer sun. You did not complain in the Sanders family. Not unless you wanted a good whupping."

Sanders was a natural athlete, and the sport he loved most was basketball. His father, however, felt that he had a better chance of winning a college scholarship if he played football, and so Barry played football. Sanders didn't see much playing time until his senior year at North High School in Wichita. In the last five games of his senior year Sanders finally saw action and came to life, rushing for more than 1,000 yards, giving him a total of 1,417 yards for the year and nearly setting a city record. His late blossoming won him All-State and honorable All-American honors, but Sanders was overlooked by many Division 1-A schools because of his small size. Just a few colleges offered scholarships to Sanders, and he accepted the offer from Oklahoma State University in parts because of its strong business program.

The demands of big-time college football came as a shock to Sanders. He later told the *Sporting News:* "I remember in my freshman year we didn't have any days off. I couldn't believe it, and it never got any better. They pretended (football) wasn't the main thing you were there for, but you were doing it 50 or 60 hours a week. I fell behind in my schoolwork." As in high school, Sanders didn't see much playing time at first. But there were glimmers of his future greatness, as he led the nation in both kick-off returns and punt returns during his sophomore year. During his junior year

At a Glance . . .

Born on July 16, 1968, in Wichita, Kansas; son of William (a carpenter and roofer) and Shirley (a registered nurse) Sanders; married Lauren Campbell, November 11, 2000; children: three children. *Education*: Attended Oklahoma State University, 1985-88.

Career: Detroit Lions, National Football League, Professional football player, 1989-98.

Awards: *Sporting News* College All-America Team; 1987, Heisman Trophy Award, 1989; *Sporting News* NFL Rookie of the Year; 1989-90, Pro Bowl selection, 1989-98; NFC Most Valuable Player, NFL Players Association, 1991; *Sporting News* Player of the Year, 1997; inducted into the Pro Football Hall of Fame, 2004.

Addresses: *Office*—c/o Detroit Lions, 222 Republic Dr, Allen Park, Michigan 48101-3650.

Sanders set 13 NCAA rushing records, including gaining the most yards in one season (2,628) and the most touchdowns in one season (39). As a result, Sanders overwhelmingly won the 1988 Heisman Trophy, becoming only the eighth junior to receive the award, and winning in the tenth-largest point margin ever.

Triumphed in the NFL

Sanders decided to forego his senior year at college and make himself eligible for the NFL draft, a move prompted by the NCAA putting the OSU Cowboys on probation after the 1988 season and Sanders' desire to relieve financial burdens on his family. His $6.1 million, five-year contract with the Detroit Lions—which carried with it a $2.1 million bonus—was one of the largest ever offered to a rookie. And as the statistics in his first year indicate, Sanders was worth the money. Although he didn't start the first two games of the season and missed parts of two others, Sanders managed to set the Lions' season rushing record and came just 10 yards short of the NFL's individual season rushing record—which he accomplished with 90 fewer carries than the winner, Christian Okoye.

People were impressed by Sanders' numbers, naturally, but they were even more impressed by the way he piled up the yards. Sanders was an amazingly difficult running back to tackle; he kept a low center of gravity and used a dizzying arrays of spins and turns to elude tacklers. "I remember bracing myself to hit him," recalled Chicago Bears defensive end Trace Armstrong in *Sports Illustrated*. "He just stopped and turned, and he was gone. He's like a little sports car. He can stop on a dime and go zero to 60 in seconds." After watching two of Sanders' performances in his first season, ex-Chicago Bear Walter Payton, then the NFL's all-time leading rusher, said of the speedy 5'-8", 200-pound running back: "I don't know if I was ever *that* good." Green Bay Packers linebacker Brian Noble similarly remarked: "He runs so low to the ground and is so strong and elusive; it makes him very difficult to get a piece of him. You never get *the* shot at him. Usually, when you get to him, he's not there anymore." Pat Jones, Sanders' college coach, had this to say in *Sporting News*: "If someone was to ask me who the most explosive back I've coached is, that would be Barry, as far as a guy who can take your breath away and is liable to score on every down.... I don't know that I've ever seen anyone like him with my own eyes."

Nearly as striking as his accomplishments on the field was Sanders' modest demeanor off the field. Sanders was notoriously reticent to discuss his play, preferring instead to divert attention toward his teammates. He told the *Sporting News* that he was "uncomfortable being valued because of how well I play football" and that he sees a liability in realizing he is an exceptional player. "If that's the case, I can prove it on the field. I don't have to talk about [it]. That's where athletes have problems off the field. People treat them differently and you start thinking you're better than everybody else. You're not."

During his second season game with the Lions, Sanders had the opportunity to enter the last game of the season and obtain the 10 yards he needed for the league season rushing record. Sanders insisted, however, that Coach Wayne Fontes continue playing back-up running back, Tony Paige. When Sanders was later asked if he had any regrets about not winning the rushing title, he told Austin Murphy in *Sports Illustrated*: "I satisfied my ego last season." A deeply religious person, Sanders also prefers to keep that side to himself. Said Fontes in *Sports Illustrated*: "He doesn't wear his beliefs on his sleeve.... Barry's not the type of guy who scores a TD and kneels down in front of everyone in the world. He's not for show, he's for real."

Retired on the Edge of Glory

Over the next nine seasons as a Lion, Sanders continued to chalk up amazing numbers. Averaging 4.5 yards per rushing attempt in 1991, he compiled a total of 1,548 yards and scored 16 touchdowns rushing. In 1992 his total rushing yardage slipped 1,352, and he averaged 4.3 yards per rushing attempt. Plagued by injury in 1993, Sanders managed to pile up only 1,115 rushing yards, yet he pushed his average per rushing attempt to 4.6 yards. Sanders broke through for 1,883 yards during the 1994 season, averaging 5.7 yards per rushing attempt but scoring only seven touchdowns rushing. The next year he averaged 4.8 yards per rushing attempt for a total of 1,500 yards and 11 touchdowns rushing. In 1996 Sanders averaged 5.1 yards per rushing attempt for a total of 1,553 yards and 11 touchdowns rushing. In 1997 he dashed for 2,053 yards, averaging a stunning 6.1 yards per rushing attempt. Sanders' rushing yardage slipped just below the 1,500-mark in 1998, when he averaged only 4.3 yards per rushing attempt. At the end of the 1998 season, Sanders had a career total of 15,269, trailing the career record of 16,726 set by Walter Payton by only 1,457 yards. Around the NFL, people spoke openly about the chance that Sanders might break the career rushing record during the 1999 season.

The expectations of the football world were crushed, however, when Sanders announced just prior to the opening of training camp in 1999 that he was retiring from football. "The reason I am retiring is simple," Sanders said in a press release, "My desire to exit the game is greater than my desire to remain in it. I have searched my heart through and through and feel comfortable with this decision." Fans and sportswriters agonized over Sanders' decision, wondering whether Sanders was just holding out for more money or was trying to get traded to a team more likely to advance in the playoffs than the perennially hapless Lions. He engaged in an acrimonious dispute with the Lions over the money remaining on his contract, and was eventually ordered to return several million dollars to the team. In the end, Sanders remained true to his word and stayed retired. His enshrinement in the Pro Football Hall of Fame in 2004, alongside Carl Eller and Bob Brown, seemed to end the persistent rumors about his return to football. In his induction ceremony Sanders proclaimed that the only thing that he missed in his career was the thrill of playing in the Super Bowl. He still lives in the Detroit area with his wife, Lauren, and their three children.

Sources

Books

Knapp, Ron, *Sports Great Barry Sanders,* Springfield, NJ: Enslow, 1999.

Sanders, Barry, with Mark E. McCormick, *Barry Sanders* (includes DVD), Indianapolis: B. Sanders with Emmis Books, 2003.

Periodicals

Detroit Free Press, December 17, 1989.

Jet, January 9, 1989; February 13, 1989; May 29, 1989.

New York Times, November 23, 1988; December 4, 1988; January 1, 1989; March 31, 1989; April 5, 1989; September 12, 1989; September 15, 1989.

Sport, November 1, 1994; September 1, 1998.

Sporting News, October 24, 1988; April 24, 1989; November 20, 1989; January 15, 1990; December 4, 1995; July 21, 1997; August 10, 1998; September 7, 1998; August 9, 1999.

Sports Illustrated, April 10, 1989; September 10, 1990; August 9, 1999; February 3, 2003; December 6, 2004.

On-line

Barry Sanders: The Official Site. www.barrysanders.com (August 4, 2005).

—Michael E. Mueller and Tom Pendergast

Isabel Sanford

1917-2004

Actress

Sanford, Isabel, photograph. EPA/Landov.

Best known for her portrayal of Louise Jefferson—Weezy—on the hit television situation comedy *The Jeffersons*, Isabel Sanford became the first black woman to win an Emmy award for best actress in a comedy series. Sanford's acting career included stage and film, as well as television stardom. In her early life as a young cleaning woman, then a housewife, and later a single mother holding down a day job, her chances of succeeding as an actress appeared nonexistent. Indeed Sanford's career did not take off until she was almost 50. She told *Contemporary Theater, Film and Television* in 2002: "If there's anything in life you consider worthwhile achieving—go for it. I was told many times to forget show business, I had nothing going for me. But I pursued it anyway."

Isabel Gwendolyn Sanford was born on August 29, 1917, in Harlem, New York, the daughter of James Edward and Josephine (Perry) Sanford. She was the last of the couple's seven children and the only one to survive infancy. Growing up poor in New York, Isabel became interested in the stage during elementary school. As a teen she sang in nightclubs against the wishes—and sometimes knowledge—of her mother. She performed at amateur nights at the Apollo Theater in Harlem, and by high school she knew that she wanted to become an actress. When her mother died, however, Sanford took over her cleaning job to help support her father.

Although her path to stardom was slow and often interrupted, Sanford never lost her interest in acting and took advantages of opportunities as they arose. Sanford's training began in the 1930s when she joined the Star Players, which later became the American Negro Theater. However when performance venues closed during World War II, the theater group languished for a time. Sanford then focused her energies on her family—her husband William Edward Richmond and their three children. But even as a housewife, she kept her eye out for acting jobs. She made her professional stage debut with the American Negro Theater's production of *On Stivers Row* in 1946 and appeared in several other Off-Broadway productions.

When her estranged husband drowned in 1960, Sanford returned to acting to supplement her income as a data processor for IBM. She went on a national tour with *Here Today* and made her Broadway debut in the

At a Glance . . .

Born Isabel (Eloise?) Gwendolyn Sanford on August 29, 1917, in New York City; died on July 9, 2004, in Los Angeles, CA; married William Edward Richmond; children: Pamela Ruff, William Eric, and Sanford Keith Sanford.

Career: Actress, stage, 1946-1993; film, 1967-1999; television, 1967-2004.

Memberships: Kwanza Foundation, corresponding secretary, 1973.

Awards: "Y" Drama Guild, New York City YMCA, Trouper Award, 1965; National Association for the Advancement of Colored People (NAACP), Image Award for Best Actress in Comedy Role, 1975; 20 Grand Salutes, Outstanding Actress, 1976; NAACP, TV Image Award for Best Actress, 1978; Emmy Award, Best Actress in a Comedy Series, 1981, for *The Jeffersons;* Hollywood Walk of Fame, star, 2004.

1965 production of James Baldwin's *The Amen Corner*. There she came to the notice of film director Stanley Kramer. He cast her as the outspoken housekeeper Tillie in the film *Guess Who's Coming to Dinner?*—a classic interracial love story starring Sidney Poitier, Katharine Hepburn, and Spencer Tracy.

Sanford moved her family to Los Angeles, California, to further her career. There she began appearing on television. Between 1967 and 1969 she performed on *The Carol Burnett Show* and made guest appearances on *Julia*, *The Mod Squad*, and *Bewitched*. Sanford continued to appear on stage and she toured the United States in *Nobody Loves an Albatross* and *Funny Girl*. She also appeared in various films including the 1972 story of singer Billy Holiday, *Lady Sings the Blues*.

In 1971 Sanford was cast as Louise Jefferson, the friend and neighbor of Edith Bunker, on the controversial hit sitcom *All in the Family*. Louise's blustery husband, George Jefferson, played by Sherman Hensley, nicknamed his wise-cracking, strong-willed wife Weezy. The couple proved so popular that in 1975 producer Norman Lear spun off *The Jeffersons* as its own series. George Jefferson's dry-cleaning establishment became a chain and the Jeffersons left Archie and Edith Bunker behind in their working-class Queens neighborhood. The newly-rich Jeffersons moved into a penthouse on Manhattan's Upper East Side. The series ran for 11 seasons before going into reruns. *The Jeffersons* was a fan favorite. In addition to her six Emmy nominations, Sanford was nominated three times for the Golden Globe Award for Best Performance by an Actress in a TV-Series-Comedy/Musical.

The Jeffersons was considered groundbreaking television. It was the first series featuring a mostly-black cast since the infamous *Amos 'n' Andy Show* was cancelled in 1953. It was the first television series to feature an upwardly-mobile black American family and its theme song was "Movin' On Up." *The Jeffersons* was a socially relevant sitcom that dealt with racial issues and tensions. American TV's first prime-time interracial married couple appeared on *The Jeffersons*. Although the black community remained divided over the show's message, it appealed to large audiences, both black and white. Sanford especially enjoyed the show's continuing appeal. She loved getting mail from fans who saw *The Jeffersons* for the first time as reruns. Her longtime manager Brad Lemack told *Hollywood Reporter* in 2004: "She was just amazed and so pleased that the show had that kind of lasting power and entertainment because she loved to make people laugh."

Isabel Sanford continued to appear on stage and in films and on television until shortly before her death. In 1993 she reunited with other cast members for a live stage production, *The Best of the Jeffersons*, in which they reenacted some of the most popular television episodes. Between 1968 and 2004 Sanford made numerous guest appearances on television series and specials and was a popular guest panelist. In 2004 her voice was heard on an episode of *The Simpsons*.

In their later years Sanford and Sherman Hensley resurrected Louise and George Jefferson in television commercials for Denny's restaurants and other sponsors. Isabel Sanford also sold Old Navy clothing and Lipton Tea on television. She was noted for her philanthropy and established a scholarship for minority students at Emerson College in Boston, Massachusetts. In January of 2004 Sanford received a star on the Hollywood Walk of Fame. *Hollywood Reporter* quoted her as saying: "Here with stars in my eyes—something that I dreamed about when I was 9 years old."

Sanford died of natural causes on July 9, 2004, in Los Angeles. She was 86. Her health had been failing during the previous months, following preventative surgery on an artery in her neck. In a tribute to Sanford in *Entertainment Weekly* at the end of 2004, Norman Lear—creator, writer, and director of *All in the Family*—wrote: "Isabel was a universal actress. She brought much more woman and mother to the character of Weezy than she did black woman or black mother. I don't think people thought of The Jeffersons as a 'black show.' They were simply tuning in to a funny show about a family they knew, and Isabel was the key to its appeal."

Selected works

Films

Guess Who's Coming to Dinner? 1967.
The Young Runaways, 1968.
The Comic, 1969.
Pendulum, 1969.
The Red, White, and Black, 1970.
Hickey & Boggs, 1972.
Lady Sings the Blues, 1972.
The New Centurions, 1972.
Stand Up and Be Counted, 1972.
Up the Sandbox, 1972.
The Photographer, 1975.
Love at First Bite, 1979.
Desperate Moves, 1981.
Pucker Up and Bark Like a Dog, 1990.
South Beach, 1992.
Original Gangstas, 1996.
Sprung, 1997.
Click Three Times (short film), 1999.

Plays

On Stivers Row, 1946.
The Amen Corner, 1965.
And Mama Makes Three, 1977.
Night of 100 Stars, Radio City Music Hall, 1982.
The Subject Was Roses, 1988.
The Best of the Jeffersons, 1993.

Television

All in the Family, 1971-75.
The Great Man's Whiskers (television movie), 1972.
The Jeffersons, 1975-85.
Honeymoon Hotel, 1987.
A Pup Named Scooby-Do (voice), 1988.
Jackie's Back! (television movie), 1999.
Intimate Portrait: Isabel Sanford, 2003.

Sources

Books

"Isabel Sanford," *Contemporary Theatre, Film and Television*, Volume 43, Gale Group, 2002.

Periodicals

Entertainment Weekly, July 23, 2004, p. 14; December 31, 2004, p. 100.
Hollywood Reporter, July 13, 2004, pp. 4-5.
Jet, August 2, 2004, pp. 61-2.
Los Angeles Times, July 13, 2004.
People Weekly, July 26, 2004, p. 69.
Washington Post, July 13, 2004, p. B6.

—Margaret Alic

Stephanie Sears

1964—

Sociology professor

Sears, Stephanie, photograph. Photo by Anthony R. Baker. Courtesy of Stephanie Sears.

Dr. Stephanie Sears, Assistant Professor of Sociology at the University of San Francisco, received a Ph.D. from Yale University in 2004 for her research and study of sociology and African-American studies. Seeking to better the lives of youth through her work, Sears' research explores empowerment and resistance in the lives of young women of color in an effort to explain the role that gender plays. Questions about race, class, and gender, and an absolute love for books and learning drive her search for answers to subjects that she finds compelling. Her exploration of these questions and her wish to better understand her own experience with adversity and loss have earned her numerous teaching fellowships, research grants, and awards at both USF and Yale.

Sears was born in Indianapolis, Indiana, on January 20, 1964, and was raised in Bloomington, Indiana, by her grandmother, Lavenia Norris, after the death of her mother, Patricia Redding Sears. Her father, Richard Sears, worked as a barber and was a former Green Beret. Sears always enjoyed school. At the predominately black St. Rita's Elementary School back in Indianapolis, students engaged in friendly academic competition. "We were all excited about getting good grades," Sears said in an interview with *Contemporary Black Biography* (*CBB*). She also had a special affection for her teachers. "I loved them because my mom was a teacher," said Sears. "I remember my mother's classroom. She wrote poems, and I'd watch her grade papers; it was a source of pride for me."

Norris would tell Sears stories of her mother's many accomplishments, her intelligence, her oratory awards, and her sense of humor. "My grandmother encouraged me to follow the same path," Sears said. "She spoke about her own life growing up during the depression and the hardships and racism she experienced. She had a sense of how racism worked at-large, and she also raised me to be aware of that, not to let that limit what I could do or who I thought I was." And she was there for Sears through the difficult days after Patricia's death. "It was my grandmother's efforts that allowed me to move through that moment," Sears said.

Sears graduated from Bloomington High School in 1982 and entered Stanford University. During this time she had begun to wonder why she had succeeded

At a Glance . . .

Born Stephanie Dawn Sears on January 20, 1964, in Indianapolis, IN; married Anthony R. Baker, 1996; children: Zoë, Asha. *Education:* Yale University, Joint PhD, African and African-American studies and sociology, 2004; Yale University, MPhil, African and African-American studies and sociology, 2001; San Francisco State University, MA, ethnic studies, 1994; Stanford University, BA, psychology, 1987.

Career: San Francisco Peer Resources, San Francisco, CA, high school coordinator, 1989-94; Girls After School Academy, San Francisco, CA, board president, 1993-94; Girls After School Academy, San Francisco, CA, board president, 1998-2000; California Association for the Education of Young Children's (CAEYC) Diversity and Equity Project, San Francisco, CA, lead researcher, 2002-03; California Tomorrow's Diversity in Health Care Project, San Francisco, CA, 2002-03; University of San Francisco, San Francisco, CA, sociology professor, 2002–.

Memberships: Delta Sigma Theta Sorority; Pacific Sociological Association; Society for the Study of Social Problems.

Awards: Yale University fellowship, 1994-98; Graduate Student Award for Distinguished Achievement in Ethnic Studies from San Francisco State University, 1995; Yale University African and African-American Studies Department Research Grant, 1999; Yale University Dissertation Fellowship, 1999-2000; Irvine Minority Scholar Dissertation Fellowship, 2002-03.

Addresses: *Office*—Sociology Department, University of San Francisco, 2130 Fulton Street, San Francisco, CA 94117.

despite her mother's death, and why some of her friends appeared to be falling apart in the wake of less tragic events. Sears decided then to major in psychology and focus on "coping strategies and resiliency among youth." Sears said, "Reading was an escape for me that allowed me to flourish academically, which then created time for me to transition. With that strong academic base I was able to maintain myself in a certain way, which then set me up well for high school and college." But her questions persisted. She wanted to understand why men and women make certain choices in their lives and was intrigued by the ability of humans to survive. "And I was curious about my mother," Sears said. "I found these questions fascinating. To better understand, Sears took African-American studies courses and several that focused on black women's experiences in the United States. She also joined Delta Sigma Theta Sorority, a predominantly black non-profit organization dedicated to supporting communities throughout the world.

Unlike the move from a predominately black Catholic school to a white public school that Sears experienced back in Bloomington, the adjustment to Stanford was not necessarily about race but about class, Sears explained to *CBB*. She learned what social wealth meant as she began to comprehend the level of society many on campus were connected to. "Prior to that I never really thought about it. Back then I thought our family was probably middle-class," she said. "At Stanford I realized that we were lucky if we were working-class. I had never been exposed to young people with that amount of money before. I saw them driving Porsches. It was mind-boggling. At first I felt out of my league; it took some time to figure out how I needed to maneuver in this environment."

She also realized that despite the enormous wealth around her there were others struggling like herself. After a couple of years navigating academic life Sears knew she had nailed it, just as her grandmother had urged. She had refused to let anything make her feel that she did not belong. "So it was also through academics that I figured out that I did fit," she told *CBB*. Stanford awarded her a bachelor's in psychology in 1987. Sears continued her studies at San Francisco State University, earning a master's degree in 1994. But she didn't stop there. She soon entered Yale University.

About entering graduate school at Yale, Sears said she was ready because of her work with young people around issues of AIDS and racism and her thesis work—the Nia Project, a rites-of-passage program for African-American girls. This project had grown out of her work with support groups for girls of color at Galileo High School in San Francisco, and became the basis for the development and implementation of an ongoing program.

The success of this early project had piqued Sears' interest. "I just wanted to learn more," Sears said. "I wanted to get a better grasp of poverty and public education and the relationship between the two. I felt like the knowledge I had couldn't explain what I was seeing anymore. I went back to school to get that larger framework to help me explain what I was experiencing when we were trying to set up the Girls After School Academy (GASA) in a public housing development. I realized that I needed a better understanding of larger structural issues, how class works on a deeper level." Sears would later become the first chairperson on the board of directors for GASA.

In 2004 Sears earned a joint Ph.D. in African and African-American studies and sociology from Yale. Sears describes her Ph D. dissertation, "Imagining Black Womanhood," as "a case study of the identity work within an Afrocentric womanist after-school program for low-income black girls." In her dissertation Sears examines "what happens when women with vision and good intentions go into low income neighborhoods to work with girls."

Along the way to her Ph.D. Sears earned a Graduate Student Award for Distinguished Achievement in ethnic studies from San Francisco State in 1995. In 1997 she was nominated for the Yale University's Prize Teaching Fellowship. Sears worked as lead researcher for the California Association for the Education of Young Children's (CAEYC) Diversity and Equity Project, as a consultant for California Tomorrow's Diversity in Health Care Project, and was a director of Programs for the Girls After School Academy.

To get beyond adversity and the rigors of academia Sears said, "One has to deal with their fears and understand that fear is natural, it is not only paralyzing but also very motivating. My friends and family helped me. I just needed to be able to voice my fears and say how challenging it was for me. Once I did that they pushed me to remember the reasons for my goals and to ask for what I needed."

Selected writings

Other

"Africentric Womanism Meets The Urban Girl," *Yale's Department of Sociology Works in Progress Conference,* 1999.

"The Included Excludeds: African American Women & the Million Man March," *Yale's Department of Sociology Works in Progress Conference,* 1995.

"Constructing Safe Space: The Organizational Power Matrix and the Facilitation of Empowerment within the Girls Empowerment Project," *Pacific Sociological Association, 76th Annual Meeting,* 2005.

Sources

On-line

"Sociology of Gender," *University of San Francisco,* http://artsci.usfca.edu/servlet/ShowEmployee?empID=239 (April 1, 2005).

Other

Additional information for this profile was obtained through an interview with Dr. Stephanie Sears on April 9, 2005.

—Sharon Melson Fletcher

John Brooks Slaughter

1934—

Electrical engineer, physicist

Dr. John Slaughter's career has in many ways traveled a wide circle, leading him from the radio repair shop that helped pay his college tuition, to high-tech electrical engineering jobs, and then back to school as the president of two nationally respected colleges. His most recent job, the presidency of the National Action Council for Minorities in Engineering (NACME) makes the circle complete. As the largest provider of scholarships for African American, Latino, and Native American students, NACME's mission is to increase the number of minorities in engineering. Slaughter is now in a position to fulfill his own mission—to help students who, like young John Slaughter, have little money or support from mainstream society, but have a fierce desire to learn engineering technology.

Experienced Segregation

Slaughter was born in Topeka, Kansas, on March 16, 1934. His father, Reuben Brooks Slaughter, was a resourceful, hard-working man who held a variety of jobs to support his family, from selling used furniture to custodial work. Slaughter's mother, Dora Reeves Slaughter, worked in the home taking care of young John and his three sisters, as well as doing occasional domestic work to contribute to the family income. Reuben Slaughter had been born in Alabama. He had come to Kansas to work in the coal mines and met Dora Reeves, whose family had lived in Topeka for several generations. After Dora and Reuben married, they lived and raised their children in the Reeves family home.

Though Kansas was a racially segregated state during the 1930s and 1940s, the Slaughters lived in a mostly white neighborhood, and young John and his sisters had both white and black friends. He attended an all-black elementary school, but his junior high and high school were mixed, with about 10 to 15 percent students of color. Though his classes were integrated, extracurricular events, such as sports and parties, were segregated. Slaughter and his friends experienced little overt racial hostility, but they did feel tension within the segregated system. "The black and white kids on the block would all start out walking to school together, but the white children went to a separate school, much closer to our homes. We would say goodbye, then proceed to Buchanan, the all-black school. We'd meet up again on the way home and often get into little fights. It was like we knew some- thing was wrong. Then, later, we'd all play ball together," Slaughter told *Contemporary Black Biography* (*CBB*).

It was in Topeka, Kansas, that the court case that ended segregation would begin, in 1952, the year after John Slaughter graduated from Topeka High School. His first cousin, Lucinda Todd, an active member of the National Association for the Advancement of Colored People (NAACP), was instrumental in the successful outcome of the case that became famous as *Brown versus the Board of Education.*

Developed Early Interest in Engineering

Slaughter enjoyed school and looked forward to going

At a Glance . . .

Born on March 16, 1934, in Topeka, Kansas; Ida Bernice Johnson August 31, 1956; children: John II, Jacqueline Michelle. *Education:* Kansas State University, BS, electrical engineering, 1956; University of California, Los Angeles, MS, engineering, 1961; University of California, San Diego, PhD, engineering science, 1971.

Career: General Dynamics Corporation, electronics engineer, 1956-60; U.S. Naval Electronics Laboratory Center, San Diego, Information Systems Technology Department, engineer and department head, 1960-75; University of Washington, Applied Physics Laboratory, director; Electrical Engineering department, professor, 1975-77; National Science Foundation, assistant director for Astronomical, Atmospheric, Earth and Ocean Sciences, 1977-79; Washington State University, academic vice president and provost, 1979-80; National Science Foundation director, 1980-82; University of Maryland, College Park, chancellor, 1982-88; Occidental College, president, 1988-99; University of Southern California; Irving R. Melbo Professor of Leadership in Education, 1999-2000, National Action Council for Minorities in Engineering, Inc. (NACME), president and CEO, 2000–.

Selected memberships: Zeta Sigma Lambda Chapter of Alpha Phi Alpha, president, 1956-60; American Association for the Advancement of Science; National Collegiate Athletic Association, chairman of the president's commission, 1986-88; Los Angeles World Affairs Council, board of directors 1990-96; National Academy of Engineering.

Selected awards: UCLA, Distinguished Alumnus of the Year Award, 1978; Topeka High School Hall of Fame, 1983; U.S. Black Engineer of the Year, 1987; American Society for Engineering Education Hall of Fame, 1993; Kansas Native Sons and Daughters, Kansan of the Year, 1994; National Academy of Engineering, Arthur M. Bueche Award, 2004.

Addresses: *Office*—NACME, Inc., 440 Hamilton Ave, Suite 302, White Plains NY 10601-1813.

to class. He loved reading, played baseball, and ran track. He developed his interest in engineering early, making many of his own toys. Fascinated to learn how things worked, he took his bicycle apart and put it back together every week. He read *Popular Mechanics* regularly, devoting many hours to building the cameras, radios, and other electronic devices he found in the magazine. By the time he was in eighth grade, he knew he wanted to be an engineer.

During his senior year in high school, Slaughter found a practical use for his hobby. He had taught himself to repair radios, and his father helped him set up a shop in his back yard. As a radio repairman, he not only honed his electrical skills, he earned the money for his higher education.

Though his family had little history of attending college, it seemed natural to Slaughter to pursue his education. Because teachers assumed that black students would not go on to college, they were frequently tracked into vocational courses. Upon graduation, Slaughter realized that he had not taken many of the science and math courses he needed for college, so he went to a local liberal arts college to take the classes he lacked. After two years at Washburn University, Slaughter was accepted into the engineering program at Kansas State University. He graduated in 1956 with a bachelor's degree in electrical engineering.

While still at Kansas State, he was offered a job at Convair, an aircraft manufacturing division of General Dynamics Corporation. The job would require moving to San Diego, California, which pleased Slaughter for two reasons. First, he felt that opportunities for advancement in technical engineering fields would be greater in California. Second, his girlfriend Ida Johnson had taken a teaching job in San Diego. Slaughter took the job at Convair, and he and Ida were married that year. While working at Convair, Slaughter returned to school, taking classes at night to earn his master's degree. Though it was not easy to go to school while working full time, Slaughter loved school and was always happiest when studying.

Advanced Working for the U.S. Government

In 1960, he left his job at Convair and went to work as a civilian at the United States Naval Electronics Laboratory Center in San Diego. He worked for the Navy for 15 years, becoming director of the Information Systems Technology Department, and earning his PhD in engineering science. Much of Slaughter's work for the Navy involved developing automatic control systems, the built-in computer controls that operate within aircraft and on ships, such as radar, navigation, and missile systems. He was among the first engineers to use digital computers to control large electromechanical devices.

In 1975, Slaughter was offered the job of director of the Applied Physics Laboratory, a U.S. Navy-supported research and development facility at the University of Washington in Seattle. He took the job and moved with his family to Bellevue, Washington, happy to be working in the university environment. After two years at the University of Washington, Slaughter received his next job through presidential appointment.

In 1977, President Jimmy Carter named John Slaughter as assistant director of the Astronomical, Atmospheric, Earth and Ocean Sciences directorate of the National Science Foundation in Washington, D.C. The NSF is the major funder for scientific research at college and university laboratories throughout the United States.

After two years on the east coast, Slaughter returned to Washington, this time to take the job of academic vice president and provost at Washington State University in the eastern part of the state. It was the first time he had been part of a college administration, and he liked the work very much. He began to feel that his experience as an African American student in a field that had long been dominated by whites could enable him to influence the direction of the university in a very positive way. However, he remained at WSU for only a year before an historical presidential appointment led him to change jobs again.

In 1980, Slaughter became the first African American to be appointed to direct the National Science Foundation. Though he was reluctant at first to leave his job at Washington State, he was unable to refuse a personal request from President Carter. Once again, he found working in the nation's capitol to be stimulating, and he enjoyed supporting academic scientific research, especially at historically black colleges and universities.

Held Top University Position

In 1982, he left the NSF to return to the academic world he loved. He became chancellor, or president, of the University of Maryland. There, he was again able to exert a positive influence on the school's development. The University of Maryland had been a segregated, all-white school until 1954. Even in 1982, when Slaughter took over as chancellor, little had been done to increase diversity among the students and faculty. During Slaughter's years at Maryland, from 1982 until 1988, he made a determined effort to introduce the idea that diversity was a positive and necessary element of any first-rate university. One of his proudest accomplishments would be the rating of the University of Maryland as a leader in diversity among major American universities.

One of the elements of college administration that appealed the most to Slaughter was the opportunity to know students and assist them personally. His next career move would be guided by this desire. In 1988 he took the job of president of Occidental College, a small, largely white, liberal arts college in Los Angeles, California. While over thirty thousand students had attended the University of Maryland, Occidental had a student body of only 1600. Though never officially segregated, minorities had not been drawn to Occidental, partly because it was an expensive private college, and partly because it had no diversity programs aimed at encouraging minority enrollment. During his 11 years at Occidental, Slaughter's programs transformed the school into a much more diverse reflection of the city that is its home. Like the University of Maryland, Occidental became a model of diversity and was named the most diverse liberal arts college in America.

In 1999 Slaughter retired from the presidency of Occidental. However, complete retirement has not come easily to the tireless engineer, administrator, and academic. That same year he took a teaching chair at the University of Southern California, passing on his own experiences by teaching courses in diversity and leadership.

But within a year, he received another call that he simply could not refuse. The National Action Council for Minorities in Engineering offered him the position of president and chief executive officer. NACME's mission of increasing the number of engineers of color was so close to Slaughter's own personal mission that he found the job irresistible. While maintaining the family home in California, he moved to Stamford, Connecticut, to help NACME in its effort to provide scholarships for African American, Native American, and Latino students. In this way, Slaughter can offer a helping hand to all the children of color who spend their weekends taking things apart to see how they work and dream of creating new technologies.

Sources

Periodicals

Chronicle of Higher Education, April 13, 1988, pp. A23-5; July 2, 1999, pp. A33-5.
Jet, April 25, 1988, p. 25.
Meet the Press, June 29, 1986, pp. 1-10.
Science, August 1, 1980, pp. 569-71.
Washington Post, November 17, 1987, p. B3.

On-line

"John Brooks Slaughter," *Biography Resource Center,* http://galenet.galegroup.com/servlet/BioRC (May 19, 2005).
"The Faces of Science: African Americans in the Sciences," *Princeton University,* www.princeton.edu/~mcbrown/display/slaughter.html (May 12, 2005).
NACME, www.nacme.org/ (June 14, 2005).

Other

Information for this profile was obtained through an interview with Dr. John Slaughter on June 14, 2005.

—Tina Gianoulis

Bruce W. Smith

19??—

Animator

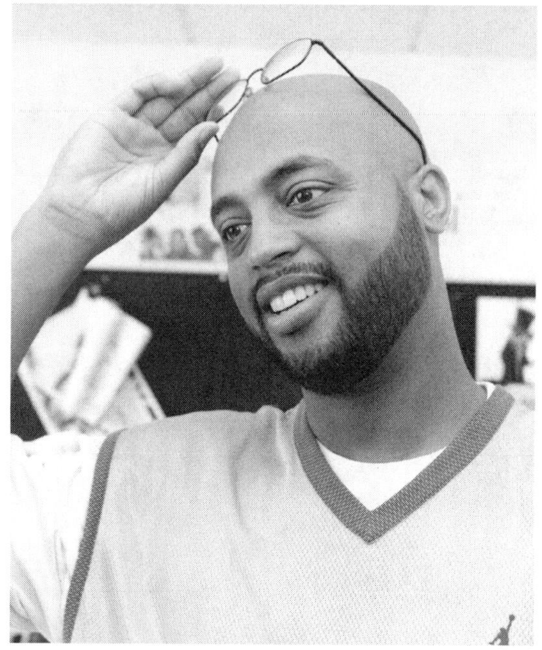

Smith, Bruce W., photograph. AP/Wide World Photos. Reproduced by permission.

Considered one of the leading talents among a new generation of animators, Bruce W. Smith has broadened the array of multicultural cartoon characters seen on television and in films. Through his Jambalaya Studio, he has created programs for children and families that focus on authentic depictions of life among racially and ethnically diverse communities.

Was a Cartoon Fanatic

Growing up in South Central Los Angeles, Smith was a "cartoon fanatic," as he noted in a *Jet* article. He loved comic books and animated television series, such *The Flintstones* and Bill Cosby's *Fat Albert*, as well as Disney animated movies. Yet he was frustrated that these shows didn't include any characters like himself or his friends. He decided that he would make his own artwork based on his own experiences. While his older brothers shot hoops, he spent his time sketching stories and creating his own cartoons. He even drew a comic strip based on the live-action sitcom *Sanford and Son*. "I was huge into the whole 'blaxploitation period,'" he admitted in a *Celebrating Children* article.

Smith began attending animation classes at age ten, after his fourth grade teacher noticed his artistic skills and helped arrange for classes. He became the designated class artist for various school projects, and by the time he was 12 had made his first animated movie. Through high school, the aspiring artist continued with extracurricular classes, intent on making art his career. "I was going to do whatever I could—even if it meant 7/11 wages or $5 an hour," he told a writer for the *Trinidad Guardian*. "It was about getting happy for doing something you love." After graduating from high school, Smith enrolled at the California Institute of the Arts. Offered a summer internship and the chance to work full-time in a studio, Smith chose to leave school before getting his degree. It was the right move, he noted in the *Guardian*, because it gave him the opportunity to work with experts at their craft.

Jobs with major studios soon followed. Smith worked as an animator on the groundbreaking film *Who Framed Roger Rabbit?*, a mix of live action and animation that was one of the top-grossing films of 1988 winning four Academy Awards. Critics raved

At a Glance . . .

Born in Los Angeles, California; married, wife's name Denise; children: four. *Education:* Attended California Institute of the Arts.

Career: Animator; Jambalaya Studio, Glendale, CA, cofounder and director, 1999–.

Addresses: *Office*—c/o Warner Brothers, 4000 Warner Blvd., Burbank, CA 91522.

about the film's creative audacity; *New York Times* writer Janet Maslin hailed its "wildly inventive" interchanges between cartoon and human characters, and praised its animators and other creative crew members for making the film's magic seem "effortless." Smith also provided animation for another Roger Rabbit film, *Tummy Trouble*. Smith then worked on character design for *Bebe's Kids*, and as animation supervisor for *The Pagemaster*, another film blending live action and animation. Subsequent projects included character design for *A Goofy Movie* and for the television series *C-Bear and Jamal*.

In 1996 Smith tackled his first directing project with the film *Space Jam*, on which he served as co-director of animation. Like *Roger Rabbit*, this film—in which Looney Tunes characters (including Bugs Bunny and Daffy Duck) convince real-life basketball superstar Michael Jordan to help them win a game against space aliens—utilized many new animation technologies. *Boston Globe* critic Jay Carr noted that the movie exploited the "antic wildness" of the original cartoons, observing that its animators "run the ball into a few new realms of animation, cleverly using the technology as opposed to letting the technology use them.... After *Space Jam*, athletes are going to start lining up outside animators' studios." Smith subsequently worked as supervising animator for the character Kerchak in Disney's *Tarzan* and for Pacha in *The Emperor's New Groove*.

Formed Jambalaya Studios

By the late 1990s Smith was growing more interested in creating his own projects. As he explained to a writer for the *Los Angeles Times*, he was aware of a "void in the market of urban entertainment, especially in the animation side.... [A]nimation was still not ready to diversify." With Hyperion Studio president and chief executive Tom Wilhite, Smith formed Jambalaya Studios, which aimed to create animated programs about ethnically diverse characters and communities. The studio's first project was the series *The Proud Family*, which Smith wrote, directed, and produced. According to Michael Mallory in the *Los Angeles Times*, the series showed that there is more to creating ethnically sensitive material than "digitally painting some characters a darker shade of skin tone and calling it diversity. It is a matter of depicting a specific American neighborhood and its people with some truth and fidelity." Indeed, Smith, the father of four children, admitted in the *Guardian* that he relied heavily on his own background in creating the series. He likened *The Proud Family*'s father, Oscar, to himself, and said that the character of Penny was modeled on his own daughter, while the mother and grandmother were based on his own wife and mother. Like many African-American families, the Proud family includes a working mother, a grandmother, and a father, who in this case is an entrepreneur. Among their neighbors is a Latino family. While *The Proud Family* was recognized for its role in promoting diverse entertainment, it was also respected as a program that could attract a wider audience. The program was nominated for an NAACP Image Award.

Another production from Jambalaya was *Da Boom Crew*, an adventure series that Smith described in *Celebrating Children* as a cross between *Star Wars* and *Boyz-N-the-Hood*. The program follows a group of orphans who make their own video game involving space aliens. A supernatural occurrence pulls them into this fictional world, where they must outsmart monsters and other villains in their search for missing boom carts. Smith was careful, he pointed out, to avoid any hip-hop stereotypes in the show. "Recreating the black experience in animated form is deeper [than that]," he explained. "And once you see *Da Boom Crew,* you see how these kids are just like you and I."

Smith also worked as an animator on *The Indescribable Nth*, which was named "Best American Short" at the BBC British Shorts Film Festival in 1999. He was lead animator for the character Pearl in *Home on the Range*. He serves on the board of directors of Animobile, a company that creates and markets "mobile entertainment" for wireless devices and networks. By the mid-2000s, Smith was widely perceived to be one of the hottest animators in the industry.

Selected works

Films

Additional animator, *Who Framed Roger Rabbit?*, Walt Disney Pictures, 1988.
Animator, *Tummy Trouble,* Walt Disney Pictures, 1989.
Character designer, *Bebe's Kids*, Hyperion Pictures, 1992.
Animation supervisor, *The Pagemaster*, 20th Century Fox, 1994.

Character designer, *A Goofy Movie,* Walt Disney Pictures, 1995.
Animation director, *Space Jam*, Warner Brothers, 1996.
Supervising animator, *Tarzan*, Walt Disney Pictures, 1999 Animator, *The Indescribable Nth*, 1999.
Supervising animator, *The Emperor's New Groove*, Walt Disney Pictures, 2000.
Lead animator, *Home On the Range,* Walt Disney Pictures, 2004.

Television

Character designer, director, *Happily Ever After: Fairy Tales for Every Child* (co-producer), HBO, 1995-2000.
Character designer, *C-Bear and Jamal*, Fox, 1996.
Director, executive producer, writer, *The Proud Family,* The Disney Channel, 2001.
Executive producer, writer, *Da Boom Crew*, WBKids!, 2004.

Sources

Periodicals

Boston Globe, November 15, 1996, p. D1.
Guardian (Trinidad), October 3, 2004.
Jet, February 9, 2004, p. 19.
Los Angeles Times, September 15, 2001, p. F2.
New York Times, June 22, 1988.

On-line

"Da Boom Crew Rockets into Space," *Celebrating Children,* www.celebratingchildren.com (April 28, 2005).
"Disney's *The Proud Family* Producer, Bruce Smith to present at Animae Caribe 2003," *Animae Caribe 2003,* www.animaecaribe.com/about/index.php?topic=news&id=0901 (June 29, 2005).
"*The Proud Family* Makes Disney Channel Its Home," *LaughingPlace*, www.laughingplace.com (April 28, 2005).

—E. M. Shostak

Will Smith

1968—

Actor, rap artist, film and television producer

On television he was the Fresh Prince of Bel Air, a streetwise Philadelphian sent to live with wealthy relatives in California. In real life he is Will Smith, a streetwise Philadelphian who has–by virtue of hard work and infectious charm–found stardom and wealth in Los Angeles. Smith has enjoyed vast success in two different fields of popular entertainment. While still too young to drink legally he released several platinum rap albums and won the first-ever Grammy Award given in the rap category.

With his accomplishment in the music industry behind him, Smith moved to television situation comedy and scored a hit with "The Fresh Prince of Bel Air." In the mid-1990s, while still a young man by any standards, Smith is in demand for television and film roles, some of which seriously test his acting talent. *Premiere* magazine contributor Veronica Chambers cited Smith for his "white-bread appeal that very few black men possess," noting that the engaging star is "Ben Franklin with a backward baseball cap."

Acting, for Smith, has often meant being his own quirky self in front of a camera. He has worked hard over the years to invest some realism into the character he played on *The Fresh Prince of Bel Air*–even if that meant flying in the face of stereotype. "Look what the Fresh Prince represents," Smith told *Essence* magazine. "He operates on several different levels–a symbol of urban youth, a symbol of Black youth and, most specifically, of Black male youth."

Grew up in a Loving Family

Willard Smith, Jr., was born on September 25, 1968, and raised in Wynnefield, Pennsylvania, a middle-class suburb of West Philadelphia. He was the oldest son and one of four children of a refrigeration engineer and a school board employee. His parents were loving but demanding, the kind who took their children to Mount Rushmore on vacation to prove that education does not end with the classroom.

"Dad was tough but not tyrannical," Smith told *Essence*. "He kept me in line. He'd get this look that said, 'One more step, Will, and it'll get ugly.' He was an independent businessman–he set up refrigeration in supermarkets–and he always provided for us. He's a steady and positive figure in my life. Mom worked as a school secretary–she's a supervisor now–and her thing was education. My folks sent me to a Catholic school because it was the best school in the neighborhood, but I felt some of the priests and nuns were racist."

As a teen, Smith attended Overbrook High, a public school in Philadelphia. His teachers there nicknamed him "the Prince" because they found him so charming. His best subject was mathematics, and he earned good enough grades to be accepted at the prestigious Massachusetts Institute of Technology (MIT) engineering program. By that time, though, fate had decreed a different path for the Prince.

Entered the Music Business as a Teen

When he was just twelve years old, Smith met Jeffrey Townes at a friend's party. Townes was better known as DJ Jazzy Jeff, and although he was only a few years

At a Glance . . .

Born on September 25, 1968, in Philadelphia, PA; son of Willard (a refrigeration engineer) and Caroline (a school board employee) Smith; married Sheree Zampino, 1992 (divorced 1995); married Jada Pinkett, 1997; children: (first marriage) Will III; (second marriage) Jaden Christopher Syre, Willow Camille Reign.

Career: Rap musician with duo DJ Jazzy Jeff and the Fresh Prince, 1986–; solo performer, 1997–; actor 1990–.

Awards: Grammy Award, for Best Rap Performance, "Parents Just Don't Understand," 1989; Grammy Award, for Best Rap Performance, for "Summertime ,"1992; National Association for the Advancement of Colored People (NAACP), Image Award for Best Situation Comedy, for *The Fresh Prince of Bel Air*, 1992; Grammy Award, for Best Rap Performance, for "Men In Black," 1998; Grammy Award, for Best Rap Performance, for "Gettin' Jiggy Wit It," 1998; ASCAP Awards, 1998, 2000; Blockbuster Entertainment Awards favorite actor (sci-fi), 1996 and 1998, and favorite actor (action/adventure), 1999; Image Award, for Entertainer of the Year, Outstanding Music Video, and Outstanding Rap Artist, 1999; BET Award, for Best Actor, for *Ali*, 2002.

Addresses: *Agent*—Overbook Entertainment, Beverly Hills, CA 90210; *Web*–www.willsmith.net.

older than Smith, he had been spinning records at parties for quite some time. Smith was just beginning to rap—calling himself the Fresh Prince—and he and Jazzy Jeff became friends. For some years they performed in different rap groups and only occasionally paired up. Then, in 1986, their partnership became more serious. "I worked with 2,000 crews before I found this maniac," Jazzy Jeff told *People*. "There was a click when I worked with him that was missing before." The two friends performed as DJ Jazzy Jeff and the Fresh Prince.

Jazzy Jeff had already released an album, so the new duo had little trouble finding a record label. In 1986 they cut their first LP together, *Rock the House*. Their first single, "Girls Ain't Nothin' But Trouble," did well on the charts. Already famous throughout the Philadelphia region, they found themselves in demand in the rest of the country as well. As the money began to roll in, Smith was able to convince his parents that college could wait. In fact, he earned a million dollars before he turned 20.

Rock the House was released in 1987 and sold some 600,000 copies. Major stardom came to Smith the following year with the double LP *He's the DJ, I'm the Rapper*, one of the first rap albums to reach platinum status with over a million copies sold. Both albums, but especially the second, offered raps about what the musicians understood best–the day-to-day troubles of modern teens. The hit single "Parents Just Don't Understand," for instance, detailed the nightmares of shopping for school clothes with a mother who is hopelessly out of touch with current styles; the Fresh Prince pleads with his mom to "put back the bell-bottom [1970s TV show] Brady Bunch trousers." This universal young adult complaint helped find a crossover audience for DJ Jazzy Jeff and the Fresh Prince. "Parents Just Don't Understand" won the very first Grammy Award given in the category of rap music.

Found Success with Clean Rap

Because their subject matter was not particularly controversial, DJ Jazzy Jeff and the Fresh Prince were afforded greater opportunities to perform their work. Promoters saw less chance for violence at their shows, so they were booked into major concert venues. Even network television executives felt comfortable putting them on the air. The "clean rap" image proved a mixed blessing, because some other rap artists criticized them for ignoring legitimate problems of black youths.

Smith's reply to detractors was that he was just responding to his own personal environment—one that did not include the stresses of a dysfunctional family, drug abuse, or violent crime. "In the beginning, following the fashion of the day, my raps had a small amount of profanity," he told *Essence*. "I'll never forget what my grandmother said when she read them: 'He who is truly articulate shuns profanity.' Man, I didn't even know what articulate meant, but I knew I wanted my grandmother's approval, just as I wanted my parents' approval."

By 1990 the Fresh Prince had released three top-selling rap albums and was one of the best-known rappers in the nation. He was also broke. "I bought everything," Smith told *TV Guide*. He had a mansion near Philadelphia, closets full of designer clothing, a fleet of expensive cars, and a jet-set lifestyle complete with fair weather friends. When the money ran out and his friends deserted him, Smith realized how foolish he had been. Already his popularity as a rapper was diminishing. Instead of panicking, however, he just cast about for a new opportunity.

Started Acting

Some Hollywood executives had already noticed Smith's stage presence and his ability to charm an audience. Beginning in 1990 he was invited to audition for small roles on *The Cosby Show* and *A Different World*, but he described himself in *Jet* as being "too scared" to keep the appointments. Finally he met Benny Medina, the head of Warner Brothers Records' black music division. Medina had moved from Watts as a teen to a wealthy Los Angeles neighborhood, and he thought that his experiences would make a funny situation comedy. Medina and Smith talked the idea over and then approached producer Quincy Jones about a pilot episode. Jones immediately sensed that a show of that nature starring Will Smith would be a hit.

The Fresh Prince of Bel Air made its debut on the National Broadcasting Company (NBC) in the fall of 1990. Smith appeared in the starring role as Will, a Philadelphia teen sent to live with his wealthy, refined, and decidedly Republican aunt and uncle in the upscale Bel Air section of Los Angeles. The show found an audience quickly, "almost singlehandedly keeping the network competitive on Monday nights," according to Gordon Dillow in *TV Guide*. For Smith, who had never done any acting before, the show was quite a challenge. "I was a nervous wreck," he recalled in *TV Guide*. "I was trying so hard. I would memorize the entire script, then I'd be lipping everybody's lines while they were talking. When I watch those [early] episodes it's disgusting. My performances were horrible."

Smith might not have been satisfied with his work, but almost everyone else was. In a *TV Guide* poll, young adults voted the Fresh Prince "hippest teen on TV." In addition, *The Fresh Prince of Bel Air* quickly became the most popular black situation comedy among white viewers, consistently placing in the Nielsen Top Twenty through its first two seasons. "Smith is such a naturally engaging comic talent that he and the show's capable supporting cast usually sidestep the treacle trap," noted Mike Duffy in the *Detroit Free Press*. "Smith never allows excess cutes to sabotage the chuckles."

Sought Film Work

An astute businessman who also seeks creative challenges, Smith began trying to broaden his horizons in Hollywood. He sought film work and has since then appeared in several movies. His most notable dramatic performance came in 1993 with the release of *Six Degrees of Separation*, a serious drama in which Smith played a gay con artist trying to fool a couple of white social climbers. "I wanted to work with [filmmakers] Spike Lee and John Singleton," Smith told *Premiere*, "and I needed to do a film like *Six Degrees* in order for those people to consider me. Spike Lee would never consider me for a role, because "The Fresh Prince of Bel Air" is all he's ever seen. How would he know that I could do what he demands of an actor?" Smith added that an intelligent choice of future movie roles could assure him a long career in show business. "Film, I think, I can do forever," he said. "As long as you're good, you can always do film," he added.

After Smith expanded his wings with *Six Degrees of Separation*, he was offered more roles in films such as *Where The Day Takes You*, and *Made In America*. But his first role as an action hero made Hollywood sit up and take notice. Smith co-starred with Martin Lawrence in the comedy-thriller, *Bad Boys*. The film was a box-office success and it set the stage for his next film, *Independence Day*.

Wanting to focus on his budding film career, in 1996 Smith decided to leave *The Fresh Prince of Bel Air* after six seasons, even though the show remained successful. The show was translated into more than a dozen languages, and Smith remembered it to *Teen People* in 2004 as "the biggest thing I ever did."

His move proved fruitful with his next film, *Independence Day*. *Independence Day* was an action-packed science fiction film with an all-star ensemble cast. Smith was one of three leads who included actors Bill Pullman and Jeff Goldblum. *ID4*, as it was nicknamed, earned more than $100 million its opening week. Smith became a bona fide action movie star. He had the sex appeal, the cockiness, and the buffed body. The downside to his success was men wanted to see if he could actually fight. He told *Jet* that as the Fresh Prince, he "was nonthreatening. So nobody wanted to fight me, but then I buffed up for *Independence Day*, came on a little cocky, and suddenly people want to knock me down."

Smith's next film was *Men In Black*. Though it was another sci-fi film, when he was asked by executive producer Steven Spielberg to take the part of Agent J, he told *Ebony*, "You just can't tell Steven Spielberg no." He teamed up with Academy Award-winning actor Tommy Lee Jones and made box office history. *Men In Black* was the number one best selling movie of 1997. It grossed over $200 million.

Nurtured Strong Family Ties

Smith, who described himself as a "one-woman man," married Sheree Zampino in 1992. Their first child, Willard Smith III, was born the following year. "She's wonderful," Smith said of his wife in *Essence*. "She allowed me to finally put down the bags of emotional stress I'd been lugging around like a fool.... I realized that physically, emotionally and intellectually she was on a higher plane than me."

Smith's life seemed to be perfect. He was a rapper, TV star, husband, father, and a blossoming movie star, but his marriage was on a rocky road. His wife soon asked for a divorce. It was finalized in 1995, and they both share custody of their son. Though devastated, Smith continued with his television, rap, and film careers.

Though Smith met Jada Pinkett when she auditioned for a role on *The Fresh Prince of Bel Air,* it was not until years later that they connected romantically. Both considered the other their soulmate. Smith told *Ebony*, "Jada is the first person I've been with willing to accept that it's not always going to be great, but that's okay." The two married on December 31, 1997; they have two children: a son, Jaden Christopher Syre, and a daughter, Willow Camille Reign.

Continued Recording Music

Though quoted as having no desire to make another record, Smith performed the title track to the *Men In Black* soundtrack. For rap fans who missed his style, it was a much-needed return. Fans who only knew Smith from TV and film were surprised; so was the music industry. His last album had bombed. The song won an NAACP Image award and garnered him his third Grammy.

In 1997, Smith released a solo album under his own name, titled *Big Willie Style*. His first single, "Gettin' Jiggy With It" was a top ten hit. He spoke with *Essence* concerning why he released another rap album, "I loved Biggie [slain rapper Notorious B.I.G.], but my son doesn't have any alternatives." *Big Willie Style* was a multi-platinum success. In 1999 he released another rap album, *Willennium,* at about the same time as his film *Wild Wild West* opened in theaters. *Willennium* was another multi-platinum success. The single "Will 2K" from the album broke into the Top 10 list and the video for the song was nominated for a Grammy Award. Continuing his outpouring of clean rap, Smith released *Born to Reign* in 2002. The album featured vocals from his wife and son, and a song about his young daughter. In 2005 he released yet another album titled *Lost and Found.*

Showed Diverse Acting Talents

Smith added two movies to his resume in 2000: *Men in Black Alien Attack*, and *The Legend of Bagger Vance,* directed by Robert Redford. In 2001 Smith stayed busy as the star of the feature film *Ali*, the story of heavyweight champion Muhammad Ali. His performance earned him his first Grammy nomination as an actor.

Sequels to Men in Black in 2002 and Bad Boys in 2003 proved box-office hits. Smith followed these blockbusters with a starring role in Isaac Asimov's classic sci-fi adventure *I, Robot*. In the 2004 film, Smith plays a skeptical police officer who "is basically Shaft, a black cop who wears lots of leather, earrings, a Mike Tyson gait, an ancient grudge and a face that says: 'I can't stand people's unquestioning faith in robots,' as James Christopher of the *London Times* put it in his review of *I, Robot.*

Smith switched gears in 2005 to star in the romantic comedy *Hitch*. In the film, Smith played a dating consultant who helped men woo the women of their dreams. *Film Journal International* found Smith the "perfect fit" for the role. And Smith told *People* that "I am Hitch in my real life." The film became an international success.

Smith told *TV Guide* that his high confidence in himself helped him to leap from local notoriety to national celebrity while still a teenager. "Confidence is what makes me different from guys at home.... I'm the one who always takes the risks." In *Seventeen*, he said: "You have to believe in something greater than yourself. You have to have faith in the power and believe it has your best interest at heart. That's how I was raised by my parents, and that's my bottom line." One thing Will Smith has proven: he has the business sense, the charm, and the talent to utilize every opportunity that comes his way.

Selected works

Albums

(With DJ Jazzy Jeff and the Fresh Prince) *Rock the House* (includes "Girls Ain't Nothin' But Trouble"), Jive, 1987, reissued, 1989.
(With DJ Jazzy Jeff and the Fresh Prince) *He's the DJ, I'm the Rapper* (includes "Parents Just Don't Understand"), Jive, 1988.
(With DJ Jazzy Jeff and the Fresh Prince) *And in This Corner*, Jive, 1989.
(With DJ Jazzy Jeff and the Fresh Prince) *Homebase*, 1991.
Code Red, 1993.
Men In Black soundtrack, title cut, 1997.
Big Willie Style, 1997.
Willennium, 1999.
Born to Reign, 2002.
Lost and Found, 2005.

Television

The Fresh Prince of Bel Air, 1990-96.
(Co-creator) *All of Us,* 2003–.

Films

Where The Day Takes You, 1992.
Made In America, 1993.
Six Degrees of Separation, 1993.
Bad Boys, 1995.
Independence Day, 1996.
Men In Black, 1997.
Enemy of the State, 1998.
Wild Wild West, 1999.
The Legend of Bagger Vance, 2000.

Ali, 2001.
Men in Black 2, 2002.
Bad Boys II, 2003.
I, Robot, 2004.
Hitch, 2005.

Sources

Books

Nickson, Chris, *Will Smith,* St. Martin's, 1999.

Periodicals

Cosmopolitan, October 1993, p. 102.
Detroit Free Press, May 10, 1993, p. E-1.
Ebony, February 1994, p. 30; August 1996, p. 34.
Emerge, September 1993, p. 11.
Essence, February 1993, p. 60-62, 118-21; July 1997, p. 60; February 2005, p. 134.
Film Journal International, April 2005, p. 118.
Hollywood Reporter, September 15, 2003, p. 19.
Jet, December 3, 1990, p. 58-61; January 10, 1994, p. 64; Jan 27, 1997.
People, September 24, 1990, p. 83-84; July 22, 1996, p. 64; February 21, 2005, p. 91.
Premiere, January 1994, p. 76-77.
Seventeen, July 1992, p. 86-87.
Teen People, August 1, 2004, p. 102.
TV Guide, September 29-October 5, 1990, p. 5; October 13-19, 1990, p. 6-9; January 23-29, 1993, p. 10-12.
Upscale, February 1994, p. 116.

On-line

"*All of Us,*" *UPN,* www.upn.com/shows/all_of_us/index.shtml (August 15, 2005).
"*I, Robot,*" *Times Online,* www.timesonline.co.uk/article/0,,7943-1202108,00.html (August 15, 2005).
"Will Smith," *Biography Resource Center,* www.galenet.com/servlet/BioRC (August 18, 2005).
Will Smith, www.willsmith.net (August 15, 2005).

—Anne Janette Johnson, Ashyia N. Henderson, and Sara Pendergast

Corinne Sparks

1953—

Family court judge

Sparks, Corrine E., photograph. Courtesy of Judge Corrine E. Sparks.

In 1987 Judge Corrine Sparks secured her spot in history by becoming the first African Nova Scotian to receive appointment to the judiciary and the first African Canadian female to serve on the bench. Sparks adjudicates family court cases relating to custody, child and spousal support, access, and child protection. She supports judicial education, developing educational programs and lecturing on that and gender and racial discrimination and the courts. Sparks works with the Commonwealth Judicial Educational Center, which promotes judicial education and her work has earned her numerous awards and recognition. Sparks' humble beginnings in segregated Nova Scotia left much to overcome. But she succeeded through hard work, a willingness to challenge, and a strong belief in her faith.

Sparks was born on August 13, 1953, and grew up in the small segregated rural area of Nova Scotia, Canada, called Lake Loon. Stressing education, her parents, Spencer and Helen Sparks, worked hard and sacrificed to provide their nine children a stable and loving home in their community of several black towns dotting the periphery of Halifax. "They took their roles as parents seriously and they did not believe in hand-outs," Sparks said in an interview with *Contemporary Black Biography* (*CBB*). Although poverty was a daily fact and schools were segregated and poor, Sparks' parents had tremendous faith and much of their family life centered on the church. "My parents' needs were secondary to their children's," Sparks said. "It was extraordinary parenting at a fundamental level. Many blacks could not afford to even look after their own children." Life was difficult for the family just as it had been for their neighbors and other blacks whose ancestors first settled in Nova Scotia during the 1700s and 1800s with promise of land and freedom. Instead, from the start African Nova Scotians were mistreated and marginalized.

Many believe the history of blacks in North America is the story of the African-American experience. Little known outside Canada is the history of the resettlement of the Black Loyalists around 1783 and the "black refugees" after 1812. Sparks traces her ancestors from both these events in African Nova Scotian history. "I would say that my family lineage is typical of most

At a Glance . . .

Born Corrine E. Sparks on August 13, 1953, in Loon Lake, Nova Scotia, Canada. *Education:* Mount Saint Vincent University, BA, economics, 1974; Dalhousie University, LLB and LLM, 1979-2001. *Religion:* Baptist.

Career: Ruck and Mitchell, Halifax, Nova Scotia, attorney, 1981-87; Nova Scotia Family Court, Halifax, Nova Scotia, family court judge, 1987–.

Memberships: Nova Scotia Home for Coloured Children, member; Canadian Assoc. of Provincial Court Judges, member; American Judges Association, member; Canadian Association of Black Lawyers, member; Canadian Chapter International Association of Women Judges, member.

Awards: Canadian Association of Black Lawyers, Service Award, 1997; National Association of Women and the Law, Frances Lillian Fish Award, 1998; Congress of Black Women, Service Award, 2002; Elizabeth Fry Society, Rebel with a Cause Award, 2003.

Addresses: *Office*—Judge of the Family Court, 277 Pleasant St. Ste. 200, Dartmouth, NS, Canada B2Y 3S2.

African Nova Scotians here in our little province," Sparks said. "But it is lamentable that we black people in the diaspora do not know enough about each other's history. Many unfortunately know very little about the many manifestations of colonialism and don't fully appreciate the fact that Nova Scotia was very segregated."

Segregation in Nova Scotia began with the first presence of black settlers. After the American Revolution, many blacks who had supported England were promised freedom, land, and safe passage from America to Nova Scotia. Thirty-five hundred slaves, indentured servants, and free men set sail for Canada only to find they were not welcome, and the harsh climate was nothing like anything they had experienced. Some had no time to build shelter and spent the winter in tents; others built pits in the ground as shelter from the cold. Very few received all the land they were promised, some received a few acres, and many received nothing. That meant little farming could be done and food would be scarce. The "black refugees" came later after supporting England during the War of 1812. They too received a cold—and many times cruel—welcome. Some settlers had to sell themselves into indentured servitude and were treated just as badly as the slaves; disease was widespread just as it had been for the Loyalists; many died. "It's a history of denial, poverty, discrimination, prejudice, and monumental barriers against our people here in Nova Scotia," Sparks said.

Race relations and slavery in Canada took their twists and turns through history, often paralleling the black struggle in the United States. By the 1970s when Sparks entered middle and high school, educational opportunities for blacks were still few. But Sparks was fortunate enough to have teachers who believed in her. "They saw my potential, something I did not recognize in myself. My elementary school teachers took an interest in me. I went to an integrated middle school where there was a fair amount of racial dissention as black and white students were brought together. But I had a number of black and East Indian teachers who took an interest. They would sometimes take me to libraries and universities. Also, my mother really valued education and knew it opened doors," Sparks told *CBB.*

From 1971 to 1974 Sparks attended Mount Saint Vincent University, where she earned an economics degree. She had gotten there by the altruism of her high school principal who, aware of her circumstances, had submitted her name to the local rotary club. She received substantial tuition assistance as a result. Also, nuns belonging to the Sisters of Charity Order supplied additional assistance in the way of tuition, room, and board. "I sometimes wonder what I would have made of my life if I had not had such good fortune," Sparks said.

Sparks went on to earn a bachelor of law degree from Dalhousie University in 1979. In 2001 she completed a master's of law degree at Dalhousie. While she studied, Sparks ran her own law practice specializing in family and real estate law and served on the boards of several organizations aiding black children and mental health before her appointment to the Nova Scotia Family Court in 1987.

Mindful of the responsibilities of one who sits in judgment of others each day, Sparks told *CBB,* "You are dealing with human beings. In order to be an effective judge you need to employ many skills on a daily basis. You need knowledge of the law, human compassion, and empathy. One has to be mindful that one is just an instrument for serving the public. In that sense, that is the most gratifying aspect of the job, the ability to serve people knowing hopefully that you are able to balance your legal knowledge with compassion and understanding with the human beings who appear before you."

Being a female whose accomplishments have earned her several "firsts" in a male-dominated field is a testament to Sparks' strength and determination. The path has not been an easy one. "I have had many, many challenges in my life, some Herculean. However, the nature of judicial office does not lend itself to a lot of outside support; you must rely on colleagues and family. Sometimes they can only understand the nuances of the obstacles I have faced professionally and otherwise. Yes, I have encountered lots of obstacles in my career and in life growing up in humble circumstances and attending segregated schools. I think it is important to confront challenges no matter how painful. You have to have coping mechanisms in this life; no one glides through it. For me it has been my faith. I am very grateful that I was raised in a Christian home."

Sources

On-line

"Remembering Black Loyalists: Who Were the Black Loyalists?" *Nova Scotia Museum,* http://museum.gov.ns.ca/blackloyalists/who.htm (04/16/05).

"Nova Scotia Family Court Judges," *The Courts of Nova Scotia*, www.courts.ns.ca/family/fam_judges.htm (04/16/05).

Other

Additional information for this profile was obtained through an interview with Judge Corrine Sparks on April 23, 2005.

—Sharon Melson Fletcher

René Syler

1963—

Journalist

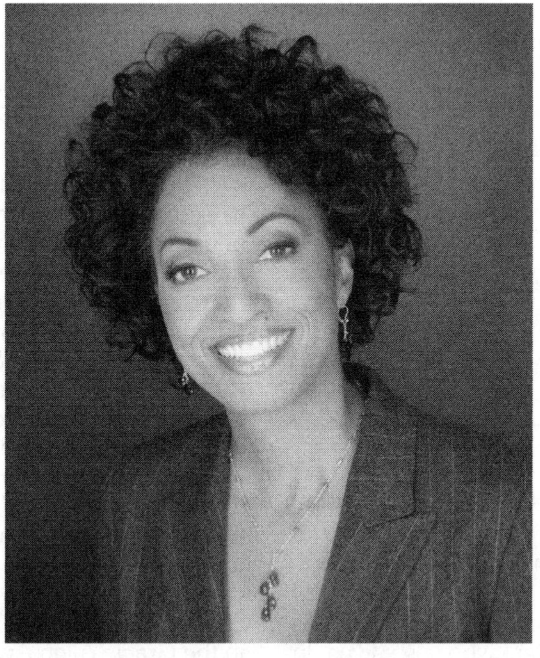
Syler, Rene, photograph. CBS/Landov.

In 2002 René Syler became the first African-American woman to host a network morning news program as co-anchor for *The Early Show* on CBS. Syler deftly handled news stories and conducted interviews with both celebrities and political heavyweights, and she won a top journalism honor for her 2003 series on breast-cancer awareness after her own health scare. "I was looking for a platform to help this cause," Syler was quoted by Yvonne Lardizabal of the Newark, New Jersey *Star-Ledger*. "If I can lend my name and face to help people listen, then that's the first step."

Syler was born on February 17, 1963, in Belleville, Illinois, near Scott Air Force Base, where her father was stationed at the time. The family later relocated to the Sacramento, California, area, and there Syler was a standout on her high school's track and field team. She enrolled in American River College in Sacramento in 1981, transferred to Azusa Pacific University three years later, and eventually earned her undergraduate degree in psychology from California State University's Sacramento campus in 1987.

That same year, Syler began graduate work in her field, but soon realized that perhaps she was not ideally suited for the career in counseling to which an advanced psychology degree seemed to lead. Around this time she read an article about Liz Walker, a Boston journalist who in the mid-1980s was the highest-paid African-American woman in television news, and decided that this might be a career option for her, too. She landed an internship at a local Fox affiliate, which gave her the necessary clips to put together a resumé reel. She then dropped it off at a Reno, Nevada, television station across the California border, and they hired her as a reporter.

Syler earned just $15,000 during her first year at Reno's KTVN-TV, and later said she kept a sack of potatoes in her desk drawer that served as her daily microwaved lunch. In 1989 she became the weekend news anchor at another Reno station, and a year later moved to Birmingham, Alabama, as the weekend news anchor for WVTM-TV. That job led to an offer from a major market, the Dallas-Fort Worth area, and she worked as a morning and noon anchor for WFAA-TV

At a Glance . . .

Born on February 17, 1963, in Belleville, IL; daughter of William Henry and F. Anne McDonald Syler; married Buff Parham (in media advertising sales); children: daughter Casey, son Cole. *Education:* Attended American River College, Sacramento, CA, 1981-83, and Azusa Pacific University, Azusa, CA, 1984-85; California State University, Sacramento, BA, 1987.

Career: KTVN-TV, Reno, NV, news reporter, 1987-89; KOLO-TV, Reno, news anchor, 1989-90; WVTM-TV, Birmingham, AL, weekend news anchor, 1990-92; WFAA-TV, Dallas, TX, morning and noon anchor, 1992-97; KTVT-TV, Dallas, noon and 6 p.m. anchor, 2000-02; CBS-TV, *The Early Show,* co-anchor, 2002–.

Memberships: National Black Journalists Association.

Awards: American Women in Radio and Television, 1997; American Women in Radio and Television, Gracie Allen Awards for Individual Achievement: National Best Anchor Award, 2004.

Addresses: *Office—The Early Show,* CBS News, 524 W. 57th St., New York, NY 10019. *Home*—Westchester, NY.

for five years. By 2002 she was married to a television advertising sales executive and was a popular local celebrity in Dallas as anchor of the noon and 6:00 p.m. newscasts for KTVT-TV, a CBS affiliate. She assumed she had reached to pinnacle of her career and was happy there. She and her sister, who also lived in Dallas, encouraged their widowed mother to relocate to the city as well; furthermore, Syler and her husband, Buff Parham, had just finished building their dream house.

Syler was stunned when CBS executives in New York called to invite her in for an interview. Her husband was wary about a possible cross-country move, but Syler went anyway and soundly chastised her husband when she returned for not being more supportive. Remorseful about the argument they had the night before she flew to New York, he told her, "'If this ever happens again I will be there,'" Syler recalled in an interview with Gwendolyn Quinn that appeared on *The Crusade,* the Web newsletter of the African American Public Relations Collective. "And don't you know, no sooner had he said that? The very next day I get the call from CBS saying, [CBS Television president] 'Les Moonves is going to be in town tomorrow and we'd like you to come up and meet with him about this show.'"

Syler began on *The Early Show* in October of 2002 as one of its new team of four anchors. The network's two-hour weekday morning broadcast, which kicked off at 7:00 a.m., had a long and troubled history as the perennial third-place loser in the morning ratings war on network news. Its various title changes and anchorperson configurations had failed to beat its two strong competitors, NBC's *The Today Show* and *Good Morning America* on ABC. Syler joined one of *The Early Show*'s holdouts from its previous incarnation, Julie Chen (who would wed Moonves in 2004), along with a CBS veteran Harry Smith and Hannah Storm, a sports broadcaster hired away from NBC. The four-anchor format was viewed by some as the network's newest attempt to lure viewers in the high-stakes morning ratings game, but *New York Times* television critic Alessandra Stanley saw it as a sign of the cutthroat nature of the news business. "Starting three women as anchors at once," Stanley observed, "could seem callous, as if signaling that if one makes it, the other two could be discarded like used rocket boosters."

Less than a year onto the job, Syler had a mammogram to screen for breast cancer—which both her mother and father had suffered—and it detected an unusual mass. She underwent four biopsies before doctors ruled that they were benign calcium deposits. During this time, she created a three-part series on cancer awareness for *The Early Show* that aired in October of 2003. The first installment came just after she was given a clean bill of health. "When they told me there was no cancer present, I couldn't stop crying," she told *Philadelphia Inquirer* writer Gail Shister. "You think, 'I'll just deal with it.' As working women and mothers, it's what we do. I don't know how to do anything but that."

Syler's series won her the National Best Anchor honors in the Gracie Allen Awards for Individual Achievement, bestowed annually by a professional organization of her peers, the American Women in Radio and Television. Her husband did comply with his earlier promise to be more supportive of her career, and the couple moved to the suburban New York City enclave of Westchester with their son and daughter. Syler's home boasts a greenhouse, where she grows orchids as a hobby, and she also enjoys scouring flea markets and estate sales for treasure. She is a member of the National Black Journalists Association, but tries to deflect attention from her historic first in the annals of television network news. Looking back to her career that began at a Fox affiliate in Sacramento in 1987, she told *The Crusade*'s Quinn that "I've seen incredible strides made in newsrooms across the country. It will be great when this is no longer an issue."

Sources

Periodicals

D, January 1, 2003.
Daily Variety, October 15, 2002, p. 2.
New York Times, October 29, 2002, p. E1.
Philadelphia Inquirer, October 14, 2003.
Star-Ledger (Newark, NJ), October 28, 2004, p. 1.

On-line

"AAPRC Weekly: René Syler," *The Crusade,* www.thecrusade.net/words/mt-archives/000722.shtml (June 21, 2005).
"Syler: A Move to the Big Apple," *CBS News: The Early Show,* www.cbsnews.com/stories/2002/10/28/earlyshow/main527260.shtml (June 21, 2005).

—Carol Brennan

Robert F. Van Lierop

1939—

Attorney, filmmaker, and diplomat

Robert F. Van Lierop's varied and distinguished career has included spells as assistant legal counsel to the NAACP in the late 1960s, as ambassador to the United Nations for the Republic of Vanuatu, as a photojournalist and film producer, and as a founding partner in the law firm of Van Lierop, Burns, and Bassett. At the United Nations during the 1980s he was influential in negotiations on important global issues, including the ending of apartheid in South Africa, and on international environmental law. He was vice president of the United Nations General Assembly in its 43rd session, Chairman of the 4th Committee (Trusteeship and Decolonization) during the 44th session, and vice chairman of the Ad Hoc Committee of the Whole during the 16th Special Session of the United Nations General Assembly on Apartheid and its Destructive Consequences in Southern Africa; he also served as the first chairman of the Alliance of Small Island States (AOSIS) from 1991 to 1994.

Van Lierop continued to pursue his legal practice during the years of his United Nations service. He has advised national governments and corporations on international law and has been an important figure in the New York City Bar Association, in particular during terms as chairman of its Council on International Affairs and as chairman of the executive committee. Van Lierop's efforts in the fight for justice and peace around the world have brought him many awards and commendations, including the Vanuatu Independence Medal, which he received from the prime minister in 1991.

Robert F. Van Lierop was born on the South Pacific island of Vanuatu on March 29, 1939; his parents were Sylvia and Edward Van Lierop. After serving in the United States Air Force from 1956 to 1960, he attended Hofstra University on Long Island, New York, graduating with a B.A. in economics in 1964. He later attended the New York University School of Law as an Arthur Garfield Hayes Civil Liberties Fellow, graduating in 1967 with a J.D. After graduation in 1967 he went to work as assistant legal counsel to the NAACP, where he was involved in litigating on civil rights issues and constitutional law. In 1968 he became an associate of the firm Fleisher, Dornbush, Mensch, Mandelstam, where he stayed until 1971.

Became a Journalist

In 1971 Van Lierop's interest in political activism and human rights causes led him to take a break from legal practice and set himself up as a freelance photojournalist and filmmaker. His first documentary film, *A Luta Continua,* addressed the struggle for independence in Mozambique, a cause he pursued until the end of the civil war in 1975; he also led delegations of African-American activists to Mozambique, Zimbabwe, and Cuba in 1977 and 1978. He made a second film about Mozambique, *O Povo Organizado*, which was completed in 1976, and he also worked on behalf of the Polaroid Revolutionary Workers Movement, which opposed corporate exploitation of South Africa. He also produced documentaries about the United Nations and South Africa as part of the weekly *Like It Is* series,

At a Glance . . .

Born Robert F. van Lierop on March 29, 1939, in Vanuatu; married Toy (a makeup artist); children: one. *Education:* Hofstra University, BA, economics, 1964; New York University School of Law, LLB (JD), 1967. *Military Service:* United States Air Force, 1956-60.

Career: NAACP, assistant counsel, 1967-68; Fleisher, Dornbush, Mensch, Mandelstam law firm, associate, 1968-71; film producer and photojournalist, 1971-76; TV producer, 1977-78; Van Lierop, Burns, and Bassett law firm, partner and attorney, 1978-81, 1994–; United Nations, ambassador and permanent representative for the Republic of Vanuatu, 1981-94.

Memberships: Lawyers Committee for Human Rights, board member; Arthur Ashe Institute for Urban Health, board member; Black Economic Research Center, board member; American Committee on Africa; National Conference of Black Lawyers; Harlem Children's Theatre; National Lawyers' Guild; New York Civil Liberties Union; American Bar Association; Association of the Bar of the City of New York, various committee chairmanships; New York State Bar Association.

Awards: Hofstra University, George M. Estabrook Distinguished Service Award, 1991; Hofstra University Award, Alumni Achievement, 1993; Vanuatu Independence Medal, 1991; Grand Cross of the Order of the Infante Dom Henrique, 1993; Hofstra University, Doctor of Humane Letters, Donoris Causor, 1994.

Addresses: *Office*—Van Lierop, Burns and Bassett, Attorney and Counselor at Law, 320 Convent Ave, New York, New York, United States 10031-6331.

which aired on WABC-TV from 1977 to 1978. The show, which Van Lierop co-produced, was a news and current affairs documentary series aimed at African Americans.

Van Lierop returned to private legal practice in 1978 when he became a founding partner in the firm of Van Lierop, Burns, and Bassett in New York City. Since its founding the firm has worked in the field of sports and entertainment law as well as advising governments and large organizations on international law, constitutional law, and civil rights law.

Became a UN Ambassador

In 1981 Van Lierop was invited to become ambassador and permanent representative to the United Nations for the island of Vanuatu, which had gained independence from Britain and France the previous year. Van Lierop held the position until 1994 and contributed to making Vanuatu a leading member of the economic cooperation organization, AOSIS, which formed in 1991 to enable small island states to work together to compete in global markets. Van Lierop became the first chairman of AOSIS and led the organization during the period of its establishment as a key negotiator in the process of developing environmental laws and conventions. In particular he was a central figure in the negotiation of the United Nations Climate Convention, which became the cornerstone of the 1992 Earth Summit in Rio de Janeiro, Brazil. By the end of his tenure at the United Nations, AOSIS had become an important voice in international negotiations on issues such as economic globalization, free trade, and climate change.

During his time at the United Nations Van Lierop held several important posts and was involved in many summits around the world. He served as a Vice-President of the 43rd Session of the United Nations General Assembly, Chairman of the 4th Committee on Trusteeship and Decolonization during the 44th Session of the General Assembly, and Vice Chairman of the Ad Hoc Committee of the Whole during the 16th Special Session of the United Nations General Assembly on Apartheid and its Destructive Consequences in Southern Africa. Van Lierop was also a non-aligned states delegate to U.N. summits at New Delhi, India, in 1983; Harare, Zimbabwe, in 1986; and Belgrade, Serbia, in 1989. In the 1980s and 1990s he also worked on behalf of the East Timorese to oppose Indonesian occupation.

Continued in Legal Practice

Van Lierop had continued to work in private practice throughout his time at the United Nations, but he returned to his successful law firm full-time in 1994, representing governments and corporations at the United Nations and advising them on international law. He has been a prominent member of many important organizations, managing to combine his activism and expertise on international affairs with high-level roles in the legal profession. For example, he was chair of the City of New York Bar Association's Committee on African Affairs (1994-97), and served on the association's executive committee (1997-2000); from 2000 to 2003 he chaired the association's Council for International Affairs.

Van Lierop has also been involved with many community and campaigning organizations and has throughout his career fought for equality and fairness in professional life and the interactions of organizations at an international level, as well as being involved in civic projects. His interests have ranged from being a board member of the Harlem Children's Theater to membership of the executive committee of the American Committee on Africa. He is a founding member of the National Conference of Black Lawyers and sits on the board of visitors for the City University of New York School of Law. He has never been unwilling to take a personal stand on important issues and in 2004 he served on the "Jury of Conscience" at the New York session of the World Tribunal on Iraq which found Western governments, in particular the United States and the United Kingdom, in breach of the Geneva Conventions, international law, and violations of human rights during the 2003 invasion and occupation of Iraq.

Van Lierop's varied career has seen him take part at the highest legal and governmental levels in the effort to reform international relations, improve international law, and fight for civil rights and equality at home and abroad. He has been instrumental in the negotiation of important international conventions on environmental protection, while as a filmmaker he was an important voice in struggles for freedom in Southern Africa. He has received many awards, including the Vanuatu Independence Medal, 1991, and the Grand Cross of the Order of the Infante Dom Henrique, 1993. His personal papers, including correspondence and writings relating to his political activism and filmmaking, are available at the New York Public Library.

Selected works

Films

A Luta Continua, 1974.
O Povo Organizado, 1976.

Television

Like It Is (series co-producer), WABC-TV.

Sources

Periodicals

Sunday Times, (London, England), June 7, 1992, p. 2.

On-line

"World Tribunal on Iraq: New York War-Crimes Hearing Finds U.S. Guilty," *International Action Center*, www.iacenter.org/wti-final.htm (June 20, 2005).

"Jury Members: Robert Van Lierop," *World Tribunal on Iraq*, www.worldtribunal-nyc.org/jury/Robert_F_Van_Lierop.htm (June 20, 2005).

"Robert Van Lierop," *Biography Resource Center*, www.galenet.com/servlet/BioRC (June 20, 2005).

"Robert Van Lierop: Personal Papers," *New York Public Library*, http://catnyp.nypl.org/search/aVan+Lierop,+Robert./avan+lierop+robert/-5,-1,0,B/frameset&FF=avan+lierop+robert&2,,2 (June 23, 2005).

—Chris Routledge

Countess Vaughn

Actress

1978—

For nine years, first on *Moesha* and then on *The Parkers,* actress Countess Vaughn was a fixture of African-American living rooms, a star on the television programs that topped measures of black viewership. The youthful Vaughn mastered a broad, sassy style of comedy with deep roots in African-American performance traditions, portraying the boy-chasing Kim Parker and developing a set of trademark mannerisms that never grew old. Vaughn, who married Joseph James in 2002, is an example of child star who grew successfully into an adult career; she began performing when she was 10.

Countess Danielle Vaughn was born in the small town of Idabel, Oklahoma, on August 8, 1978. Her parents, Leo and Sandra Vaughn, were schoolteachers. At age three she began singing with her church choir. "I never imagined being on television, acting, singing, doing the whole entertainment thing," she told Mike McDaniel of the *Houston Chronicle.* But while she was still a child it became clear to everyone around her that her voice was something special. The family had records by some great vocal models around the house—gospel queen Mahalia Jackson, as well as a jazz singers like Dinah Washington and pop diva Whitney Houston.

When Vaughn was nine, someone—she didn't know who—sent a tape of her singing to the producers of television's *Star Search* program, and she was selected to appear on the show in 1988. Her rendition of the Dionne Warwick hit "What the World Needs Now" earned her the titles of junior vocalist champion and overall junior champion. She also had the presence of mind to mention during her performances that the situation comedy *227* was her favorite show, and that led to a year-long role on the program. Guest slots on *Thea* and on *The Fresh Prince of Bel-Air* opposite Will Smith followed, as did recurring roles on *Hangin' with Mr. Cooper* and *Roc*. In 1992 Vaughn released an album entitled *Countess* on the Virgin label. The album featured a ballad, "Unconditionally," co-written by one of the leading vocal stars of the day, Michael Bolton. Executives had been trying to persuade her to record ever since her *Star Search* turn, but Vaughn waited until her voice was more mature.

Vaughn performed on the *Today Show* and various television specials, and she tried her hand at live theater with a role in the musical *Mama, I Want to Sing, Part 2.* In 1996 she made her big breakthrough as she was cast in the UPN series *Moesha* as Kim Parker, opposite teen star Brandy Norwood in the title role. The bubbly four-foot-ten Vaughn made the party girl Kim Parker an appealing character, impressing *Entertainment Weekly* critic Ken Tucker with her depiction of the character's "attempts to transcend her up-from-the-ghetto roots" with mangled pronunciations of words that she tried to give what she thought were classy inflections. *Moesha* remained a hit through the late 1990s, and Vaughn earned an NAACP Image Award for best supporting actress in a comedy series in 1998. Several other awards came her way, including a Proven Achievers Award from Los Angeles radio station KJLH in 2000, and a nomination for an International Black Comedy Award that same year.

The show made Vaughn a genuine star. She finished high school coursework with tutors, never attending

At a Glance . . .

Born on August 8, 1978, in Idabel, OK; daughter of schoolteachers Leo and Sandra Vaughn; married Joseph James, January 16, 2002; children: Jaylen James.

Career: Actor, 1990s–; recording artist, 1992.

Selected awards: NAACP, Image Award, for outstanding supporting actress in a comedy series, 1998; Los Angeles radio station KJLH, Proven Achievers Award, 2000.

Addresses: *Studio*—c/o United Paramount Network, 11800 Wilshire Blvd., Los Angeles, CA 90025.

school. "I don't regret that at all," she told McDaniel, pointing out that her parents had never pressured her to pursue television stardom. "We all have decisions to make, and I chose to make something out of my career." Crowds mobbed Vaughn and Norwood as they toured malls around the United States, making promotional appearances. "It was truly an ego booster," she told McDaniel, "although I didn't like my shirt getting torn, and my mom fell. It was an ego booster, but it got scary." The only downside, she went on, was dating: "It's genuinely hard to find someone who cares for me and not what I do." In addition to promotional appearances, Vaughn made time for benefits like one for Clean Slate '98, a Pittsburgh drug-awareness event.

As *Moesha* neared the end of its run, Vaughn was given a starring role of her own in a spin-off of the series. The premise of *The Parkers,* which premiered on UPN in 1999, was that Kim Parker had graduated from high school and enrolled at Santa Monica Junior College—and that her mother Nikki Parker, who hadn't been a part of the *Moesha* cast of characters, took the opportunity to get a college education at the same time. Cast in the role of Nikki was the successful plus-sized comedienne Mo'Nique. One indicator of Vaughn's talent was that she and Mo'Nique displayed convincing chemistry as Nikki Parker's antics, such as her constant pursuit of Professor Stanley Oglevee (Dorien Wilson), caused unending embarrassment for her daughter. Many viewers, in fact, believed that the two actresses really were mother and daughter, although in real life they were only ten years apart in age.

"The show is something positive," Vaughn pointed out to *Jet.* "It shows two women getting along. I like that with a mother and daughter getting along and not always screaming at each other." It was often silly, but for Vaughn that was a virtue. "Sometimes we don't want you to focus on the serious stuff because it's so much of that in the world. We just want you to get away from that and laugh," she told *Jet. The Parkers* became the top-rated show among African-American households, and although both Vaughn and Mo'Nique felt frustrated that it failed to cross over substantially to a white audience, it was a hit by any standard. *The Parkers* ran for five seasons, following Kim Parker through such adventures as a marriage and later an annulment, finally going off the air in the spring of 2004.

By that time, Vaughn had gone through new changes in her life. In 1999 she appeared in the hip-hop film *Trippin',* and after a cameo in the Disney production *Max Keeble's Big Move* she was looking to new film roles in the mid-2000s. On the personal side, her marriage resulted in a son, Jaylen James, born in the summer of 2003. She took a maternity leave from *The Parkers* and was temporarily written out of the script but returned in time for the series finale. As of the mid-2000s, Vaughn hoped to record a second album and find new acting opportunities.

Selected works

Albums

Countess, Virgin, 1992.

Films

Trippin', 1999.

Television

227, NBC, 1991.
Moesha, Fox, 1995-99.
The Parkers, Fox, 1999-2004.

Sources

Periodicals

Entertainment Weekly, April 19, 1996, p. 62; September 10, 1999, p. 129.
Houston Chronicle, July 3, 1997, YO section, p. 3.
Jet, April 10, 2000, p. 58; October 23, 2000, p. 60; May 10, 2004, p. 54.
Knight Ridder/Tribune News Service, October 7, 2003, p. K1699.
Pittsburgh Post-Gazette, April 8, 1998, p. D1.
Times-Picayune (New Orleans), August 22, 1999, p. T10.

On-line

"Danielle Vaughn," *Biography Resource Center Online,* www.galenet.com (June 27, 2005).
"*The Parkers*: Countess Vaughn James," *UPN,* http:

//www.upn.com/shows/parkers/cast_01.shtml (June 27, 2005).

—James M. Manheim

Bernita Walker

1946—

Social activist

Walker, Bernita R., photograph. Courtesy Bernita R. Walker.

For more than two decades, Bernita R. Walker has dedicated her life to the support of families escaping domestic violence. She is co-founder and executive director of Project: Peacemakers, Inc., a non-profit public benefit corporation in Los Angeles that provides intervention and education for those escaping domestic abuse. Walker, a retired Los Angeles deputy sheriff and a domestic abuse survivor, has overseen the training of more than 1,000 community members in the fight against abuse. In addition, Walker is co-founder of Jenesse Center, a shelter for domestic abuse victims and their children. Walker is an advocate for the cause, choosing it as her life's work, advising governmental agencies and spreading the word through community education.

Born on August 20, 1946, in Los Angeles, California, Walker seemed meant to do great things. She grew up in a show business family, watching and learning from relatives with special talents. Her father, who hailed from a musical family, was Aaron (T-Bone) Walker, a blues singer credited with the invention of the electric blues style of guitar playing that some called the "California style of Blues." T-Bone started in the 1930s and wrote popular tunes like "Stormy Monday," "Mean Old World," and "Jealous Woman." His riffs and showmanship influenced the likes of B.B. King, Jimi Hendrix, Eric Clapton, and Chuck Berry. T-Bone is also an inductee to the Rock & Roll Hall of Fame. Walker's mother, Vida Lee Lashley Walker, was known on the circuit as a "good musician's wife," Walker said in an interview with *Contemporary Black Biography* (*CBB*). Her role was vital to the family as they all traveled from one performance to the next on the back roads of the segregated South. It wasn't easy and Walker remembers being confused by the racism. There were the "whites only" signs and filling stations that would sell them gas but wouldn't allow them to use the restrooms. "As a child I remember being very hungry after getting off a flight to New Orleans. I watched as my father pleaded with a white woman to allow us to buy a hot dog at the snack bar. But she refused us anyway." This was Walker's first memory of the unfair and harmful actions people take to deliberately harm others; not unlike the unfairness of the domestic abuse she would later experience and work to eliminate.

In 1964 Walker graduated from Thomas Jefferson High School and entered California State University at Los Angeles. This time in her life was a difficult one as

At a Glance . . .

Born on August 20, 1946, in Los Angeles, CA; children: Kelie. *Education:* California State University, BS, public administration, 1991. *Religion:* Christian.

Career: Los Angeles County Sheriff Department, Los Angeles, CA, deputy sheriff III, 1968-78; Jenesse Center, Inc., Los Angeles, CA, executive director, 1980-95; Project: Peacemakers, Inc., Los Angeles, CA, executive director, 1995–; Long and Walker Publishing, founder, 1989–; Oluremi Longhouse, founder, 1992–.

Selected memberships: LAPD's African-American Community Forum; 77th Division Community Police Advisory Board; Los Angeles City Domestic Violence Task Force; Golden State Grand Chapter, Order of the Eastern Star, PHRA.

Selected awards: Luella B. Hilliard Lifetime Achievement Award; California Attorney General's Community Service Award; Los Angles Police Commissioners Community Service Award; Agape Foundation Community Service Award; Eta Phi Sigma Sorority-Kappa Chapter Service Award.

Addresses: *Office*—Project: Peacemakers, 1826 W. 54th Street, Los Angeles, CA 90062-2601.

she worked a series of jobs and long hours to make ends meet after the birth of her daughter Kelie. In 1968 she joined the Los Angeles County Sheriff's Department as a deputy assigned to the Sybil Brand Institute for Women, a women's jail. Later Walker transferred to special investigations. During the years she served as a deputy, Walker learned valuable lessons about human nature, violence, and prison. Although she was surprised at the attitude of some of the officers she worked around, there were also lots of good people working there, she said. Walker did realize, upon seeing several old schoolmates in the women's prison, that it could easily have been herself, incarcerated.

In 1978 when Walker retired due to a knee injury, she was well aware that a child exposed to violence at home could end up lost behind bars. "Violence," Walker told *CBB*, "is a learned behavior. Children who experience it in their early years are more likely to commit violence against others or allow themselves to be abused."

After leaving the Sheriff's Department, Walker searched for her calling as she worked and returned to school. At the time, Walker and four friends would sometimes visit a local night spot in the neighborhood, but their kids began to feel left out. "The kids made it clear that they wanted more time with their mothers," Walker recalled to *CBB*. To solve their dilemma the women formed a social club that included the kids. The women also decided they'd donate some of the club's earnings, so they named it Jenesse Social and Charity Club. They just needed to find a worthy cause. The group searched for an organization to support, but could find none in South Central Los Angeles. So Jenesse started its own. The members of Jenesse learned to write proposals to seek grant money and received help from a local minister. He called the group one day to offer the use of the church rectory to house the center. One day an acquaintance told the women about new legislation that would generate revenue to fund battered women's shelters from a marriage license fee increase; they had found their cause. The Jenesse Center, dedicated to helping battered African-American women and their children, opened in 1980, with Margaret Cambric as its first executive director and Walker as assistant director. The group expanded the center in 1981 to include a shelter. Walker became executive director in 1993. In 1995 Walker resigned from the position.

The day after Walker resigned from Jenesse, she started Project: Peacemakers, Inc. As its executive director she continued her mission against violence through crisis intervention and prevention education. Project: Peacemakers has a multi-program set-up which includes D.A.R.T., CalWorks, G.R.O.W., and L.A. Bridges. D.A.R.T—The Domestic Abuse Response Team—is a group of trained volunteers who partner with the 77th Police Division to respond to incidents of abuse. CalWorks is a federal program partnering with Project: Peacemakers to offer anger management, domestic violence, and parenting classes, as well as counseling and support groups, to parents who have been victimized by domestic violence. The G.R.O.W. program assists adults without children or who have lost custody of their kids, as they transition from public assistance to the labor market. L.A. Bridges is an after-school program which uses the assistance of families, schools, and community to prevent gang violence.

Walker also founded the Oluremi's Longhouse program, a center for sober living, in 1992. The facility accommodates 14 residents, all men trying to stay sober and get on their feet while learning mutual respect. Out of this program came one of the largest Alcoholic Anonymous groups in the country, noted Walker.

In addition to this work, Walker also runs the family business—Lord and Walker Publishing, a company Walker created in 1989 to manage her father's music. Walker also sits on several boards around the state and teaches domestic violence related courses.

Walker is tireless and seems fearless. She said the

strength she displays protecting families from the menace of domestic abuse was inherited from her multiethnic heritage. "My mother was the granddaughter of an Irish slave owner, my great grandmother was believed to be Native American or Mexican. My grandmother was a very dark African American," she said. Walker learned fortitude from their collective struggle against slavery, encroachment, and war. The ability to face the enemy is in her blood. Perhaps what keeps her going are the stories of the women who took their lives back after living in fear. She meets them often and knows their gratitude.

Acknowledging how faith can give someone courage enough to escape a toxic relationship, Walker put it simply: "You know God did not give us a spirit of fear." Walker worked diligently to try to eliminate the violence, but remarked that to rid families of such violence cultural changes needed to occur. "We need to teach our boys to respect girls and teach our girls to respect themselves," Walker told *CBB*. "We need to learn it as a culture." Walker stressed her point, noting that 90 percent of the convicted felons in the United States were either abused as a child or saw it in the home regularly, and adding that this is also true for 100 percent of inmates on death row. Guided by her desire to remedy these cultural ills, Walker continued to press on with her work.

Sources

On-line

Project: Peacemakers, Inc., www.projectpeacemakersinc.org (June 12, 2005).

Other

Additional information for this profile was obtained through an interview with and materials provided by Bernita R. Walker on June 13, 2005.

—Sharon Melson Fletcher

Willard White

1946—

Bass-baritone opera singer, actor

Widely considered one of the greatest singers of his generation, Jamaican-born bass-baritone Willard White made his professional operatic debut with New York City Opera, where he played the character of Colline in *La Bohème* in 1974. His European debut was with Welsh National Opera in Cardiff, Wales, where he played Osmin in Mozart's *The Abduction from the Seraglio* in 1974. He has since gone on to perform in the world's major opera houses and his powerful voice and commanding stage presence have made him a popular and admired singer across a wide range of musical styles. White is best known for performing as Mephistopheles in *The Damnation of Faust*, a role he has played many times. Besides the traditional classical repertoire he is celebrated for his performances as Porgy in *Porgy and Bess.* White was honored as a Commander of the Order of the British Empire (CBE) in 1995 and received a knighthood from Queen Elizabeth II in 2004.

Willard White was born on October 10, 1946, in St. Catherine, Jamaica, the son of a dockworker, Egbert, and Gertrude White. His supportive but non-musical family recognized his talent and White attended the Jamaican School of Music before moving to New York and the Juiliard School, where he studied with Maria Callas. He married Gillian Jackson in 1974 and they have three sons and a daughter; he also has three children from his second marriage. White made his first professional appearances in 1974 when he performed with the New York City Opera in *La Bohème*, and with Welsh National Opera, playing Osmin on Mozart's *The Abduction from the Seraglio.* In 1976 he performed for the first time with English National Opera and also made his first appearance at the Glyndebourne Festival in 1978 as the Speaker in *The Magic Flute*; he returned to Glyndebourne in 1986 as Porgy in George Gershwin's *Porgy and Bess*.

White's reputation as a singer rests on his warm, powerful voice and his stage presence, but his career is also remarkable for the range of music he has performed successfully. He has become world famous for his menacing Mephistopheles in Berlioz's *The Damnation of Faust*, as well as other major roles from the classical operatic repertoire. But he is also celebrated for his stage performances and his recording as Porgy in *Porgy and Bess*, and for solo performances in 1999 and 2000 at the BBC's "The Last Night of the Proms" concert in London, the biggest event of the British classical music calendar, and one that reaches a global audience of many millions. He has also performed in numerous concert performances of operatic arias, and songs, including singing at the opening of the Millennium Dome as part of London's celebrations at the start of the twenty-first century.

White's career as an opera singer has taken him to the great opera houses of the world, including those in London, New York, Salzburg, San Francisco, Sydney, and Milan. He has sung with the world's most celebrated orchestras, such as the London Symphony Orchestra, the Los Angeles Philharmonic Orchestra, and the Berlin Philharmonic Orchestra, and performed most of the major operatic roles for bass-baritone. White's versatility extends beyond music into stage acting and he has appeared as Othello with the Royal

At a Glance . . .

Born Willard Wentworth White on October 10, 1946, in St Catherine, Jamaica; married Gillian Jackson, 1974 (marriage ended); married second wife; children: (first marriage) three sons and one daughter, (second marriage) three children. *Education:* Jamaican School of Music, Jamaica; Juilliard School, New York, New York.

Career: Opera singer, 1974–; actor, 1980s–.

Awards: Commander of the Order of the British Empire (CBE), 1995; Knighthood, 2004, for services to music.

Addresses: *Office*—c/o 10 Montague Ave., London SE4 1YP, England.

Shakespeare Company to considerable acclaim; after Paul Robeson he is reputedly only the second singer to play Shakespeare's most famous black character. In fact White has often been compared with Robeson and has paid tribute to him with a series of concerts based on his repertoire, entitled "An Evening with Willard White—A Tribute to Paul Robeson." In particular the song "Ol' Man River," which Robeson made famous, has become one of White's trademarks.

White is a popular performer with a reputation for bringing emotional and intellectual intensity to the projects in which he is involved. He has been married twice and has seven children; he lives in London.

Selected works

Opera Performances

La Bohème, New York City Opera, 1974.
The Abduction from the Seraglio, Welsh National Opera, Cardiff, England, 1974.
L'incoronazione di Poppea, English National Opera, London, 1976.
The Magic Flute, Glyndebourne Festival, 1978.
L'africaine, Covent Garden, London, 1978.
Orfeo, Salzburg Festival, 1980.
Porgy & Bess, Glyndebourne Festival, 1986.
Pelleas et Melisande, toured United States, 1995-2000.
Semele, Aix-en-Provence, France, 1996.
Nabucco, Cardiff, Wales, 1996.
La damnation de Faust, Empire Theatre, London, 1997 .
Flying Dutchman, Coliseum, London, 1997.

Plays

Othello, Royal Shakespeare Company, 1989.

Television

Paul McCartney's Liverpool Oratorio, Great Performances, PBS, 1991.
Porgy and Bess, American Playhouse, PBS, 1993.
King Balthazar, Amahl and the Night Visitors, NBC, 1978.
The Love for Three Oranges, 1982.
Porgy and Bess: An American Voice, 1998.

Sources

Periodicals

Ebony, November 1991, p. 24.
Jamaican Observer, June 14, 2004.
Opera News, April 2000, p. 28; September 2003, p. 88.
Time, February 20, 1995, p. 73.

On-line

"Knighthood of Opera Star White," *BBC News*, http://news.bbc.co.uk/1/hi/entertainment/arts/3798349.stm (May 6, 2005).
"Opera Star Performs at Opening Concert," *BBC News*, http://news.bbc.co.uk/1/hi/wales/2716283.stm (May 6, 2005).
"Willard White," *Biography Resource Center*, www.galenet.com/servlet/BioRC (accessed May 5, 2005).
"Willard White," *Jamaica's Classical Musicians*, www.joyousjam.com/jamaicasclassicalmusicians/id3.html (May 6, 2005).

—Chris Routledge

Marco Williams

1956—

Filmmaker

Marco Williams's documentaries offer an unflinchingly look in the face of hard issues like racism, injustice, and the black American experience. In filming personal issues such as the search for his father or the repercussions of a black man's murder at the hands of white racists, Williams has created a body of work that rises above its subjects. "The personal is the universal, the specific is the universal, not the general," he explained to *Contemporary Black Biography* (*CBB*).

Discovered Desire to Direct in College

An only child, Marco Williams was born on October 31, 1956, in Philadelphia, Pennsylvania. His father was long gone by then, but his mother—heir to four-generations of fatherless families—was resilient and strong. She moved Williams to Manhattan's Lower East Side when he was very young and made sure he received a top-notch education, including high school at the Buxton School, a progressive prep school in Massachusetts. Like many kids, Williams had a childhood full of friends, street games, and reading. Unlike many future filmmakers, he grew up without a television set and rarely went to the cinema. "I didn't know anything about movies, really," he told Billy Frolick in the book *What I Really Want to Do Is Direct: Seven Film School Graduates Go To Hollywood*.

When Williams was 18 his mother packed up for Paris to train as a French chef. Williams returned to Massachusetts and his freshman year at Harvard University. He had also been offered scholarships to Yale, Brown, and the University of Pennsylvania. Harvard did not pressure freshman to choose a major immediately, and Williams explored several areas. But one class stood out: "It was a survey of Alfred Hitchcock's films," Williams told *CBB*. "I was really impressed by the intentionality in his work, that things were not accidental, that you could create suspense through camera angle, camera choice, juxtaposition."

After his freshman year, Williams took two years off . "When I returned, I knew I wanted to make films," he told *CBB*. In the interim he had dabbled in poetry and photography and as he explained to Frolick, "I imagined that film was a synthesis of photography and poetry. So I went back to Harvard determined." Williams joined the school's visual and environmental studies program and as a junior directed his first film, *From Harlem to Harvard*, a half-hour film that explores race and class on the Harvard campus as it documented the experiences of a freshman from Harlem.

Debuted at Sundance with Two Films

In his senior year at Harvard, Williams had the chance to meet his father. It gave him the motivation for his next film, *In Search of Our Fathers*. "I started to feel that this was amazing—two adult men about to meet each other for the first time," Williams told Frolick. "I thought this should be documented." Over the next ten

At a Glance . . .

Born on October 31, 1956, in New York, NY. *Education:* Harvard University, BA, visual and environmental studies, 1981; University of California, Los Angeles, MFA, film and television, 1991; University of California, Los Angeles, MA, Afro-American studies, 1992.

Career: Filmmaker, 1980–; North Carolina School of Arts, Winston-Salem, NC, filmmaker-in-residence, 1994-98; Duke University, Durham, NC, guest lecturer, 1995; New York University, New York, NY, assistant professor, 1998–; Two Tone Productions, New York, NY, 2000s–.

Awards: National Educational Film and Video Festival, Silver Apple Award, for *In Search of Our Fathers,* 1994; IFP/New York, Anthony Radziwill Documentary Achievement Award, for *Two Towns of Jasper,* 2002; Hot Docs Canadian International Documentary Film Festival, Silver Award, Best International Documentary, for *Two Towns of Jasper,* 2002; Pan African Film Festival, Best Documentary, for *Two Towns of Jasper,* 2002; Peabody Board, Peabody Award, Excellence in Electronic Media, for *Two Towns of Jasper,* 2003.

Addresses: *Office*—Two Tone Productions, 426 Broome St., New York, NY, 10013.

years, Williams compiled footage with his father and his mother, and slowly put together the 70-minute documentary. Along the way, the film became less about Williams's meeting his father and more about what constitutes the black family.

When *In Search of Our Fathers* was released in 1992, it earned international acclaim and several awards. It was shown on PBS's renowned series, *Frontline*, and was selected for the 1992 Sundance Film Festival, one of the most important film events in the world. It was also screened in places as far-flung as Australia, Africa, South America, Asia, and Europe. "For me, the greatest satisfaction was that even though this is a film about the American experience, black America, this film at its core is about family," Williams told *CBB*. "And I discovered that...people across borders, across nationalities, were really receptive to it. They were receptive to the personal nature of it. It was a personal story, but it had transcendent qualities."

During the decade that it took to make the film, Williams moved to the West Coast and enrolled in the University of California, Los Angeles. In 1991 he earned a master's of fine art in film and television, and in 1992 he earned a master's in Afro-American studies. In 1990 he had been selected out of hundreds of applicants to direct a half-hour short film for the Discovery Program and Chanticleer Films. *Without a Pass*, released in 1992 was shown on Showtime and was nominated for CableAce awards for Best Director and Best Theatrical Special. The film was also selected for 1992's Sundance Festival, making Williams the only director that year with two films in the Park City, Utah festival. "It was an affirming time for me," Williams told *CBB*. "I was presented to the film community as a storyteller. That was a great personal pride for me."

Murder Led to Racially Probing Film

Williams spent several years in California trying to break into Hollywood as a feature film director. When that did not pan out he accepted a teaching position with the North Carolina School of Arts in 1994. "It's not what I have been dreaming of doing," he told Frolick. "Even though the components are attractive, it's not by my own design that I'm leaving. I would have rather made a film and taken the opportunity to teach second." At North Carolina, Williams kept open his options to direct and within a year he was summoned to San Francisco to film *Making Peace: Rebuilding Communities,* part of a PBS series documenting grassroots efforts to curb violence. Williams filmed groups in Columbus, Ohio, and Chicago, Illinois. "These films were me trying to fit into a series," Williams told *CBB*. "It has my imprint, but it is not me." After the film wrapped he returned to North Carolina to finish out his teaching contract.

In 1998 Williams returned home to New York and became an assistant professor in the film and television department at New York University. That same year, a black man named James Byrd was chained to the back of a pick up truck by three white supremacists in the town of Jasper, Texas. Byrd was dragged until he was beheaded, his body torn apart. Whitney Dow, a white filmmaker who had known Williams since his days at Buxton contacted Williams about the murder. "While Whitney was shocked and surprised, I was disturbed but neither shocked nor surprised because black people have been brutally murdered in America for over three hundred years," Williams said in a "Behind the Lens" interview posted on the PBS Web site. "With our differences so vivid, I thought that by collaborating with Whitney on a film about race, one that embraced the idea that black and white Americans see the world differently, we might be able to be part of bridging that difference."

Williams and Dow spent a year filming in Jasper with two separate film crews—Williams's was black, Dow's white. "[This approach] was a result of conversations between Whitney and I, a black man and a white man, and recognition that there are some topics, particularly racial division, that we're more comfortable to speak about with people who are like ourselves, with people who have a common or shared experience," Williams explained on NPR's *All Things Considered*.

Worked to Improve Race Relations

2002's *Two Towns of Jasper* revealed the depths of racism in a way that few films had done before. It also earned Williams the most accolades of his career. In addition to film festivals worldwide, including Sundance, the film was shown on PBS's *P.O.V.* series and featured on *The Oprah Winfrey Show* and ABC's *Nightline with Ted Koppel*. Williams and Dow earned several awards for the film, including the prestigious Peabody. Williams also found a way to give back with the film. "[It] has also allowed me to do community outreach," he told *CBB*. "The film is screened in places working to deal with race relations."

Williams next film was 2003's *MLK Boulevard* for the Discovery-Times Channel. "It explored why we name streets for King, and what those streets signify," Williams told *CBB*. "Have we come a long way in this country or not? Do these streets honor an American hero or an African-American icon?" To make the film Williams traveled to dozens of MLK boulevards across the country. "So it was also a road trip movie." Williams followed that up with another film touching on black themes in America—*I Sit Where I Want: The Legacy of Brown v. the Board of Education*. Set in a Buffalo, New York, school, "It is about race relations through the eyes of high school students," Williams told *CBB*. The film was highly praised by the press and went on to become part of race relations programs at schools nationwide.

By 2005 Williams was running Two Tone Productions and had several film projects in the works, including *Banished: How Whites Drove Blacks Out of Town in America*, a documentary exploring the forcible expulsion of blacks from dozens of American towns following the Civil War. "It asks how do we reconcile the atrocities of the past?" Williams told *CBB*. Williams also continued to teach at NYU while seeking his break into feature films. "I have lots of ideas for film," he told *CBB*. "I have not reached the pinnacle of my career but I feel good about the work that I've done. I feel like I am making a contribution to society."

Selected works

Films

Director, *From Harlem to Harvard*, 1980.
Script supervisor, *The Brother from Another Planet*, 1983.
Director, *In Search of our Fathers*, 1992.
Director, *Without a Pass*, 1992.
Director, *Making Peace: Rebuilding Our Communities,* 1995.
Co-director, *Two Towns of Jasper*, 2002.
Director, *MLK Boulevard*, 2003.
Director, *I Sit Where I Want: The Legacy of Brown v. the Board of Education*, 2004.

Sources

Books

Frolick, Billy, *What I Really Want to Do Is Direct: Seven Film School Graduates Go to Hollywood,* Dutton, 1996.

On-line

"Behind the Lens: Filmmaker Interview," *PBS: P.O.V.*, www.pbs.org/pov/pov2002/twotownsofjasper/behindlens_filmmaker.html (May 29, 2005).

Other

"Whitney Dow and Marco Williams Discuss Their Film Project, a Documentary Called the "Two Towns of Jasper," *All Things Considered*, National Public Radio (NPR), January 17, 2003.
Additional information for this profile was obtained through an interview with Marco Williams on July 1, 2005.

—Candace LaBalle

Stevie Wonder

1950—

Singer, songwriter

In the course of following Stevie Wonder on his relentless travels, journalists come to realize just how beloved an entertainer he is. "It dawned on me," wrote Giles Smith in the *New Yorker*, "that a substantial part of Stevie Wonder's public life consists of the voices of complete strangers telling him they love him." *Rolling Stone*'s David Ritz had a similar epiphany. "Following Stevie Wonder around New York is exhilarating work," he wrote. "I get the feeling that he loves being Stevie Wonder. He loves the attention, the adulation, the chance to perform." What's more, Ritz remarked, Wonder's "optimism is infectious." Such optimism may spring from a deep spiritual wellspring, but it is also sustained by decades spent creating indelible, meaningful music.

It is estimated that Wonder—born Stevland Judkins Morris in Saginaw, Michigan—was blinded by a surfeit of oxygen in his incubator shortly after his premature birth. "I vaguely remember light and what my mother looks like," he ventured in a 1986 *Life* interview, "but I could be dreaming." His father left the family early on, and he and his five siblings were raised by their mother. She moved the clan to Detroit, where they struggled mightily to survive. Though he has groused good-naturedly in adulthood at the limitations his sightlessness has placed on him, Wonder told Ritz that as a child he soothed his mother's tears by telling her that he "wasn't sad." He recalled, "I believed God had something for me to do." Along with his siblings, he paid musical tribute to the Almighty in the Whitestone Baptist Church Choir, along with his vocal prowess demonstrating a gift for piano, harmonica, and drums by age 11.

Thanks to the intercession of a friend, Stevland was brought to the attention of Berry Gordy, president of Detroit-based Motown Records, and Gordy's producer Brian Holland. Gordy placed the exceptional youngster's career in the hands of his associate Clarence Paul, whom he designated as Stevie's mentor. Paul told *Rolling Stone*'s Ritz that Gordy had instructed him, "Your job is to bring out his genius. This boy can give us hits." Handed the show business moniker "Little Stevie Wonder," the talented adolescent—signed to the Motown offshoot label Tamla—did indeed produce a stunning string of hits.

Wonder's fourth single, "Fingertips, Pt. 2," appeared in 1963 and became the first live performance of a song to reach the top of the U.S. pop charts. Also that year, Wonder became the first recording artist to reach the top position on the Billboard Hot 100, R&B singles, and album charts simultaneously. Unable to attend a regular Detroit school while becoming a pop sensation, Wonder was sent to the Michigan School for the Blind at Motown's expense.

"Motown meant discipline to me," Wonder recalled to Ritz. "The attitude was 'Do it over. Do it differently. Do it until it can't be done any better.'" Under such demanding circumstances the young performer grew up fast. In 1964 he put aside the "Little" label and let fans focus on the Wonder; over the next few years he churned out pop-soul smashes like "Uptight," "Nothing's Too Good for My Baby," "I Was Made to Love

At a Glance . . .

Born Stevland Judkins Morris, May 13, 1950, in Saginaw, MI; son of Lulu Mae Morris; married Syreeta Wright (a singer), 1971 (divorced, 1972); married Karen "Kai" Millard; children: seven children (five outside of marriage).

Career: Recording artist, Motown Records, 1963–. Founded Black Bull Music publishing company, 1971; sponsored Stevie Wonder Home for Blind and Retarded Children, 1976; founded Wondirection Records, 1982; activist for and contributor to various political and social causes, including Mothers Against Drunk Driving, the establishment of a national holiday honoring Martin Luther King, Jr., the anti-apartheid movement, AIDS awareness, and Charge Against Hunger program; KJLH radio station, Los Angeles, owner.

Awards: 15 Grammy awards, including those for best male vocalist in both pop and R&B categories, best pop song, and best album; Distinguished Service Award, President's Committee on Employment of Handicapped People, 1969; Academy Award for best song, 1985, for "I Just Called to Say I Love You"; inducted into Rock and Roll Hall of Fame, 1989; Whitney M. Young Award, Los Angeles Urban League, 1990; Carousel of Hope Award, Children's Diabetes Foundation, 1990; Honorary Global Founder's Award, Mothers Against Drunk Driving, 1990; *Essence* magazine award, 1995; inducted into Songwriters Hall of Fame, 2002; National Academy of Popular Music/ Songwriters Hall of Fame, Johnny Mercer Award, 2004; Billboard Music Awards, Century Award, 2004.

Addresses: *Office*—c/o Motown Records, 1350 Avenue of the Americas, 20th Floor, New York, NY 10019; 5750 Wilshire Blvd., Los Angeles, CA 90036.

Her," and "For Once in My Life." By 1968 his label had amassed enough chart-toppers to fill his first Greatest Hits album.

In 1969 Wonder met President Richard Nixon at the White House, where he received a Distinguished Service Award from the President's Committee on Employment of Handicapped People. Meanwhile, he continued to pile up hits, as "My Cherie Amour" sold over a million copies and "Signed Sealed Delivered (I'm Yours)" vaulted up the charts. 1970 saw Wonder marry Syreeta Wright, a Motown employee and aspiring singer; the two wrote together, and Wonder produced several successful records for her. The marriage was short-lived, however; they divorced in 1972. By all accounts, they remain friends.

Wright has said that Wonder's music was her chief rival. "He would wake up and go straight to the keyboard," she recalled to Smith of the *New Yorker*. "I knew and understood that his passion was music. That was really his No. 1 wife." Wonder fathered children by three other women over the next couple of decades, though he did not remarry. "I was at the birth of two of my children," he confided in *Life*. "I felt them being born—it was amazing." In a 1995 *Rolling Stone* interview, the 44-year-old artist did express a yearning for matrimony, calling it "the space where we're most relaxed and able to give and receive maximum love. I'm not there yet—but soon. It's one of my goals."

When Wonder turned 21 in 1971 he was due the money he had earned as a minor (this arrangement had been stipulated in a previous agreement). But Motown only paid him $1 million of the $30 million he'd earned during that time. After considerable legal wrangling he managed to attain a unique degree of artistic and financial autonomy. "At 21, Stevie was interested in being treated well and in controlling his life and in presenting his music, and all those things were extraordinary things for a young man to ask at that point," explained Johanan Vigoda, Wonder's longtime attorney, to Smith of the *New Yorker*. "It wasn't the freedom to be dissolute or undisciplined. He wanted to be free so that he could bring the best of himself to the table."

What Wonder brought to the table—with the establishment of his own music publishing company and near-total creative freedom—was an increasingly sophisticated body of work that managed to fuse the high spirits of classic soul, the down-and-dirty syncopations of funk, exquisite melodies, and his own introspective and increasingly politicized lyrical sensibility. From a sonic standpoint, too, he was a trailblazer, demonstrating the versatility of the synthesizer when it was still something of a novelty instrument in the R&B world.

Wonder's momentum was almost stopped permanently by a 1973 automobile accident that nearly claimed his life and left him with deep facial scars. If anything, however, this event provoked him to redouble his efforts. Virtually all of Wonder's work during the early to mid-1970s is essential pop, most notably his albums *Talking Book*, *Innervisions*, *Fulfillingness' First Finale*, and the epic *Songs in the Key of Life*. His songs from this period—including the percolating funk-rock workouts "Superstition" and "Higher Ground," the effervescent "Boogie on Reggae Woman," the jubilant paean to classic jazz "Sir Duke," the grittily nostalgic "I Wish," and the breezy chart-buster "You Are the Sunshine of My Life"—left most of

Wonder's competition in the dust both artistically and commercially. "What artist in his right mind," mused singer-songwriter and soul icon Marvin Gaye in the presence of *Rolling Stone*'s Ritz, "wouldn't be intimidated by Stevie Wonder?"

1979 saw the release of Wonder's musically beguiling *Journey Through the Secret Life of Plants*, the theme of which many listeners found a little eccentric, to say the least. "It was a consideration of the physical and spiritual relationships between human beings and plants," Wonder explained to Ritz, quipping that "some called it shrubbish." Though he increasingly failed to match his creative and sales peaks of the preceding decades, Wonder was still a giant presence in the world of pop. His *Hotter Than July*, with its reggae-driven hit "Master Blaster (Jammin')," indicated his continuing creative restlessness. And "That Girl," the unstoppable love song "I Just Called to Say I Love You"—which won an Academy Award for best song and stands as Motown's top-selling single internationally—and his duet with ex-Beatle Paul McCartney on the anti-racism anthem "Ebony and Ivory" all burned up the charts.

Over the years Wonder also became progressively more involved in politics, lobbying for gun control, against drunk driving and the apartheid system enforced by South Africa's white minority, and on behalf of a national holiday in recognition of civil rights martyr Martin Luther King, Jr. He played a number of benefits and made public service announcements, often winning honors for his advocacy. The slogan underneath his picture on a poster for Mothers Against Drunk Driving read: "Before I ride with a drunk, I'll drive myself." He also contributed his labor to the Charge Against Hunger campaign organized by American Express.

By the late 1980s, Wonder had become less prolific than he had been in the past, but he was still phenomenally successful. He received a Grammy for 1986's *In Square Circle* and in 1989 was inducted into the Rock and Roll Hall of Fame. He won plaudits for his work on the soundtrack to Spike Lee's 1991 film *Jungle Fever*, allegedly composing the material for it in the space of three weeks. "Movies are always a good challenge," he told Neil Strauss of the *New York Times*, "because it's taking what's happening visually and, even though I'm not able to see it, getting a sense of the movie and finding a new way to work with it." His work for *Jungle Fever* had preempted a collection of songs he'd been crafting while living in the African nation of Ghana; the resulting disc would not hit stores for several years.

In 1992—by which time multimillion-dollar deals had become commonplace—Wonder signed a unique lifetime pact with Motown. "This is a guy you don't ever want to see recording for anyone else," company president Jheryl Busby told the *New Yorker*'s Smith in 1995. "I worked hard to make Stevie see that we had his interests at heart. Stevie is what I call the crown jewel, the epitome. I wasn't looking at Stevie as an aging superstar but as an icon who could pull us into the future." Wonder himself seemed to share this sense of his eternal newness: "I'm going to be 45," he reflected to Ritz in *Rolling Stone*, "but I'm still feeling new and amazed by the world I live in. I was in the Hard Rock Cafe in Tokyo last week, and they started playing my records, and I started crying, crying like a little kid, thinking how God has blessed me with all these songs."

When *Conversation Peace*—the album on which Wonder had been working for nearly eight years—was released in 1995, it garnered a range of reactions. *Vibe* deemed it "a decidedly mixed bag, leapfrogging back and forth between divine inspiration and inoffensive professionalism"; reviewer Tom Sinclair took particular exception to the "cloying sentimentality" of some of the songs, as did other critics. *Entertainment Weekly* praised the album's sound, but noted that "the song selection here, while frisky, is thin, making this comeback small Wonder." *Time*'s Christopher John Farley, however, while allowing that the recording "isn't a slam dunk," called it "another winner for Wonder." Regardless of their respective verdicts, most reviewers concurred that Wonder's versatility, passion, and chops remained intact.

Wonder proved the validity of these observations during his 1995 concert tour. "Running 2 1/4 hours, it was an outstanding show—full of pure, old-fashioned R&B," declared *Los Angeles Times* writer Dennis Hunt of Wonder's performance at the Universal Amphitheatre. Pondering the performer's endurance and the disappearance of most of his contemporaries from the scene, Hunt observed, "Some may point to exquisite taste as the key to Wonder's success, but the real secret is his ability to stay current, to be fluent in the R&B style of the moment." Not surprisingly, critics were virtually unanimous about Wonder's 1995 live double CD, *Natural Wonder*, which *Rolling Stone* called "an important and revelatory statement."

It took ten years for Wonder to release his next album—ten long years, in the opinion of his label, which went through troubled times over those years, including several changes in management. By mid-2005, Wonder had released the first single from the album, a funky number called "So What the Fuss" which featured Prince on guitar. The video for the single was greeted with acclaim as the first-ever video with descriptive narration for the visually impaired. The narration, voiced by rapper Busta Rhymes, describes the actions that accompany the song, including comments on what Wonder is wearing and what instruments are being played. The album, *A Time 2 Love*, was expected to follow by mid-summer 2005, yet Wonder kept delaying its release, to the frustration of Motown execs. *Newsweek* quoted wonder as saying: "The reason they haven't got it is I'm not ready to give it to them. However long it takes me, I'm giving the very best that I can... I won't settle for less." It remains to be seen how this album will fit into the Wonder pantheon of music.

Wonder has clearly slowed down the pace at which he releases albums, though he continues to consider himself both a musician and an activist. He conducts an annual holiday benefit concert to provide toys to underprivileged children, he performed at the Live 8 benefit concert in 2005, and he owns a Los Angeles radio station, KJLH, that is dedicated to serving L.A.'s black community. Asked by *Billboard* whether he had become more activist than musician, Wonder answered: "I'm more musician. My way of expressing how I feel when I'm talking about political or social positions is better served when I do it through my music. It's not to say I can't express myself verbally. But music is the vehicle I've been given as a way to do that." Wonder's plans for the future include a variety of projects. "I plan to do a book," he told *Billboard,* "and I'm excited about the prospects of a film.... It would be very inspirational in the things that I went through growing up as a little boy being blind and the things my mother had to contend with.... Then maybe there would be another film about the second half of my life.... More than anything, I want to do a musical. I'd also like to do an acting role. I have a couple of ideas I've been working on, film storylines that are pretty good." Though many in the music industry view Wonder as one of the forefathers of modern funk and R&B, Wonder insists that his musical career is far from over: "For me to say I've reached my peak is to say that God is through using me for what he has given me the opportunity to do. And I just don't believe that."

Selected discography

Albums (On Motown, unless otherwise noted)

Little Stevie Wonder: The Twelve-Year-Old Genius, 1963.
Recorded Live (includes "Fingertips, Pt. 2"), 1963.
Uptight (includes "Uptight"), 1966.
Down to Earth, 1967.
I Was Made to Love Her (includes "I Was Made to Love Her"), 1967.
Stevie Wonder's Greatest Hits, 1968.
For Once in My Life (includes "For Once in My Life"), 1969.
My Cherie Amour (includes "My Cherie Amour"), 1969.
Stevie Wonder Live, 1970.
Signed Sealed and Delivered (includes "Signed Sealed Delivered [I'm Yours]"), 1970.
Where I'm Coming From, 1971.
Greatest Hits, Vol. 2, 1972.
Music of My Mind, 1972.
Talking Book (includes "You Are the Sunshine of My Life" and "Superstition"), 1972.
Innervisions (includes "Higher Ground"), 1973.
Fulfillingness' First Finale (includes "Boogie on Reggae Woman"), 1974.
Songs in the Key of Life (includes "Sir Duke" and "I Wish"), 1976.
Journey Through the Secret Life of Plants, 1979.
Hotter Than July (includes "Master Blaster [Jammin']"), 1980.
Stevie Wonder's Original Musiquarium (includes "That Girl"), 1982.
In Square Circle, 1985.
Characters, 1987.
Jungle Fever (soundtrack), 1992.
Natural Wonder, 1995.
Conversation Peace, 1995.
At the Close of a Century (boxed set), 1999.
The Definitive Collection, 2002.
A Time to Love (includes "So What the Fuss"), 2005.

Duets

With Paul McCartney, "Ebony and Ivory," *Tug of War*, Columbia, 1982.
With Chaka Khan, "I Feel for You," *I Feel for You*, Warner Bros., 1984.
With Dionne Warwick, "That's What Friends Are For," 1986.
With Lenny Kravitz, "Deuce," *Kiss My Ass*, 1995.
Also contributed songs to albums by Rufus, Minnie Riperton, and other artists.

Sources

Books

Love, Dennis, and Stacy Brown, *Blind Faith: The Miraculous Journey of Lula Hardaway, Stevie Wonder's Mother,* New York: Simon and Schuster, 2002.
Lodder, Steve, *Stevie Wonder: A Musical Guide to the Classic Albums,* San Francisco, CA: Backbeat, 2005.
Werner, Craig Hansen, *Higher Ground: Stevie Wonder, Aretha Franklin, Curtis Mayfield, and the Rise and Fall of American Soul,* New York: Crown, 2004.

Periodicals

Billboard, May 13, 1995, p. 26; December 11, 2004, p. 15.
Ebony, July 2004, p. 24.
Entertainment Weekly, March 31, 1995, p. 61.
Jet, May 8, 1995, pp. 56-58; May 22, 1995.
Life, October 1986, pp. 67-74.
Los Angeles Times, January 16, 1995, p. F1.
Newsweek, June 20, 2005, p. 44.
New Yorker, March 13, 1995, pp. 78-87.
New York Times, January 25, 1995, p. C15.
Rolling Stone, July 13, 1995, pp. 82-85, 126; January 25, 1996, p. 72.

Time, September 4, 1995, p. 76; April 10, 1995, p. 88.
Vibe, March 1995, pp. 97-98.

On-line

Stevie-Wonder.com, www.stevie-wonder.com (August 11, 2005).
Stevie Wonder Official Site, www.steviewonder.net (August 11, 2005).

—Simon Glickman and Tom Pendergast

Emmanuel Ofosu Yeboah

1977—

Athlete, activist

Saddled with a useless right leg, abandoned by his father, orphaned by his mother's death, and living in a country where physical deformities have traditionally been considered a curse, Emmanuel Ofosu Yeboah faced odds that would intimidate any Westerner. The best a disabled Ghanaian could hope for in a country with an annual income of less than $500 was to eek out an impoverished living as a street beggar. Yeboah had a better idea—he would take a bike ride. With just one good leg, he pedaled around the sub-Saharan nation in an effort to open his countrymen's eyes to the fact that disability does not mean inability. His 400-mile journey took Yeboah worlds away from his final destination. He was thrust into international celebrity, featured in a documentary, and given a brand new leg. Since then he has embarked on a new journey—transforming the lives of Ghana's estimated 2 million disabled people. "In this world, we are not perfect," Yeboah humbly told the *New York Daily News*. "We can only do our best. I just want to make life better, and help people benefit from my experience."

Countered Disability with Mother's Comfort

Emmanuel Ofosu Yeboah was born in rural Ghana in 1977 with a missing right tibia, or shin bone. His foot dangled uselessly from the curled up stump of his lower leg. Yeboah told *Sports Illustrated* that in the deeply superstitious country of Ghana, "when you are a deformed child, people think your mother sinned." His father, ashamed of the child, abandoned the family soon after Yeboah's birth. Friends and family urged Yeboah's mother to abandon or even kill the baby. Comfort Yeboah, a proud woman with a deep sense of human dignity, did neither. Instead she lived up to her name by nurturing her son. "She gave me the idea that I could go to school and become a great man," Yeboah told *Sports Illustrated*.

Yeboah and his mother lived in a tiny home that lacked electricity and plumbing. His bed was the dirt packed floor. Despite this poverty, as a Ghanaian, he had access to free public education. Though disabled children rarely took advantage of this opportunity, Comfort insisted that Yeboah be educated. At first she carried him two miles each way to school. Later, when he was old enough to get to school on his own, he recalled to the *New York Daily News*, "I'd hop on my leg." Of 240 students, Yeboah was the only disabled child. He was teased by the other children and, of course, sidelined from sports.

At the age of 13 Yeboah dropped out of school against his mother's wishes. She had fallen ill and he decided to travel to Accra, Ghana's capital, to earn some money. Though the streets were teeming with disabled beggars, Yeboah preferred to work. He set up a little shoe shine box and earned $2 a day shining shoes. During a holiday visit home, Yeboah's mother died. It was Christmas Eve, 1997. Right before she died she pulled Yeboah to her side and told him, "Don't let anybody put you down because of your disability," Yeboah recalled to the *New York Daily News*. They were words that would change his life. "What my mother told

At a Glance . . .

Born in 1977 in Ghana, Africa; married Elizabeth (2003); children: Linda.

Career: Athlete and activist; Emmanuel Education Fund, Ghana, founder, 2004–.

Memberships: Right to Play International, athlete ambassador.

Awards: Challenged Athlete Foundation, Most Inspirational Athlete of the Year, 2003; Nike, Casey Martin Award, 2003; Cinequest, Life of a Maverick Award, 2005.

Addresses: *Office*—c/o Challenged Athletes Foundation, 2148-B Jimmy Durante Blvd., Del Mar, CA, 92014. *Home*—Koforidua, Ghana.

me was a gift. I want to show everyone that physically challenged people can do something."

Planned a Bike Ride for Disabled Rights

After his mother's death Yeboah returned to Accra. Shining shoes on the streets day after day, he witnessed the resigned desperation of the other disabled people around him. Somewhere in the midst of their hopeless begging and the constant back and forth rustle of his shoe brush, an idea was born. Yeboah decided he would bike around Ghana to raise awareness of the plight of the disabled. "I wanted people to know that if you are a disabled person in your leg, you're not a disabled person in your mind," he told *The Mercury News*. First, he needed to find a bike.

A doctor told Yeboah about the California-based Challenged Athlete Foundation (CAF), an organization that supports disabled athletes. Yeboah had never written a letter before, yet he carefully prepared a request to the organization explaining his idea and asking for a bike. Bob Babbit, founder of CAF, was so impressed with Yeboah's vision that he not only sent over a new mountain bike, but also threw in biking gear and $1,000.

Yeboah's friends were skeptical. "Riding a bicycle 600 kilometers on one leg—who ever heard of that before?" Gordon Abodoe told the *New York Daily News*. However, when Abodoe and his friends saw Yeboah take the new bike out for its first spin, they gave him a rousing ovation of applause. "Emmanuel has a very strong spirit to do whatever he wants to do," he added in the *New York Daily News* interview.

Broke Disability Myths in 380 Miles

For several months after receiving the bike, Yeboah juggled training with seeking governmental support. He tried several times to get a meeting with Ghana's King Osagyefuo, but was turned away at the palace doors. Disabled people were believed to be too unworthy to step onto royal property. Finally the king agreed to meet Yeboah. It was the first time a disabled person had been allowed entrance to the palace. Yeboah told the king of his plan and the bike he had received from CAF. According to an article on the Orthotics and Prosthetics (OandP) Web site, the king asked, "Why do you want to do such a thing, and what do you want from me?" Yeboah responded, "I want to prove that just because you have a disability does not mean you can't use your God given gifts, and I need your support." The king complied.

In 2001 Yeboah began his journey. He was 24. Over several months he rode 380 miles through Ghana, wearing a bright red shirt that read "The Pozo," Ghanaian slang for a disabled person. Along the way he stopped to meet villagers, speak with disabled children, and give speeches to dignitaries, church leaders, and the ever-present media. He was not afraid to speak out against the government's policy on the disabled, and politely, consistently requested that the disabled be given the same respect as the able-bodied. As a result, Emmanuel became a one-named celebrity in Ghana.

CAF officials closely followed Yeboah's journey and after he finished, they invited him to California to participate in the 2002 Triathlon Challenge, CAF's primary fundraiser. Yeboah took seven hours to complete the 56-mile bike leg of the event. After the race, *Sports Illustrated* recalled him saying, "I did not know San Diego was so hilly."

Received a New Leg Up on Life

While in California, Yeboah was examined by doctors at the Loma Linda University Orthopaedic and Rehabilitation Center. They determined that he was a good candidate for a prosthetic leg and asked him if he would like to undergo an amputation to be fitted for the device. "At the Triathlon, I saw athletes like Rudy Garcia-Tolson and Paul Martin running and biking on a prosthesis," Yeboah recalled to OandP. "I accepted the offer so maybe I too could run, ride my bike with two legs, and even someday wear pants."

In April of 2003, Loma Linda performed the operation free of charge. Normal costs for such a procedure would have reached into the tens of thousands of dollars. In addition, when the staff at the hospital heard Yeboah's story, they opened their wallets to provide him with daily living expenses during his stay in the United States, as well as provide his family back in Ghana with the equivalent of the income lost during his absence.

The operation was a success. Not only did Yeboah get to wear pants and a pair of shoes for the first time in his life, six weeks after the operation, he returned to San Diego to compete in the CAF triathlon. With two legs, he was able to shave three hours off his time, finishing the course in four hours. Back home in Ghana, he donned a tan suit and walked on his own two feet into his church for the first time in his life. He quickly adapted to a life free of crutches and soon began to run and even play soccer. To cap off an amazing year, in December of 2003 he married a woman named Elizabeth. When the couple later had a daughter, they named her Linda after the hospital that gave made Yeboah's new life possible.

Founded Educational Fund for Disabled Ghanaians

Yeboah's achievements did not go unnoticed. In 2003, CAF named him the Most Inspirational Athlete of the Year. Actor Robin Williams presented him with the award along with a state-of-the-art running leg. From California he traveled to Oregon and the corporate headquarters of Nike, where he received the prestigious Casey Martin Award, given to honor an athlete who has overcome physical, mental, societal, or cultural challenges to excel in their sport.

The Nike award came with a check for $25,000. CAF matched that gift with another $25,000. Yeboah used the money to create the Emmanuel Education Fund in Ghana. "My goal is to make sure that children with disabilities get an education, receive proper medical care, and play sports whenever they want," he told OandP. He has committed to putting 15 disabled students through school each year and has helped organize the distribution of hundreds of wheelchairs to his countrymen.

His actions have won him the respect of fellow Ghanaian, United Nations Secretary General Kofi Annan as well as King Osagyefuo, who has adopted Yeboah's cause. The king has provided financial and managerial support for the Emmanuel Education Fund and has arranged academic and athletic training for Yeboah. The king described Yeboah to OandP as "a man who leads by example and who is not driven by self, but driven to help others." The praise was not lost on the international sporting community which elected Yeboah to represent Ghana in the 2004 Olympic Torchbearer Relay.

Shared Gift of Pride with a Nation

Yeboah's rise from a one-legged orphan to a surefooted athlete and disabled rights activist was the kind of human tale that begged to be told. Fortunately, talented twin-sister filmmakers Lisa Lax and Nancy Stern heard about the tale in 2003 from a friend at the CAF. They spent several months filming *Emmanuel's Gift* in the United States and Ghana. They were there as Yeboah oversaw the distribution of 100 wheelchairs to Ghanaian street people. "Those people were literally crawling on their hands and knees," to get to the chairs, Lax told *The Mercury News*. "I was shooting as the scene unfolded, and I had to put my camera down because tears were streaming down my cheeks. People's lives were literally changing in front of your eyes." The documentary, narrated by Oprah Winfrey, garnered early critical acclaim and began the round of film festivals in 2005.

Meanwhile Yeboah continued changing people's lives. He has established cycling and running teams, and a wheelchair basketball team. He is negotiating funding for a Sports Academy for disabled athletes in Ghana and trying to form a Ghanaian team to compete in the 2008 Paralympic Games in Beijing. Having worked closely with the Minister of Education to pass governmental legislation for disabled rights, Yeboah has expressed interest in running for a parliamentary post in Ghana.

All of Yeboah's work on behalf of the disabled in Ghana is double-sided. On the one hand he has shown able-bodied Ghanaians, from paupers to princes, that the disabled are as normal as any one of them. On the other hand, he has taught disabled Ghanaians to believe in themselves, to pick themselves up off the ground and be proud. "His impact has been very tremendous," his friend Abodoe told the *New York Daily News*. "He's affected the lives of so many people who otherwise would've lived very depressed lives." All that as a result of a mourning boy's desire to fulfill his mother's dying wish. That is the gift of his disability.

Sources

Periodicals

Sports Illustrated, November 15, 2004.

On-line

"Disabled Athlete's Gift of Inspiration," *The Mercury News*, www.miami.com/mld/mercurynews/entertainment/columnists/bruce_newman/11059313.htm (April 10, 2005).

"Ghana: From Rags to Riches," *New York Daily News*, www.nydailynews.com/sports/story/289363p-247720 c.html (April 10, 2005).

"King of Ghana Visits Ossur North America and the Challenged Athletes Foundation," *Orthotics and Prosthetics*, www.oandp.com/edge/issues/articles/NEWS_2004-08-12_04.asp (April 10, 2005).

—Candace LaBalle

Cumulative Nationality Index

Volume numbers appear in **bold**

Zairean

Zambian

Zimbabwean

Cumulative Occupation Index

Volume numbers appear in **bold**

Dance

Education

Fashion

Film

Government and politics--international

Government and politics--U.S.

Law

Military

Music

Religion

Science and technology

Social issues

Sports

Television

Theater

Writing

Cumulative Subject Index

Volume numbers appear in **bold**

Cumulative Name Index

Volume numbers appear in **bold**